American Examples

American Examples

New Conversations about Religion

volume 3

EDITED BY
CODY MUSSELMAN, ERIK KLINE,
DANA LLOYD, AND MICHAEL J. ALTMAN

THE UNIVERSITY OF ALABAMA PRESS   TUSCALOOSA

The University of Alabama Press
Tuscaloosa, Alabama 35487-0380
uapress.ua.edu

Typeface: Scala Pro

Cover design: Michele Myatt Quinn

DEPARTMENT of RELIGIOUS STUDIES
THE UNIVERSITY OF ALABAMA

Published with the support of the University of Alabama Department of Religious Studies

Cataloging-in-Publication data is available from the Library of Congress.
ISBN: 978-0-8173-6127-3
E-ISBN: 978-0-8173-9480-6

Contents

Preface

Michael J. Altman

This is the third volume of *American Examples*, and the second volume compiled during the COVID-19 pandemic. These chapters, like so many other things back in 2021, began on Zoom. The authors presented them from offices, living rooms, couches, and backyards at the American Examples research workshop over two weekends in February and March, 2021. That year was the virtual American Examples program. We adapted our usual workshop format to the new Zoom medium. Pets and children offered welcome interruptions. Discussions happened in the chat, while others went on across the tiles of faces on our screens. We checked in on each other during each of the workshops across 2021 as some of us in the group moved from virtual to hybrid to even in-person teaching. Despite the distance and the screens and the weirdness of 2021, another cohort of American Examples came together and built a scholarly community. This book is a testament to how hard everyone in that group worked amid everything that was happening. I am so proud of these early-career scholars and so thankful for everything they did to make American Examples a success in 2021.

For all the challenges that American Examples faced in 2021, it also found new opportunities. Because we shifted to a virtual format, lodging and airfare costs were not limiting factors on the size of our group. This led to the biggest cohort of participants in the program's short history. That also means there are more essays in this volume than in either of the previous two. The shift to a virtual format also allowed us to experiment with new forms of public humanities scholarship. We tried to learn animation on the fly and produced a YouTube video series (1-800-REL-HELP, a hotline for answers to all your religious studies questions). We got better at audio editing and made a few podcast episodes, too. We tried to build stuff and make stuff. Not all of it worked. But, to me, that's the thing at the center of American Examples: try stuff, build stuff, make stuff, experiment.

As I write this preface, we are just over a month away from the final in-person workshop for the 2022 American Examples cohort. After a virtual teaching workshop in March, we held an in-person research workshop in Tuscaloosa, Alabama, in April. It was the first in-person American Examples event since March 2020. It was excellent. We threw a party on the last night and ate barbecue from a local food truck. The papers from that workshop will fill volume 4 of *American Examples*. We are also headed toward an in-person workshop series in 2023. We are excited to begin this new era of American Examples.

None of this would be possible without the support of many different people. We are once again most grateful to the Henry Luce Foundation for the funding that makes these volumes, these workshops—and that barbecue—possible. Jonathan VanAntwerpen has been flexible and helpful as we navigated all the changes the pandemic brought to our program. I am deeply grateful to my colleagues in the Department of Religious Studies at the University of Alabama who also make this program possible. Steven Ramey and Vaia Touna mentored the research workshop where these chapters began. Merinda Simmons, Russell McCutcheon, Richard Newton, and Nathan Loewen all pitched in on the other virtual workshops in 2021. Erica Bennet, Ciara Eichhorst, and Sonya Harwood-Johnson worked hard as the American Examples Fellows, and I am grateful for the ways they made the program run smoothly and helped this book make it to press. I am also grateful to Dan Waterman and Kristen Hop at the University of Alabama Press for their support and work on these volumes. American Examples has been successful because all these people are part of it.

The prefaces to these volumes have become an annual moment to take stock of this thing we have all imagined together—and by "we" I mean all those people mentioned above and all the current and previous program participants. Four years and three anthologies into this thing, I think American Examples has become a place for people to do work in the study of religion that they might not be able to do somewhere else. I have heard people describe this or that dissertation or book manuscript as an "American Examples project." I am still not sure exactly what that means, but I hope it means that American Examples is here for the projects, the ideas, the arguments, and the scholars who might not find an audience in other parts of the study of religion or the study of religion in America. If that is the case, that is something everyone involved with American Examples should be proud of.

American Examples

Introduction

Situating American Examples

CODY MUSSELMAN, ERIK KLINE, AND DANA LLOYD

In its third year, American Examples has yet again brought together a cohort of young scholars to put the "examples approach" into practice in the study of American religion. As Michael Altman explains in the introduction to the first *American Examples* volume, the "examples approach" uses different instances of "something someone calls religion somewhere someone calls America" to interrogate the first-order terms—for instance, "religion" and "America"—that set the boundaries of religious study in the Americas and to theorize anew the parameters of the American religious history subfield.[1] Rather than approaching their subjects of study as if the religiosity or Americanness of their examples was taken for granted, American Examples scholars have sought to reanimate the terms of their study and use their subjects to rethink both what counts as religion and what counts as America. By moving beyond these first-order concerns, the essays and examples throughout the series aim to raise questions and offer insights that are transferable to other times and places. The present volume continues this line of inquiry and broadens the dialogic scope between various disciplines.

This rethinking and retheorizing has not happened within a vacuum, however, as this interdisciplinary group of scholars have likewise been responding to recent calls from American studies to expand the study of the Americas beyond its geographical boundaries and to think about America through its tendrils of empire, military power, political influence, and commerce that have spread throughout the world.[2] In this line of thinking, America not only becomes a location of transnational and transhemispheric consequence, but also begins to resemble a many-headed beast. These calls highlight how the concept of "America" is multifaceted and can mean different things at different times in different places to different people. Likewise, "religion" is a historically difficult concept to contain, define, and examine, and the field of religious studies is continually at odds over how to manage religion's tendency to exceed its definitional bounds. In short, neither religion nor America now serves as the neat conceptual containers they were once thought to be. And yet, embracing the messy complexity of these terms opens up new space for thinking about how they operate and, crucially, for analyzing their relationship to each other. While the contributors to this third volume of *American Examples* resist any assertion of American exceptionalism, the essays collected here—and indeed, the series as a whole—highlight how dislodging the first-order terms underlying the study of religion in America generates a fecund space for reconsidering religion and place.

THE EXAMPLES APPROACH

The overarching goal of the *American Examples* series is to collectively raise a new set of big questions through a close analysis of specific examples. Such questions are, as Altman explains in his introduction to the first volume of the series, about "how society works, how social groups work, how difference is managed and disciplined, how identities are formed and re-formed, how movements form and disperse, how the nation-state governs, how truth regimes are authorized," and not least of all how the categories of "religion" and "America" are made and remade.[3] In their contributions to *American Examples,* American religion scholars use the "examples approach" to arrive at and interact with the aforementioned big questions through what we call the "third thing"—a concept that grew out of discussions of what Jonathan Z. Smith called the "third term."[4] As Altman detailed in the introduction to volume one, the "third thing" asks scholars to examine both their object (thing one) and their analysis of their object (thing two) and seek "a more generic pattern" that is portable, such that other scholars and thinkers from different disciplines, time periods, and geographies can find utility in it. The purpose of identifying the "third thing" is to create broader conversations within the academic study of religion and reach toward common curiosities, conceptual problems, and theories. In a sense, by focusing on the "third thing," American Examples scholars are seeking to refurbish a kind of comparative religions approach for the twenty-first century. By acknowledging that both "religion" and "America" are open-ended categories that various parties are invested in producing, emphasis on the "third thing" helps to make conversations that might once have been thought of as particular to American religious history into shared conversations with scholars in other disciplines. In short, the "third thing" honors specificity and expertise, yet underscores the importance of transportable and comparable ideas for opening up a broader dialogue around some of humanity's most pressing questions.

While we recognize a great deal of promise in the examples approach, we note that, at times, focusing on the restricted scope of one example may appear limiting and myopic. Prea Persaud and Samah Choudhury highlight this shortcoming in their introduction to volume two of the *American Examples* series. They call attention to how the essays featured within the volume do not adequately address or reflect the environment of protest, racial violence, and political fervor that animated the 2020 context during which the essays were revised. In their efforts to make ideas about American religion transportable and comparable, the contributors missed an opportunity to reflect upon how their own social locations, identities, and races would necessarily influence their selection of "third things" and inform the big questions they asked. Persaud and Choudhury's critique highlights how the works of scholarship within the American Examples approach are shaped by the conditions of their construction. This important insight prompts us, as editors, to reflect upon the context in which the contributors to the present volume conducted their research, wrote and reflected upon their examples, and arrived at their "third things."

"THIRD THINGS" IN CONTEXT

For the past several years, one event, more than any other, has provided the backdrop for all other reflection and analysis: the COVID-19 pandemic. This is particularly noteworthy because this third volume of *American Examples* features the first cohort of scholars to come together in an entirely virtual setting. Even though much of the research presented in the following essays predated the pandemic, we couldn't help but see the influence of life's uncertainty under COVID-19 in the essays collected here. In reading and organizing them, we noticed how the authors paid special attention to temporal and spatial boundaries. We began wondering if this focus on space and the past, present, and future resulted from the precarity of our contemporary moment, a moment that in all our quarantine and isolation has demanded reevaluation of one's place in time and culture.

Quarantining and following social distancing practices necessitated confining one's physical self to a circumscribed area, whether a neighborhood, a house, an apartment, or even just a room. Space began to take on new importance, with an increase in home renovation projects, a swell of city-dwellers swapping out their small apartments for suburban or country homes, and a constant evaluation of how much space or distance to put between oneself and the nearest other person. Concerns of space were ever present. And just as space contracted, so too did time. The predictable routines of everyday life were upended, making time feel foreign.

The present never quite felt present in quarantine. Rather, we lived presently by remembering what people called the "before-times," or imagining some fleeting future when everything would be "back to normal." The longer we endured quarantine, though, the further away—and fuzzier—the before-times became; it also became clearer that returning to "normal" was something not just unachievable, but undesirable. Amid the Black Lives Matter protests, a heated election that resulted in an insurrection at the nation's capitol, unprecedented climate crises including southern hurricanes and western wildfires, and, of course, a pandemic that only emphasized the fatal shortcomings of the US healthcare system, we doomscrolled through our isolated days with a recognition that those romanticized before-times had led us to this anxious present. As time wore on, conversations shifted away from efforts to get "back to normal" and toward embracing a "new normal." This phrase, "the new normal," reflected a reluctant acceptance of the grip the virus held over our lives and routines, yet it also evoked confusion and contemplation: What was the timeframe of normal? What was the feeling of normal? And if we didn't like this timing, this feeling, or this normal, then what might we do to imagine a different future with a different kind of normalcy?

The pandemic underscored how existential questions about space and time are an enduring part of the human experience, even when they are temporarily dulled by the doomscrolling, made subconscious by our workaholism, or sidelined in service of more urgent caregiving duties. Yet the disruption caused by the pandemic also created new opportunities for reflection on the big questions that animate life. In this way, the contributors to this volume could see the goal of American Examples reflected in our culture at large. What was "America," in a country divided over masking and vaccines? What was "America," when its purchasing power and rampant consumerism was impeded by global supply chain problems? What was "religion," when it went online? To what did we ascribe meaning, when life began to feel meaningless? How was difference managed and disciplined, when a recognition of our commonality and shared suffering was essential for survival? And for each of us: how should we be spending our time on this earth? In the depths of the COVID-19 pandemic, big questions that had always existed under the surface bubbled up with a new urgency.

TIME AND SPACE IN *AMERICAN EXAMPLES*

Some essays in this volume raise time or space as their "third thing" more clearly than others. For example, Chelsea Ebin's essay, "Tomorrow's Past Today," looks at the interplay between imagined pasts and futures in the US Christian right movement, arguing that the movement's idealization of a politically conservative past is a fundamentally modern and future-oriented stance. Addressing revivalism's divine rupture into time, Michael Baysa's "Managing Revival," meanwhile, examines how eighteenth-century ministers debated whether or not the religious revivals of the 1740s counted as true religion. Revivals, with their emotional and performative displays of religious feeling, encouraged a direct and unmediated connection to the divine and, in doing so, introduced a new temporality to popular religious practice in America. In his essay, Baysa highlights the importance of print texts for solidifying the role of revivalism in colonial America's shifting relationship to religion and time. Similarly, Hinasahar Muneeruddin's essay "The Rhythyms of Ritual" argues that the rhythms of poetic ritual offer transformation in a particular moment in time. Finally, Sean Sidky's "We Have No More Prayers" looks back to the Holocaust and examines how Jewish catastrophe literature and Yiddish Holocaust poetry both challenge contemporary literary-religious categorizations and create a community in which future generations can participate. For these essays, considerations of time orient the authors' reflections on religious practice and change in America.

Space was also a major theme, and several of this volume's essays highlight the fraught spatial boundaries inherent to the empire-building project of a colonized America, while others examine the cyberspatial boundaries of modern life, the built environment, and the fragility of borders. Lauren Horn Griffin, in "The Illusion of a #RadTrad Identity," finds that social media spaces like Twitter provide space for imagined communities such as radical traditionalist Catholics. Meanwhile, in "Becoming Hindu in the Greater Caribbean," Alexander Rocklin is similarly interested in how space and identity constitute each other. He looks at how Hindu South Asian merchants navigated strict immigration laws in Panama at the beginning of the twentieth century, and parses out how they equated their religious identity with an elevated racial status to secure free and unencumbered movement throughout the Caribbean and recognition as members of higher rungs within Panama's ethnoracial religious hierarchy. Jaimie Crumley similarly traces movements across borders and racial boundaries in her essay "The Black Queer Theological Tradition of Abolition." She dissects the nineteenth-century memoir of a boundary-defining Black itinerant female preacher, Zilpha Elaw. Crumley follows the peripatetic

Elaw in her transatlantic journey, and identifies in Elaw's theology a queer abolitionist impulse. Similarly, Christopher Bishop's essay "Vessels of Salvation" focuses on a Southern Methodist manual for church architecture from the 1870s. The manual, Bishop argues, codified white southern middle-class standards of taste in its standardization of sacred space. All these essays highlight how space, and the freedom to construct it and move about in it, informs religious identity formation in American history. They also illuminate how paying attention to space can help scholars of religion locate markers of race, gender, class, and status in theorizing religious community and experience.

Some essays move beyond a more conventional spatial analysis and leverage spatial metaphors, like Joshua Urich's essay "Truth Is Never Ridiculous." In this piece, Urich looks at the affect of ridicule in two case studies to show how nineteenth-century Americans were emotionally processing and physically responding to new territorial maps, social boundaries, and claims of religiosity in a century of imperial expansion and scientific innovation. Urich, with his emphasis on P. T. Barnum's "Feejee Mermaid" hoax, demonstrates how the period's affect of ridicule directs readers to geographic limits of "normal" and "other." Lucas Wilson's essay, "Guilt, Anxiety, and S(h)ame-Sex Attraction," examines how gay men occupy heteronormative scripts in overly conservative evangelical spaces, such as Liberty University. He shows how the university's gay conversion therapy program sought to regulate and control queer expressions of sexual desire and gender. While Urich's and Wilson's essays may seem quite different in subject matter, they similarly indicate how different structures of affect and emotion across time functioned in constructing community, identity, and behavioral norms.

No study exists outside of time and space, and the original research and essays featured in this volume are no exception. These essays and their contributors nevertheless reflect a pandemic moment that is uniquely characterized by spatial-temporal stretching and compressing. No aspect of life was untouched by the pandemic, least of all religion. The essays in this volume draw our attention to how different ways of occupying, shaping, and thinking about space and time impact the practice and place of religion.

CONCLUSION

In his foundational work *Critique of Everyday Life,* Henri Lefebvre highlights how scientific and cultural paradigm shifts affect modern existence.[5] He notes that even unremarkable practices often morph into something we might identify as religious community: "human activity tends to become codified in practice, so that festivals, and even the gestures and speech of everyday life, become ritualized."[6] The pandemic changed and upended many activities of everyday life in 2020, making the usual patterns of life irrelevant and forcing new rituals to emerge out of a limited range of activity. While the long-term impact of the pandemic is yet unknown, one reliable constant is an ever shifting conception of "something someone calls religion somewhere someone calls America." As a whole, the American Examples project tracks the evolutions of that slippery concept "American religion" and uses "third things" to identify larger shifts in identity, culture, practice, and community. The essays in this volume collectively rely upon time and space as "third things" to orient their reflections and questions about religious life in America.

Still, a collection is more than the sum of its parts. Just as the individual essays point toward an illuminated "third thing," collecting them and reading them together prompted us to wonder if there might not be some third thing for the volume as a whole. If the examples ultimately highlight third-order concerns that can be transportable, what does their positioning with one another, when collected, highlight? More than just a metatextual concern, the question underscores wider applicability of the examples approach. As discussed earlier, Persaud and Choudhury, in their introduction to volume two, show how this collective third thing—the not-always-visible connective tissue of these studies—can sometimes reveal underlying power structures within and between the collected examples. In other words, when we step back to view the whole, we can see something perhaps not immediately evident at the individual level.

Responding to that question, one possible answer we arrived at is how these chapters variously point to empire generally and to the long reach of America's imperial history specifically. Religious scholars know very well the historical connections between empire and religion, and how religious thought and practice have been wielded for imperial and colonial control. Some of the essays here point to this influence explicitly, but all do so implicitly. Indeed, the ways in which American empire often lurks behind the scenes reflects the historical tendency of the United States to mask its imperial ambitions behind both conceptual myths and geographic demarcation. In *How to Hide an Empire* Daniel Immerwahr reminds us that "*empire* is not [only] about a country's character, but its shape."[7] As we examine the spatial and temporal shape of American religion, we necessarily learn about the shape of the American empire. Throughout the essays gathered here, we see how this space changes in geographic, technological, and conceptual iterations.

Still, what distinguishes the American Examples approach is its conscious attention to portability. While we see the imprint of American empire throughout the collection, we cannot claim that it is the sole—or even primary—unifying thread. Students and scholars alike can approach the series with an eye for both the broad and particular; indeed, the American Examples ethos invites new ways of observing, connecting, and theorizing the very fluid terms of religion (whatever that is) in America (wherever that might be). With that spirit in mind, we invite readers to consider the examples in this volume and to continue the conversations about the many third things they find.

NOTES

1. *American Examples*, vol. 1, ed. Michael Altman (Tuscaloosa: University of Alabama Press, 2020), 1.

2. For more on the transnational turn in American studies, see Shelley Fisher Fishkin, "Crossroads of Cultures: The Transnational Turn in American Studies: Presidential Address to the American Studies Association, November 12, 2004," *American Quarterly* 57, no. 1 (2005): 17–57; Nina Morgan and Alfred Hornung, *The Routledge Companion to Transnational American Studies*. (New York: Routledge, 2015); Shelley Fisher Fishkin, "From the Editors," *Journal of Transnational American Studies* 1, no. 1 (2009).

3. *American Examples, Vol. 1*, 19–20.

4. Jonathan Z. Smith, *Drudgery Divine: On the Comparison of Early Christianities and the Religions of Late Antiquity* (Chicago: University of Chicago Press, 1990), 33, 99.

5. Henri Lefebvre, *Critique of Everyday Life: The One-Volume Edition*, translated by John Moore and Gregory Elliott (New York: Verso, 2014), 150.

6. Lefebvre, *Critique of Everyday Life*, 224.

7. Daniel Immerwahr, *How to Hide an Empire: A History of the Greater United States* (New York: Farrar, Straus, and Giroux, 2019), 400.

We Have No More Prayers

Speech, Silence, and Communal Identity in American Yiddish Holocaust Poetry

SEAN SIDKY

Scholarship on Holocaust literature in the United States through the late 1950s and into the 1960s was primarily interested in the mechanisms by which survivors attempted to communicate their experiences of concentration camps, thought by scholars of the time to be incommunicable, even unimaginable to any who did not experience them.[1] This position holds that the Holocaust is historically and even ontologically unique and, as such, fundamentally exceeds the possibilities of artistic or linguistic communication. Shared by scholars and survivors alike, this position quickly became a central feature of public discourse surrounding Holocaust memory and memorialization in the United States.

The extreme nature of this representative claim has not limited its popularity among writers, though its presence in scholarship has diminished in recent years. Numerous post-Holocaust writers, especially in the United States, have insisted on the need for what survivor Elie Wiesel called a "fresh vocabulary, a primeval language."[2] Yet, writers consistently draw on metaphors, genres, and forms whose history is either embedded within the European history that led to the Holocaust, or (and the two are not exclusive) part of a long tradition of Jewish literary responses to catastrophe.

The centrality of survivor testimony continues to shape the landscape of the field, though the concerns of Holocaust literary scholarship have changed significantly in the intervening decades. It was not until the late 1970s that studies of Holocaust literature began to seriously engage with poetry as a medium for responding to the Holocaust, with scholars such as Lawrence Langer and Alvin Rosenfeld focusing in particular on the nonreferential functions of poetic language. This capacity of poetry to be nonrepresentative allowed these scholars to avoid the still present assumption of unrepresentability that underwrote and motivated much of their scholarly work.[3]

In 1984, the parallel publication of Alan Mintz's *Ḥurban,* and David Roskies's *Against the Apocalypse* shifted the field toward a historically embedded approach that emphasized the place of Holocaust literature within its literary and cultural traditions.[4] By tracing the development of literary forms and themes from their earliest instantiations in the Bible to the literature of the post-Holocaust period, these two texts have allowed us to recognize common features that make up a diachronic tradition of Jewish literary responses to catastrophe. Though Mintz and Roskies both see the Holocaust as distinct in some ways from other historical catastrophes, they foreground the role of literary tradition in shaping the linguistic and artistic mechanisms by which writers are able to confront the Holocaust. That is, whatever the nature of the Holocaust, writers have a limited toolbox out of which to respond to the events. As such, their works revive, recall, and transform traditional modes of literary expression in order to draw connections between past and present in forming their responses to the Holocaust.

For the Jews of Europe, the tragedies of the past, memorialized in literature and integrated into patterns and rituals of Jewish remembrance and mourning, served for generations as a heuristic for interpreting the complex events of the present. This was especially true for the Jews of Eastern Europe through the nineteenth and early twentieth centuries, who were "schooled in the exercises of collective memory," as Roskies puts it, by a century of state oppression and pogroms. Many elements of the Holocaust—ghettos, exile, mass murder, even the yellow stars—were part of recognizable patterns of oppression.[5] Far more than previous persecutors, the Nazis paid particular attention to Jewish history in constructing the symbolic landscape of the destruction. All of this is part of the religio-cultural memory that became textualized, and thus evoked, in literary responses to the Holocaust as writers, faced with the resurgence of Jewish catastrophe history enacted in the Holocaust, turned to historical texts as models for their own writing.

Holocaust literature in Yiddish is inseparable from this tradition of interpretation. This is equally true of the Yiddish Holocaust literature composed in the United States. Written in response to incomplete news arriving in irregular bursts, and motivated by the dual need to interpret that information and to understand its implications for Jewish life and communal existence in the

United States, the American Yiddish Holocaust poetry that I will examine here is not interested in questions of unspeakability, driven as it is by the *need* for speech. Embedded in Jewish literature, history, and theology, this poetry understands the Holocaust both in the context of and as a challenge to the interpretive frameworks that Jewish tradition offers.

Yet, as a result of the historical development of the field of Holocaust literature, as well as the reception history of the Holocaust in the United States, distinct hierarchies remain among the texts and witnesses to the Holocaust that exclude this American Yiddish literature. This reflects a hierarchy that developed within the postwar community. As historian Raul Hilberg notes, there was an "unmistakeable rank order among the Jews who lived through the wartime Nazi years. In this hierarchy, the decisive criteria are exposure to risk and depth of suffering. Members of communities that were left intact and people who continued to live in their own homes are hardly considered survivors at all. At the other end of the scale, individuals who emerged from the woods or the camps are the survivors par excellence."[6] Despite continuing efforts at expanding the borders of the genre, this hierarchy continues to shape the boundaries over what constitutes and counts *as* Holocaust literature.

David Roskies and Naomi Diamant's recent attempt at redefining the genre makes clear moves to expand its scope.[7] Their definition is the most inclusive offered thus far: "Holocaust literature comprises all forms of writing, both documentary and discursive, and in any language, that have shaped the public memory of the Holocaust and been shaped by it."[8] Yet, in several ways it acts to reinforce the essentializing binaries established by prior scholarship. In particular, in their survey of wartime literature they remain fixed on a geographical binary between what they call the "Jew Zone" of Nazi-controlled Europe, and the oddly titled "Free Zone" that comprises the entire rest of the world. For wartime literature in the "Free Zone," such as American Yiddish poetry, to *count* as Holocaust literature, it must satisfy the additional criterion of aiming to motivate political action. Their framework relies on retroactive judgment of a text's reception and its impact on public memory, rather than its content or composition, as the primary criterion for its inclusion within "Holocaust literature." It thereby limits us to engaging with only the most widely read texts, thus reinforcing the boundaries of the established literary canon.

No works of American Yiddish Holocaust literature can be said to have had a significant impact or influence on the public memory. Even the most widely read American Yiddish poem, Yankev Glatshteyn's "Good Night, World" (1938), is limited to a secular Yiddish-speaking readership and a small number of Yiddish literature or Holocaust literature scholars.[9] Neither can these writers, who composed their texts as responses to the influx of limited information from Nazi-controlled Europe, have been significantly influenced by public memory, nor were they working within a space of remembrance as later survivor writings would. Finally, and crucially, we also cannot say with any certainty that the writers of these poems had political mobilization as their aim, given that they were writing in Yiddish for a diasporic and largely politically disenfranchised Yiddish-speaking community, whose members were all at least as aware of the events in Europe as the poem's authors.

The poems discussed in this essay present a distinctive challenge to the systems of categorization that inform even the most inclusive scholarly definitions of Holocaust literature. Drawing on established forms and discourses within the tradition of Jewish catastrophe literature, the poems I examine here are monologues articulated by speakers witnessing and responding to the destruction of Europe's Jews from positions of relative safety. At the same time, they recognize, and feel, the existential threat the destruction poses to the Jewish community as a whole, to *Jewishness* itself, and refuse any sense that the Holocaust's impact is limited to its physical destruction. This essay argues that these poetic speakers recognize and acknowledge the duality of their positions: they are both members of, *among*, the community being destroyed, and enabled by their physical safety to speak. They are not survivors, nor are they the dead, but they understand the extent of the destruction to encompass the entirety of the Jewish community, religion, history, and futurity, and they write from within this space.

Following a discussion of the origins of the Jewish catastrophe tradition as a foundation for the rest of the argument, this essay will offer close readings of three American Yiddish Holocaust poems: two by Kadye Molodovsky (1874–1975), who began her career in Warsaw before relocating to New York in 1935. The two poems I discuss below are taken from her collection of Holocaust poetry, *Only King David Remained*, written beginning in 1941 and published in 1946.[10] The third poem is Yankev Glatshteyn's (1896–1971) aforementioned "Good Night, World," first published in 1938. Glatshteyn, who was born in Lublin and emigrated to New York in 1914, was, like Molodovsky, a prolific poet, editor, and major figure in the New York Yiddish literary milieu.

To illuminate the complexity of this position, I read these poems as *monologues*. They all take the form of first-person speeches given by a single speaker and directed at a specific, identifiable addressee. This addressee is not given voice within the poem, and a response from them is either not expected or, as we will see below, entirely structurally precluded. As an interpretive framework, encountering these poems as monologues allows us to foreground several aspects: first, we can recognize and engage with the construction of the poetic speaker themselves. Though scholarship on Holocaust literature is especially prone to collapsing the speaker into the identity of the author, the voice discernible within a given work of literature is as much a constructed feature as meter or rhyme. Understanding these poems as monologues allows us to see the uncertainty that informs a poetic speaker's construction of their own position, both in relation to their silent addressee and in relation to the community among which they place themselves and from which they speak. It allows a speaker to give voice to their thoughts and emotions, and, crucially, to give those emotions direction and form.

Second, monologue emphasizes the diegetic construction of the poem's addressee: monologues require the existence of a rhetorical addressee, but do not necessarily require the addressee to be responsive, or even to be listening. They are a function of the poetic language. This is particularly useful because the most common monologic forms in Jewish catastrophe literature closely resemble prayer and liturgy and, as such, are directed toward God. In part this is because the monologue form is foundational to the history of Jewish catastrophe literature: from its initial instantiation in the book of Lamentations, Jewish poetic responses to catastrophe have taken the form of speeches directed at an absent divine.

Finally, by employing recognizable and historically prevalent forms, these poems draw parallels in the minds of their readers between individual poems and the literary tradition from which those forms are drawn. Although it assumes much on the part of the reader, form is another critical tool by which readers can draw connections between texts, and by which the conceptual and thematic world of a poem is expanded. Like biblical reference or allusion, like the language of prayer and liturgy, within the tradition of Jewish catastrophe literature, the monologue is another critical point in a constellation of references, a shared vocabulary through which readers can identify with the poetic speaker and begin to recognize *themselves* as among the community of suffering for which the poem speaks.

This essay argues that the monologic structure of this poetry allows the speaking voices to draw from and transform traditions of Jewish response to catastrophe in order to articulate their distinctive positionality. These poetic responses to catastrophe create spaces of communal engagement and identification grounded in but not reducible to the religious and literary traditions that inform their construction. The speakers of these poems speak from within a community under threat. Though theirs is a position of relative safety, as a result of that safety, they are forced to encounter the Holocaust as a threat to the possibility of Jewish existence itself, to their own identities as individuals and as communities.

This essay demonstrates that literary responses to catastrophe function as a process of articulation and rearticulation, an ongoing dialogue between present experience and inherited tradition (in this case both religious and literary) into which readers enter as they engage with the text. American Yiddish Holocaust poetry models one way in which a collective is constituted in the face of catastrophe, through the invocation of a shared literary and religious tradition, in order to form a common vocabulary for voicing the experience of witnessing that destruction from a distance, and with that, creating the possibility for a communal identity to emerge, grounded in the literary response to catastrophe itself. Literary response to catastrophe thus creates space for new forms of communal identification among its readership, emerging from a recognition of one's own position in relation to the destruction, a geographically and temporally unbounded space of identification in which even future generations might participate, recognizing themselves in the act of reading as implicated in the suffering here being given voice.

ANCIENT INHERITANCES

Lamentations, the ur-text of Jewish catastrophe, is an extended poetic response to the destruction of Jerusalem in 587 BCE. The importance of this disaster, especially the loss of the Temple of Jerusalem, is hard to overstate: it remains one of the chief elements, if not the centerpiece, of the Jewish liturgical tradition. The Holocaust is often referred to in Yiddish as "the third destruction," placing it on a continuum of destruction that began with this event, followed by the destruction of the Second Temple in 70 CE. The centrality of this event to Jewish communal memory is due in no small part to the intensity of the rhetorical and dramatic movement of Lamentations itself.

Lamentations 3, in particular, is a turning point in the poem's narrative and a marked shift in the perspective of the poem as a response to catastrophe. The first line of the chapter introduces the poetic speaker as a definable figure and feature of the poem rather than a disembodied omniscient voice: "I am the man who has known affliction under the rod of his wrath" (3:1).[11] Both speaking for Israel as a whole, and establishing their own identity within the narrative of the poem, at this line a single, identifiable voice suddenly reframes Lamentations as an extended monologue. Thus, Lamentations 3 introduces, as a foundational concern of Jewish catastrophe literature, the complex duality of the catastrophe speaker's position as individual witness affected by disaster and as speaker for the nation.

The development of this position over the course of Lamentations 3 is complex: as the individual speaker enumerates the list of troubles they have suffered at the hands of God, the poetic "I" is gradually replaced by the nonspecific "man," the generalized object of God's wrath. When the first-person voice resurfaces at the culmination of a long theological monologue that attempts to find reason for God's punishment, it has transformed once again. Coinciding, crucially, with the desperate insistence that there *must* be some reason for this destruction, even if it remains unknown, it is not the poetic "I" that returns, but the collective "we." "Let us search and examine our ways, and turn back to the Lord" (3:40).

Mintz reads this as a transformation of the speaker's relationship to the people. He argues that, at the opening of Lamentations 3, the speaker acts only with a mind to their own suffering and that over the course of the chapter they discover a "capacity for empathy" that leads the speaker to assume "the role of an advocate of his people's cause before God."[12] Ultimately, this leads to a total sublimation of the individual speaker into the collective. This is the *aim* of Lamentations, Mintz claims, uniting the people into a singular expressive voice, in the service of the book's broader attempt to find an explanation for God's actions in the face of his absolute silence.[13]

Reading Lamentations as the beginning of a continuum of *monologic* catastrophe poetry, however, reminds us of the importance of retaining the identity of the individual speaker even as they serve as representative for the collective. Where Mintz sees the transformation as culminating in an act of "self-transcendence," I argue that the opening lines of this chapter, the long list of sufferings the speaker has endured, *enable* the emergence of the collective voice alongside the speaker's.[14] Looking outward from Lamentations 3 to engage the entirety of Lamentations as a monologue, we can read these moments of self-description not as an inability to imagine anything beyond their own persecution, as Mintz puts it, but rather as a recognition that they *have also been persecuted*.[15] Rather than reading Lamentations 3 as the *sole* site of critical poetic reflection, understanding it as an extended monologue retroactively marks the first two chapters as part of a developing narrative of the speaker's self-awareness. No longer is the poetic voice of the first two books *merely* a passive observer, as it had seemed in the description of the terrible fate that befell Zion and its people; now we understand these chapters to be recounting a fate in which the speaker is *both* witness *and* victim.

The collective "we" remains prominent through the final chapters, though the focus can no longer be solely on the fate of the nation. Instead, the poem-as-monologue pushes us to reconsider the distinction between the individual and the collective, because the collective experience of destruction *necessarily* includes the individual. Only the most cynical reader would read an individual victim's lament as negating the suffering of others in their community. Rather, the poetic "I" enables the people to have a voice for their collective suffering, because the poetic speaker is also one of the victims and, as such, is *always* speaking for the community, even when speaking of themselves alone.

This carefully held dual positioning characterizes the speaker of Molodovsky's accusatory prayer-poem, "Havdole," acutely aware of both their role as speaker for the community and their own physical distance from the destruction to which they respond.[16] "Havdole" is directly addressed to God, calling on him to create a new world in which the Jewish people will no longer be among the other peoples who have betrayed and destroyed them. "God of Abraham, / Make us a second Creation."[17] For Yiddish-speaking readers, the title situates the poem immediately within a liturgical tradition. "Havdole," for which the poem is named, is a set of prayers that mark the conclusion of the Sabbath, and thus the distinction between the sacred, set-aside time of rest, and the mundane time that begins at the setting of the sun that evening.

The first line of the poem confirms the choice of title: the opening epithet "God of Abraham" belongs to a specific Havdole prayer, a *tkhine*, or Yiddish-language women's prayer, that entreats God to continue to protect the Jewish people. Within the tradition of Jewish catastrophe literature, as we will see below, it is implicitly understood that God will not respond to even the most intense cry. And here, paired with the impossibility of the request for a "second Creation," and the deep tragedy of the events that inspire the poem, the destruction called the Holocaust, the invocation of a prayer for protection must be read as both deeply despairing and painfully ironic. Writing is "rooted in ancient inheritances," Molodovsky wrote in 1971.[18] By beginning with such an address, and ironically employing this piece of common liturgy, this poem announces itself as embedded within the traditions of Jewish catastrophe literature, and also as sitting in complex relation to that tradition, part of a parallel history of utilizing liturgical modes of expression against the divine.

Though I focus on the diegetic speakers of these poems, given the history of the field, it is nearly impossible to encounter American Yiddish Holocaust poetry *without* being reminded that the author did not directly experience the Holocaust. A careful reading of "Havdole" reveals the presence of a speaker acutely aware of their own separation in time and space from the portion of the collective who suffers the terrible fate they recount. This kind of poetic speech is enabled by such physical distance. Rather than claiming to have been present within the ghettos and camps, Molodovsky's speakers position themselves within, and speak on behalf of, a collective that contains not only those who died or are dying at the hands of the Nazis but also those who remained outside of Europe, on whose shoulders the burden of memory and memorialization now falls. Here is the full text of the poem:

HAVDOLE

God of Abraham,
Make us a second Creation.
May no sun shine there—
The light has betrayed us anyway.
May the wind not sing there—
Together with the Germans it has driven
Our people to the slaughter-workshop
May no greener sea roar there—
It sank the ships—planks
With our last escapees.
May the mountains there not rip the sky with their peaks—
They did not block the way for the murderers,
To protect a small child.
We renounce beauty.
We renounce courage.
We renounce hymns.
May Einstein leave no heir.
We are excommunicated together
With the divine naïve one, Spinoza.

Make us a world with a strip of sky
And once a year a star should shine there,
And make *Havdole*, and divine interpretation:
This is a second Creation,
Outside the world of the Germans,
Outside the wisdom of blood.
And the children under this strip of sky will
Answer: Amen and Amen.

The insistence on the collective is a purposeful reminder against a reading that would dismiss a poem because of its having been written, for example, in the United States during the Holocaust. To do so would undercut the significance of the communal destruction insisted on therein: it is *we* who have been destroyed, not *them*. Even at its most distant the poem refuses to allow the reader to imagine themselves as separate from the collective, claiming ownership of those who have been murdered. Taking the poem as monologue, as speech, reaffirms the importance of the communal identity being here constructed, grounded in the need for the poetic speaker to be *both* distanced from the destruction *and* caught up in it as a communal catastrophe. Moreover, in explicitly claiming its own distance from Europe, the poem forcefully reminds us that the scope of this collective "we" contains more than the direct victims and survivors; it includes the readers of the poem as well, Yiddish-speaking Jews in the United States.

This is the specific burden that American Yiddish Holocaust poetry must bear: it is written for, and thereby works to *construct*, a community of readers who do not yet understand their own relationship to the Holocaust. In fact, the ability of these poems to function as catastrophe literature at all requires their readership to be sufficiently familiar with the events to which they refer, and also with the religious tradition within which they operate, to recognize the complexity of the collective position being articulated by the poetic speakers, as well as their own relationship to or within that collective. That is to say, these monologue poems require the readership to first recognize this form, the unanswered monologue to God, as part of the liturgical tradition that begins in Lamentations. The recourse to traditional form and simultaneous insistence on collective speech thus enables both the speaker and the poem's readers to reconcile their own physical position with their experience of a larger, existential catastrophe that necessarily includes the entire Jewish community.

WE HAVE NO MORE PRAYERS

The most noticeable *thematic* feature of "Havdole" and Molodovsky's other direct renunciation of the divine, "God of Mercy," is that they are addressed to God who does not and will not answer.[19] In addition to an identifiable speaker, monologue poems require a specific, diegetic addressee, someone within the framework of the poem itself to whom the monologue is being delivered. Despite the silence of the addressee, they remain a crucial enabling force within these poems, providing direction and focus to the poetic voice's articulated thoughts and experiences: even if the addressee's actual existence is in doubt, their purpose is to *be spoken to*.

Though both of Molodovsky's poems take the form of prayers, prayer is not necessarily monologic. Rather, this feature has emerged out of the conditions that have produced Jewish catastrophe literature. Within the framework of the Bible, prayers could be and often were answered, both verbally and with action. God could reasonably be assumed to be listening, or even to be actively present. This is the central theological problem of Lamentations: the destruction of the Temple brought with it the loss of the people's mechanism for communicating and thus reconciling with God. It is *this* loss, more than the physical destruction, that created the need for a text like Lamentations. Without a means of reconciliation and dialogue with the divine, the destruction cannot be made to fit into the cycle of sin, punishment, and redemption that characterizes a Jewish theological conception of history.

Lamentations is unable to reclaim active dialogue with God. Rather, its success, according to Mintz, lies in the transformation of the speaker's experience of the first two chapters—*absolute* rejection by God—so as to recover God as "an addressable other."[20] Yet, as Mintz concedes, this "can distract but momentarily from the unmoved fact that God neither speaks nor acts. Nowhere in Lamentations is there the least trace of a divine response."[21] The most we can say that the poetic speaker of Lamentations achieves is establishing a paradigm of expression in which God *might* speak: Lamentations ultimately grants the last word to a God who even then remains silent.

The silence of God within Lamentations created a new communicative paradigm within Jewish literature as the first instance of prayer untethered from God. By the time that modern writers are composing their responses to the Holocaust, even the vestigial hope that is retained in Lamentations is rarely imaginable. In fact, through centuries of continued destruction, the tradition of Jewish catastrophe literature had already become characterized by an assumption of God's absence, with each successive catastrophe reinforcing the inevitability of silence. Thus, when these poems mirror the structure of prayers, they speak from within a long tradition built on the understanding that God will not respond to their pleas.

Both of Molodovsky's poems take this assumption and extend it into the demands they make of God: words alone could not suffice as a response to either "Havdole" or "God of Mercy," poems that call for action. Not *just* action, either, but a reimagination of the very terms of Jewish existence and, in the case of "Havdole," of the world itself. In the face of such demands, speech without accompanying action would serve only to exacerbate the crises faced by the speaker, reminding them of the failure of God to act.

There is no *need* for a divine response in "Havdole." The poem carries a single thought from beginning to end: the first half recounts the failures of the world and the reasons for the speaker's desired separation, and the second half lays out the kind of world that would be acceptable as recompense. The new world is noticeably more distant from the world of recognizable prayer and liturgy: "Havdole" comes only once a year; the Jews are no longer part of the broader world, and, presumably, prayers for protection like the *tkhine*, referenced by the first line, are no longer necessary. In this way, the poem's closing moments are thematically analogous to the better known "God of Mercy," over the course of which Molodovsky entreats God to take away the chosenness of the Jews.

In addition to ending with calls to action that preclude verbal responses, both poems structurally resist the possibility of God speaking. "Havdole" closes with the familiar phrase, "amen and amen," the general function of which is to mark prayer as complete. Here it is tinged with irony, as the world in which the words will be uttered is one in which God is effectively removed from daily life. Where the conceptual development of Lamentations is incomplete because it rests on the minuscule possibility of God responding, insofar as "Havdole" mirrors the structure of a prayer, it leaves no space for any other voice. Transforming the rhetorical traditions of Lamentations, then, these poems ironically employ the language of prayer and liturgy in the form of *monologue* because to do otherwise (to invite, or even leave open the possibility for dialogic response) would be to cede consolatory authority to a disinterested, absent, or even nonexistent God.

Molodovsky's best-known poem, "God of Mercy," follows a parallel thematic development to "Havdole."[22] It begins by laying out the terrible fate that has befallen the Jewish people, before proposing to or entreating from God a solution that effectively ends the relationship between God and the Jewish people as we know it. Much like that of "Havdole," the monologic structure serves first to heighten the thematic development that the ironic epithet of the title seems to express: God is being admonished, mocked even, for his actions that led to the Holocaust.

Building toward the dramatic final lines, the tone of the poem grows more mocking, angrier, or perhaps just more desperate. At bottom, each stanza is little more than a list: the first, a list of things the Jewish people can no longer do (having been destroyed); the second, a list of the horrors they have faced; and the third, a sardonic list of the ways in which God marks his chosen people. With each repetition, as the collective pile of tragedies grows, it becomes more difficult to read the epithet "God of Mercy" as earnest. Here is the full text of the poem:

God of Mercy

God of Mercy
Choose another people,
Choose.

We are tired of dying and death
We have no more prayers.
Choose another people,
Choose.
We have no more blood
To be a sacrifice.
Our house has become a desert.
Earth is too scarce for our graves,
There are no more lamentations,
No more elegies
In the old books.

God of Mercy,
Sanctify another land,
Another mountain.
We have covered all the fields and every stone
With ash, with holiness.
With the old,
And with the young,
And with babies paid
For every letter of your ten commandments.

God of Mercy,
Lift your fiery brow,
And see the peoples of the world—
Give them prophecies and the days of awe,
In every language they babble your word—
Teach them the acts,
The ways of temptation.

God of Mercy,
Give us simple clothes,
Of shepherds with sheep,
Of blacksmiths at their hammers,
Of washers, of hide-skinners,
And give us one more blessing:
God of Mercy,
Take back from us the divine presence of genius.

Even the final stanza offers a list, this one of mundane (perhaps non-Jewish) occupations that would grant the Jewish people safety in obscurity.

The final instance of the title epithet, in the penultimate line, breaks with the regular structure of beginning each stanza with an entreaty to God. Thus, this final cry is both more dramatic than its previous instantiations and more forceful, marking the request or demand that follows with a level of intensity as yet unseen. It is difficult to imagine a verbal response emerging from this situation, certainly not one that is satisfying to a speaker and people who are asking to be *removed* from the special relationship that is required for such direct communication.

The relationship of this poem to Jewish liturgy is one of the few aspects of any Yiddish-language Holocaust poetry that has been examined by scholars. Here, I draw in particular on the work of David Roskies, who borrows the phrase "sacred parody" from scholarship on British devotional poetry in order to illuminate the relationship that each generation of Jewish catastrophe literature cultivated with the texts and traditions that preceded it. "It is a parody in the double sense. Most directly the sacred text is put to irreverent use, but what triggers this response on the part of the individual sufferers is their desire to imitate the sacrilege, to disrupt the received order of the text in the same way as the enemy, acting at the behest of God, interrupted the order of the world."[23] Parody, Roskies asserts, may be destructive, but it can also be an act of faith if undertaken reverentially, with "self-imposed limitations."[24] How we, as readers, are meant to discern destructive from faithful parody remains unclear but for the caveat that a "faithful" parody should act to "expand the meaning of the text"—in contrast, perhaps, to other forms of parody that impose a singular interpretation.[25]

Though Roskies and others utilize the concept of sacred parody as a means to examine Jewish writers' relationships to their own religious upbringings, this notion of parody—destructive as a means to being generative—serves as a useful analogy for the complex relationship of poetic witnesses to the historical events about which they speak. The desire to be rid of the conditions that produced the Holocaust, such as the chosenness of the Jews, along with the need to express this using tools (language, forms, genres) that are themselves products of those conditions, is a struggle that plagues many Holocaust texts and has been raised by many writers of Holocaust literature.[26]

Both of Molodovsky's poems model themselves on prayer and liturgy as a means to ensconce themselves within a long tradition of Jewish liturgical writing and to employ a language recognizable to a Yiddish-language readership. Recognizing the poem as positioning itself within a tradition of Jewish catastrophe literature is crucial in order to grasp the stakes of the unanswered cries and also to see the community-building function of these impossible requests. These poems muster the form and language of prayer against itself, and against the divine, as a means to open a space for communication about the destruction, God's role in it, and the future of the Jewish people that does not rely on the promise of response implicit in commonplace prayer. Within a Jewish theological framework, as Mintz notes, lamentation is the people's attempt to articulate their response to God's absence, but consolation must be given from the outside: "the discourse of lamentation is the discourse of Israel; consolation is God's."[27] These poems, therefore, reject the idea that the meaning-making capacities of the language of prayer rest on the hope for a response and, as such, attempt to reclaim consolation as a function of the act of articulation itself and, in doing so, to reassert the speaking voice's position within the community for which they speak.

Holocaust poetry is, in some ways, *always* a form of sacred parody, because it fundamentally rests on and derives from a tradition that already sits in ambivalent relationship to its tools. It operates from within a tradition that it claims is insufficient for expressing its present experience, while simultaneously employing that lack as a space for generating meaning, and for forming connections between text and reader. American Yiddish Holocaust poetry purposefully disrupts its received religious and literary traditions, and the interpretive frameworks that they bring, in order to transform it into something concrete and expressible. In the remainder of this essay, I explore one example of sacred parody that extends this disruption beyond Jewish religious and literary traditions, Yankev Glatshteyn's 1938 poem "A gute nakht, velt" [Good Night, World], which takes as its target the enterprise of modernity itself, and the place of the Jewish people within it. First, however, I briefly consider what sacred parody offers beyond the specific case study of American Yiddish Holocaust literature.

At the heart of sacred parody is an intense uncertainty about whether there is any kind of consolatory power left in the traditions of writing, speech, and expression available for use in literary responses to destruction. Sacred parody, considered generally, thus helps to illuminate the double-edged approach of catastrophe literature to the mediums of its expression. Sacred parody might then be thought of as the formal expression of this ambivalence, a continual process of rejecting, utilizing, and transforming the available tools for responding to catastrophe without fully rejecting or accepting any singular system of interpretation or form of response.

It is this relationship, ultimately, that I aim to retain from Roskies's notion, and that I believe offers a model for the category of catastrophe literature more broadly. Sacred parody serves as a shorthand for the ways in which catastrophe literature invokes its inherited traditions, forms, and language in order to destabilize in the minds of readers the connotative baggage those literary features bring with them, thus reflecting in a given form, reference, or allusion, the complexity of the communal position from which a text speaks. To read catastrophe literature, then—that is, recognizing a given text *as* catastrophe literature—is necessarily to bring to bear the reader's own relationship to the traditions invoked and transformed, reimagining the implications and outcomes of that sacred parody in such a way as to position oneself among, and within, the community being created in responding to catastrophe.

I WALLOW IN YOUR DUST

The tone of "Good Night, World" differs dramatically from the poems discussed earlier in this essay: the speaking voice is full of hatred and disgust. Neither the modern world nor the ghetto to which they call for a return are free from their disdain: the modern world is unclean and stinking, the ghetto is full of refuse and dirt. The latter, however, offers a solace that the former does not. There is safety, the poem says, in isolation and separation from the world. The "ghetto" of which the poem speaks is not the ghetto of the Nazis (the first of which was established a year after the poem was written), but the historical ghettos of medieval Europe. Despite all the restrictions they carried for those living within the walls, to the poetic speaker in 1938, the ghetto offered an image of stability and security in separation that was lacking from the world within which they found themselves.[28]

The speaker of this poem is decidedly solitary, searching for a community and a respite from the multiple worlds they find themselves inhabiting. The ambivalent relationship they feel with respect to both the present, modern world and the Jewish past now only existing in their memory gives rise to the tension and anger that move the poem forward. The poetic speaker insists, in fact, on their autonomy and isolation ("At my own command / I go back to the ghetto"), though that claim to autonomy is undone immediately by the repeated reminder that the world has been "devastated" by the "piggish German, hateful Pole, / Amalek thief." The speaker attempts, unsuccessfully, to claim agency, while simultaneously revealing that their yearning for the ghetto is a direct response to the state of the modern world.

Though it lacks the same commitment to the collective voice, "Good Night, World" models a parallel self-transformation to that of the Lamentations speaker. The overt and insistent isolation of the poetic voice here, and their distaste for the "Jewish life" that offers them their only respite, transforms over the course of a few lines into a direct assertion of the importance of membership within a community. Though the poetic speaker insists throughout on their own independence and singularity, the transformative joy that accompanies their final move toward "Jewish life" models for its readership the symbolic formation of a new communal identity. The poetic speaker here does not long for a return to some idealized past; in fact, the ghetto seems an entirely arbitrary image, a recognizable metaphor drawn from Jewish history that serves to represent a world separated, free from the taint of modernity.

Good Night, World

Good night, wide world
Big, stinking world.
Not you, but I slam the gate.
With my long robe,
With my flaming, yellow patch,
With my proud step,
At my own command—
I go back to the ghetto.
Wipe out, trample all converted traces,
I roll around in your refuse,
Praise, praise, praise,
Hunchbacked Jewish life.
A ban, world, on your unclean culture.
Although everything is devastated,
I wallow in your dust,
Sad Jewish life.

Piggish German, hateful Pole,
Amalek thief, land of swilling and gorging,
Limp democracy, with your cold
Sympathy-compresses.
Good night, electrical-insolent world.
Back to my kerosene, tallowy shadows,
Eternal October, minute stars,
To my crooked streets, hunchbacked lanterns,
My torn-out pages, my bible books,
My Talmud, to the difficult
Subjects, to the bright Hebrew-Yiddish,
To law, to deep meaning, to duty, to justice.
World, I stride with joy to the quiet ghetto lights.

Good night. I give you, world, a donation
All my liberators.
Take the jesusmarxes, choke on their courage.
Die over a drop of our baptized blood.
And I have hope that although he lingers,
My waiting goes up day-after-day,
Green leaves will still rustle,
On our tree, withered.
I do not need consolation,
I go back to my four cubits,
From Wagner's pagan-music to melodies, humming.
I kiss you, messy Jewish life.
It cries in me the joy of coming.

The final renunciation must necessarily be symbolic, not only because that world is historically inaccessible, and undesirable, but also because Jewish life *itself* has been hobbled and altered by its own history and interaction with the world. Unlike the political speeches that the poem's tone and structure recall, "Good Night, World" is *not* a call to specific action: the singularity of the voice, the metaphorics of the return, and the impossibility of its achievement work to prevent a tangible path forward. The poem, then, is a call to reconnect with communal histories and traditions at the cost of participation in the modern world.

The most fascinating feature of this poem, when read as a monologue, is that the speaker explicitly addresses the non-Jewish world in a language that the world cannot understand. Anita Norich takes this to indicate that the speaker is *not* in fact addressing the non-Jewish world, but rather speaking figuratively *about* that world to the community of Yiddish readers around them. Norich argues that the poem is a critique of modern Jewish life, pointing to a failure of Jewish artistic, religious, and cultural projects that the speaker locates in the relationship of the Jewish community to modernity itself.[29] As such, she claims, the speaker is calling on the Jewish people to reject the modern, Western world; the poem ought then to be understood as a response not so much to the specific events taking place in Europe that surrounded its composition as to the broad failure of modernity to provide a space for, to recognize, Jewish cultural and artistic projects.

It is possible, however, to take the poem at its word, and to read it as choosing to speak to the non-Jewish world in Yiddish *because* it cannot understand. The speaker's monologue paints a picture of having been shunned by the world, responding to the world's apathy and disdain by (perhaps preemptively) rejecting it in favor of a return to an imagined possibility of Jewish communal isolation. The insistence in the first stanza on the speaker's autonomy reads as bitter and defensive, marking the lines that follow, the celebration of the dirtiness of the ghetto, as gleefully ironic, especially when calling the non-Jewish world "unclean" by contrast. All of this is contained, or perhaps represented, in the irony of an emotional speech directed at an audience who cannot understand a word of it: in calling out to the non-Jewish world in Yiddish, the poetic speaker is actively recognizing the insurmountability of the apathy or rejection that motivates their speech, and formally reifying it.

There is no need for the world to be able to comprehend the words of the poet's rejection because, as readers will inevitably understand, the poem insists that this rejection is, ultimately, *not* "at [their] own command" but instead is the doomed attempt to take control of a situation that is out of their hands. In this way, the poem's rejection of the world is rhetorically identical to the speakers of Lamentations, and of both of Molodovsky's poems: an emotionally charged monologue directed at an addressee who is not listening and will not respond.

As noted above, within the tradition of catastrophe literature that begins with Lamentations, the rejection of consolation *is* a rejection of the promise of God's intervention. Insofar as "Good Night, World" has historically been read as a rallying cry for a return to Jewish self-sufficiency, this line can be read as the most extreme rejection of the possibility of external consolation, implicitly refusing even the tentative promise that is offered at the close of Lamentations. "I do not need consolation," the speaker proclaims finally. Yet, in voicing this despair and frustration, the poem reaches out to its readership: drawing from a constellation of familiar historical reference points and experiences, the speaker offers a model for a *kind* of consolation through the active and agential re-creation of communal identity.

The speaker here thus musters the full weight of the tradition of Jewish catastrophe literature behind their rejection of the divine and the world, and as evidence for the need to reclaim the *search* for communal identity, or the process of articulating a communal identity as an end in and of itself. The monologic structure of this rejection serves to reaffirm its intended audience (distinct from its addressee), and the reflexive aim of the poem that reveals itself fully in the final lines—which turns away from the world for the first and only time to focus on an entirely internalized emotion—as if joy is only possible once that retreat from the world is complete. That is, because the world can offer nothing in response to the speaker's cries, nor indeed can they even understand them, by the final line of the poem, this rejection of the world seems to be less an end itself than a means through which to illuminate for themselves and their audience the value of the turn *toward* the "Jewish life" the speaker had earlier (tentatively) dismissed. It does not matter, ultimately, that the world cannot understand, only that the speech was made, that its readership can engage with it, and that the poetic speaker was able to give voice to their desire to leave the world and the emotions that inspired it.

Norich is particularly taken aback by the dissonance of the poem's title. This is a domestic, mundane farewell, "the last words a person may hear at night, the words a parent speaks to a child."[30] The sudden "apposition of the 'world,'" she claims, is "shocking," revealing a finality akin to death, "a suicidal desire that the line barely masks."[31] Though this reading is at odds with the expressive joy that characterize the final lines of the poem, Norich points to a critical appositional mechanism that motivates any reading of Glatshteyn's poem. I argue, however, that this dissonance occurs most intensely not within the first line, but between the first and second. Although bringing the world into the mundane frame of the opening line is odd, it still suits the kind of nursery, lullaby-like affect of that address. There is comfort in the line still, as if the world is at rest along with the poetic speaker; it hardly prepares us for the intense affective shift that characterizes the rest of the poem. The nostalgic comfort of the opening phrase is *immediately* undone by the second line, a sudden tonal shift that enacts in the affective realm the same betrayal attested to by the poetic speaker: the illusion of comfort and solace, followed by the revelation of depravity and filth.

Each of the poems discussed in this chapter enacts an analogous transformation, and all do so within their first two lines. The opening lines of these poems are loaded referents for the Yiddish reader, connoting an entire history of liturgy, prayer, and communication with the divine or with the world. The speed with which these poems signal their departure from, or transformation of, those traditional modes of expression is surprising, true. For the reader encountering these poems in the context of their original publication, however, either during or immediately after the Holocaust, or within the author's published collection of Holocaust poetry, and familiar with the very traditions that these lines invoke, that shift is part of the encounter with catastrophe literature. Here I present the opening lines of the three together, for comparison:

> God of Abraham,
> Make us a second Creation.[32]
>
> God of Mercy
> Choose another people,[33]

Good night, wide world
Big, stinking world.[34]

The tradition is grounded in a dissonance between inherited modes of expression and demands made by the experiential intensity of the present. All three of these poetic speakers intentionally draw on and manipulate these recognizable forms of literary expression as a means to frame the reader's encounter with the text, and to reenact in the textual realm the radical disruption to which the poems themselves respond.

Reading these poems together allows us to recognize and highlight the parallel structural, thematic, and rhetorical movements that shape their narratives. The dissonance between form and content with which these poems both ground and signal their relationship to their addressee helps us to understand the critical role that structure, form, and voice play in shaping our encounter as readers with these poetic texts. This realization is enabled, ultimately, by engaging with these poems through the lens of monologue.

There is nothing about the framework of monologue that is *essential* to comprehending the workings of these poems: a careful reading with a mind to the relationship of the speaker and addressee, the assumption of a response, and the place of the reader within the poetic frame is perfectly possible without recourse to the idea of monologue. Monologue is useful as an interpretive lens not because it reveals something that was not there, but because it brings into focus essential features of these poems that had been previously overlooked in favor of broad symbolic, religious, political, or biographical readings. Monologue is valuable as a way of approaching this poetry because it prioritizes the role of the poetic speaker *in relation* to an addressee, and a readership, upon whose textual existence the entire poem turns. The addressee need not be real, but the speaker of the monologue relies on their rhetorical presence to allow them *to be heard*: the poems discussed in this chapter are the outpouring of emotions that need to be given direction in order to be expressed.

In the Jewish literary tradition that began with Lamentations, the most common and effective place to direct these emotions is toward God, not because He may respond but because doing so allows the speakers to draw from a shared network of poetic structures, language, and reference that the biblical text and tradition have inspired. These poems transform this tradition, true, but they do not leave the reader with any new or concrete formations upon which to draw: each of the poems in this chapter rejects the possibility of outside consolation, of a response, instead gesturing toward a nebulous future in which speech itself is the only mechanism for comprehending the destruction, and toward the new communal identity formations that will necessarily emerge from that destruction.

As a collection of speakers who find themselves tasked with processing their own experiences of the Holocaust as an ongoing event, the impact and extent of which will remain unknown for many years, each turns to tradition as a springboard for the creation of something new, and something distinctly *communal*. God will not respond, He won't undo covenant or make a new world; no one can return to the isolated community of the premodern ghetto. The only *possible* path forward from these poems is the reaffirmation of communal identity in the face of radical, external threats. Despite the uncertainty that permeates these poems, the speakers of all three are deeply committed to their role as representatives for, and members of, the community as a whole, both those who have been murdered, and those who remain.

This American Yiddish Holocaust literature thus models one expression of literary response to catastrophe, offering its readership a shared vocabulary drawn from Jewish religious and literary tradition through which to form a connection to the poetic speaker and, in doing so, to join a community of suffering within which their complex and emergent response to the destruction of the Holocaust can begin to be articulated. However, this example also illustrates the extent to which the creation of new modes of communal and collective identification is a *necessary* part of any attempt to respond to catastrophe, an ongoing process of articulating and rearticulating one's relationship to that destruction. In the encounter with such texts, readers are made acutely aware of their own position in relation to the catastrophe, drawn into the dialogue created by the text between the literary and cultural traditions within which it speaks, and the necessity of formulating an immediate response to the destruction. In the case of the Holocaust, the reader must confront their own position within the discourse of tradition, God, and the unclear, nebulous Jewish futurity to which all these poems gesture. In the encounter with any catastrophe literature, however, the act of reading is as critical as the act of speaking; the reader comes to occupy the dual position of witness to the speaker's experience of processing the destruction and must contend with the fact that they are now, themselves, implicated within a community struggling to give voice to its suffering.

NOTES

1. George Steiner, *Language and Silence: Essays on Language, Literature, and the Inhuman* (New York: Atheneum, 1967); George Steiner, "The Long Life of Metaphor: An Approach to the 'Shoah,'" in *Writing and the Holocaust*, edited by Berel Lang (New York: Holmes and Meier, 1988), 154–71.

2. Elie Wiesel, "Why I Write," in *Confronting the Holocaust: The Impact of Elie Wiesel*, edited by Alvin H. Rosenfeld and Irving Greenberg (Bloomington: Indiana University Press, 1978), 200–206. See also Aharon Appelfeld, "After the Holocaust," and Cynthia Ozick, "Roundtable Discussion: Cynthia Ozick," in *Writing and the Holocaust*, 83–92 and 277–84.

3. Lawrence L. Langer, *The Holocaust and the Literary Imagination* (New Haven: Yale University Press, 1975); Alvin H. Rosenfeld, *A Double Dying: Reflections on Holocaust Literature* (Bloomington: Indiana University Press, 1980).

4. Alan L. Mintz, *Ḥurban: Responses to Catastrophe in Hebrew Literature* (New York: Columbia University Press, 1984); David G. Roskies, *Against the Apocalypse: Responses to Catastrophe in Modern Jewish Culture* (Cambridge, MA: Harvard University Press, 1984).

5. Roskies, *Against the Apocalypse*, 13, 191.

6. Raul Hilberg, *Perpetrators Victims Bystanders: The Jewish Catastrophe, 1933–1945* (New York: HarperPerennial, 1993), 187.

7. David G. Roskies and Naomi Diamant, *Holocaust Literature: A History and Guide* (Waltham, MA: Brandeis University Press, 2012).

8. Roskies and Diamant, *Holocaust Literature*, 2.

9. Yankev Glatshteyn, "A gute nakht, velt" [Good Night, World], *Inzikh* 8, no. 3 (April 1938): 66–67.

10. Kadye Molodovsky, *Der meylekh dovid aleyn iz geblibn* [Only King David Remained] (New York: Papirene Brik, 1946).

11. *Ani hagever ra'ah oni beshevet evrato.* I am using the 1985 Jewish Publication Society translation, the standard translation in Jewish studies scholarship and, in the case of Lamentations 3:1, identical to the translation Mintz uses or offers.

12. Mintz, *Ḥurban*, 38–39.

13. Mintz, *Ḥurban*, 40.

14. Mintz, *Ḥurban*, 39.

15. Mintz, *Ḥurban*, 38. "In his isolation he imagines that he alone has been singled out for victimization."

16. Kadye Molodovsky, "Havdole," in *Der meylekh dovid aleyn iz geblibn* [Only King David Remained] (New York: Papirene Brik, 1946).

17. All poetry translations are my own.

18. Kadye Molodovsky, "Mayn elterzeydns yerushe" [My Great-Grandfather's Legacy], *Svive*, January 1971, 60; as quoted by Heather Valencia, "Only King David Remained: Reactions to the Holocaust in the Poetry of Kadya Molodowsky," in *The Fourteenth Avrom-Nokhem Stencl Lecture in Yiddish Studies, Occasional Papers* 7 (Oxford: Oxford Centre for Hebrew and Jewish Studies, 2006), 12–13.

19. Molodovsky, *Der meylekh dovid aleyn iz geblibn*, 3–4.

20. Mintz, *Ḥurban*, 37.

21. Mintz, *Ḥurban*, 41.

22. Kadye Molodovsky, "El Khanun" [God of Mercy], in *Der meylekh dovid aleyn iz geblibn* [Only King David Remained] (New York: Papirene Brik, 1946).

23. Roskies, *Against the Apocalypse*, 20.

24. Roskies, *Against the Apocalypse*, 20.

25. Roskies, *Against the Apocalypse*, 20.

26. This particular problem of poetic language also undergirds Adorno's oft-cited "*Nach Auschwitz Gedicht zu schreiben, ist barbarisch* [After Auschwitz, to write a poem is barbaric]." See Theodor W. Adorno, "Cultural Criticism and Society," in *Prisms* (Cambridge, MA: MIT Press, 1981), 34.

27. Mintz, *Ḥurban*, 41.

28. Glatshteyn, "A gute nakht, velt"; Yankev Glatshteyn, "A gute nakht, velt," in *Gedenklider* [In Remembrance] (New York: Yidisher Kemfer, 1943), 41–42. When the poem was first published in the April 1938 volume of Glatshteyn's journal *Inzikh*, it did not carry a date (the date was clearly visible paratextually above), but when it was published in Glatshteyn's first collection of Holocaust poetry, *Gedenklider* [In Remembrance], the poem itself carried the date "April, 1938."

29. Anita Norich, *Discovering Exile: Yiddish and Jewish American Culture during the Holocaust* (Stanford: Stanford University Press, 2007), 47.

30. Norich, *Discovering Exile*, 49.

31. Norich, *Discovering Exile*, 49–50.

32. Molodovsky, "Havdole," ll. 1–2.

33. Molodovsky, "El Khanun," ll. 1–2.

34. Glatshteyn, "A gute nakht, velt," ll. 1–2.

The Illusion of a #RadTrad Identity

Lauren Horn Griffin

In the aftermath of the election of Donald Trump to the US presidency in 2016, political observers scrambled to explain what happened. Much of the focus revolved around understanding "evangelicals" in an attempt to figure out why so many white Christians supported Donald Trump despite his many publicized moral shortcomings.[1] News articles, academic books, and social media conversations tried to get at exactly who these "white evangelicals" were and why they did this. The presupposition was that an identifiable evangelical identity existed, and that their "culture" was the reason for their political action.[2] Many religious studies scholars attempted to point out how "evangelical" had become an overused, misunderstood, and largely incoherent term in modern American political and religious discourse.[3] But in the runup to and aftermath of the US presidential election of 2020, similar pieces just kept coming. This time, though, they began to expand their questioning to conservative Catholics in addition to conservative Protestants.[4] For example, one NPR piece on traditionalist Catholics posited that "for Trump, conservative Catholics are the new evangelicals."[5] Though the target is slightly different, the framework remains the same: traditionalist Catholics must be identifiable, and their culture spurred (or will spur) their political action. As they did with regard to conservative Protestants, political commentators, including scholars, have reduced traditionalist Catholics in some political rhetoric to "new right Catholic," while at the same time many self-identified "trads" fear being treated as one-dimensional fundamentalists. In an attempt to understand this aspect of the American cultural landscape, scholars, pundits, and the general public have begun to discuss, and thus construct, "rad trads" as an object of study.

The term "traditionalist Catholic" has been used for decades to refer to those

Catholics who prefer the liturgy and/or social teachings of the Church before (what they see as) the "modernizing" reforms of the Second Vatican Council (or Vatican II, 1962–65).[6] Sometimes "radical" is added to identify those who go further in their reaction to or rejection of Vatican II. The Southern Poverty Law Center describes "radical traditional Catholicism" as antisemitic and antidemocratic, and lists eleven "radical traditionalist" organizations as hate groups.[7] The term "rad trad," which has since become an internet meme, emerged in the early 2000s with Web 2.0, growing and changing within the Catholic blogging community. One of the earliest instances of the term that I have seen appeared in the London *Times* in 2008, in an article titled "American Catholics Must Stop and Listen to the Pope," in which an American priest, Father Dwight Longenecker, bemoaned the "rad traddies." He defined them as Latin Mass fanatics who "support schismatic groups opposed to modernising the Church" and wish to "turn back the clock to some golden age before the Second Vatican Council." His usage of the term was hotly debated in the comments of "Insight Scoop," a blog of the authors and staff of Ignatius Press, a well-known Catholic publishing house. One commenter, Catholic author Sandra Miesel, claimed to have coined the term and quibbled with Fr. Longenecker's usage, arguing that "rad trad" involves "other social and political freight." Others in the forum asked Miesel, as the inventor of the term, to lay it to rest, as they found it "smug" and inadequate to articulate the difference between mainstream lovers of Catholic tradition and those further out on the ecclesiastical and political fringe.[8] Even in the blogs and forums of 2008, the term was already being debated and expanded to include more or less than some core users had hoped. The word was already getting away from them and, as this essay will show, has morphed even more in the internet culture of the 2020s.

In *The Illusion of Cultural Identity*, Jean-François Bayart argues that the very idea of cultural identity prevents us from grasping the cultural dimensions of a variety of phenomena we are curious about, from major political events to other social and economic phenomena.[9] Continued efforts to understand "religion" in America, or even "American religion," often focus on identifications. Scholars want to know what groups there are, how many practitioners are in them, and how these groups overlap with other identifiers like race, gender, sexuality, and class. In trying to identify and classify, scholars (along with journalists and other observers) actually produce the groups they are trying to analyze. This essay examines the contest over identifications, particularly in the context of subcultures within an established and legible "religion" like Catholicism and investigates how discourse on the category itself contributes to the production of a subculture. I use "trad" and especially "rad trad" Twitter content (specifically, the discussion surrounding radical traditionalist Catholics on Twitter) as an example of the ways in which identities are created in discourse and, moreover, the ways in which we implicitly and explicitly treat these identities as an explanation for a particular behavior or action. An online "trad" subculture has been variously imagined by Church leadership, journalists, scholars of religion, and users of Twitter (and other social media). The conversations surrounding #RadTrad, however, say more about the concerns of the social actors engaging in the conversation than about any essential components of a "trad" identity, and ultimately demonstrate the equivocality of cultural identity. Journalists most often focus on the relationship of rad trads to the Trump movement, while Catholic leadership focuses on their relationship to Vatican II. Susan Harding's well-known essay "Representing Fundamentalism: The Problem of the Repugnant Cultural Other" (1991) addressed in detail how scholars themselves shape their objects of study, particularly those they find "repugnant" or harmful and which they wish to address for the social good.[10] In trying to articulate contemporary US Christianity's relationship with right-wing populism, "religion" as an independent variable often still proceeds untroubled in scholarship.[11]

Social media are prime spaces to apply this type of discourse analysis because such spaces are solely dedicated to performing and consuming imagined identities. It is sometimes fun and always profitable to try to identify and name social media subcultures. While the majority of social media data collection and analysis is done by those looking for a market for their products, users themselves identify and name subcultures they see arising from the content they are fed through the algorithms of the applications they are using. Consumption, then, creates the idea of subcultures. In her *New York Times* article on Catholic Twitter, Tara Isabella Burton compares social media platforms to fertile soil for some communities, allowing users to locate like-minded individuals.[12] But what if, instead of imagining social media as the "fertile soil" for the "communities" that organically grow there (as if these identities existed and simply needed a space to find each other for a community to take root), we instead thought of social media and religious identities as co-constitutive? Because of the interaction between human and machine through the generation of catchy names, hashtags, images, and algorithms on social media, the more a term is used and explained, the more it attracts the types of people who might be drawn to it, constantly constructing, reflecting, and reconstituting itself.

While the representation of what constitutes a rad trad is created by scholars, Catholic leadership, and journalists, this essay focuses on how the term has been used and consumed on social media, specifically Twitter. To get a sense of what those posting on #RadTrad Twitter say about themselves, I used a combination of quantitative and qualitative methods to analyze the Twitter data. I retrieved tweets that contained "#radtrad," "rad trad," or "radtrad" from a two-year period between January 1, 2019, and December 31, 2020, resulting in a corpus of 6,684 tweets.[13] I will focus on two issues revealed by the word frequency analysis: First, gender roles are a central feature of rad trad conversations online, but one that has not been highlighted by Catholic leadership, news media, or scholarship. Second, a large portion of the conversation surrounding rad trad is self-referential, or a theoretical discussion of the category itself. This is, of course, due in part to my methodology—searching for the term in isolation is naturally going to pull tweets that are talking *about* the term itself. But that is exactly what we are after here: getting a glimpse into contemporary debates over the term demonstrates the fluid and contingent nature of these categories, which in turn highlights the pitfalls in assuming a stable "religious culture" that might explain political action.[14]

Like all Twitter subcultures, #RadTrad Twitter is an imagined community. But how is it imagined, and to what social ends? I focus here on the semantic dimensions of algorithmic culture by emphasizing digital rhetoric and its uses on social media.[15] Interrogating representation itself, just as Harding did with "fundamentalists," we may ask how #RadTrad Twitter was manufactured, what categories and assumptions were imposed upon it, and what trajectories are implicit in its narrative representations. This theoretical approach is not new, but it is still not consistently applied to "religious" objects—which shows how these culturalist assumptions still operate uncritically within contemporary discourses on "religion." Thirty years after Harding's essay, we now live in what some call the digital society or the information society, and new media processes have drawn new boundaries and created new affinities.[16] One tweet that stands out in demonstrating this point comes from a user bemoaning what she sees as the overly committed users on her timeline, noting that it was full of kpoppers, e-girls, normies, ancap, radtrads, and MGTOWs.[17] In this user's list, identities that we might call religious, political, or cultural are not cordoned off—these are all "very online" identifiers, blurring our presupposed categories. In complicating what it means to be a present-day "rad trad," this essay demonstrates yet again how terms demarcate groups and, in doing so, reduce their complexity; moreover, it serves as a specific instance of how internet technologies (particularly social media) have transformed how we communicate and how we imagine our communities. This all-encompassing digitality must be central to the study of communities we call religious.

METHODOLOGY

In my corpus of 6,684 tweets, 24 languages were detected. The largest group (54 percent) were in English, followed by Portuguese (34 percent), while 5 percent were in Spanish, 2 percent were in German, and 1 percent were in Tagalog. The remaining 4 percent were in other languages, but no other language made up a significant portion of the corpus. Determining where the tweets came from is difficult because not everyone lists their location in their bio, but rad trad tweets in English came from Canada, Britain, Australia, Europe, Latin America, and South America. However, the clear majority of rad trad tweets in English, based on what I could determine from Twitter profiles and the content of the tweets, came from the United States. A large portion of the conversations revolved around the US Church (mentioning US clergy, public figures, parishes, and so forth) and US politics.[18]

Conducting a word frequency analysis of just the English usages showed that—after self-referential words like "catholic," "traditional," and "twitter"—the most frequently utilized words in conjunction with rad trad were "pope" (141), "god" (90), "latin mass" or "TLM" (67), "love" (67), and "women" (61). Conducting a sentiment analysis showed that #radtrad (with the hashtag) was used more positively than the term alone, without the tag, which trended toward negative usages.[19] Though the "rad trad" sobriquet has pejorative uses, many self-described rad trads have claimed it and displayed it proudly with the hashtag. There were some ironic and critical usages of the hashtags, but most were intentional signals of a person's identification with the imagined subculture. The most commonly used tags in conjunction with #radtrad (which did not include some variation of "catholic[s]," "tradition[al]," or "twitter") were #popefrancis, #latinmass, #sspx, #proudboys, #knightsrepublic, #prolife, and #stevebannon.[20]

Many of the concerns and fixations described in the news media and academic articles were not emphasized in the Twitter data. For example, in a recent and very thorough exposé for *Vanity Fair*, Kathryn Joyce describes rad trads as mapping Catholicism onto existing alt-right conspiracy theories that center on fears about "globalism," freemasonry, and communists. Thus, racism figures centrally into Joyce's profile, creating an image of online Catholics anchored by white supremacy and (specifically) antisemitism.[21] Others have focused on Islamophobia, especially in the years following President Trump's 2017 restrictions on travel from some predominantly Muslim countries. Archbishop Vigano (a figure who is heavily emphasized by Joyce) is only mentioned ten times in conjunction with "rad trad" in my corpus of tweets (and all mentions were in English). In those tweets, users debated whether or not he was of "rad trad" identity. While a few tweets saw him as a very extreme figure, some talked about him not being extreme enough, viewing him as a latecomer to "radtradism." Islam is only mentioned eight times in my corpus of tweets—not an oft-discussed topic, especially in comparison with their main social issue: the roles and rights of women.[22] Islamophobia was likely a hotter topic in 2016 and early 2017, but my Twitter dataset does not include those years. Of course, the Crusader imagery that appears in some posts and as profile pictures could certainly be considered in an analysis of antisemitism, Islamophobia, and white supremacy on #RadTrad Twitter, but my dataset focuses on rhetoric (thus, without commentary these images are left up for interpretation). The point here is that, while Islamophobia is unquestionably present in some self-identified rad trad groups and individuals, it is not an essential—or defining—component of #RadTrad Twitter. It may well have been more discussed in 2016–17 #RadTrad Twitter, but that reinforces the contingent, fluid, and situated nature of "rad trad culture."

ORTHODOX OUTLAWS AND "TRADWIVES"

The word "pope" is by far the most used word in conjunction with "rad trad," and #popefrancis was the most used hashtag in conjunction with #radtrad. Not only Pope Francis, but also the theoretical role of the pope, the authority of the pope, the history of the papacy, and past popes loom large in rad trad conversations on Twitter, highlighting the centrality of authority in these discussions. The sentiments on papal authority and Pope Francis, though, vary widely. Some self-identified rad trads express enthusiasm about Pope Francis, others recognize him as pope but are highly critical, and yet others believe not only that the papal seat is vacant but that "Bergoglio" (often referred to by his surname as a slur) is an antipope. Many nontrads (sometimes called "normies") attempt to describe rad trads as rejecting Pope Francis, which then leads to a discussion in which rad trads appear in their mentions to clarify their own position on the pope. These conversations, however they end up, often contain a common theme: rad trads feel misunderstood, marginalized, or angry in relation to conversations about authority. One user laments that their personal Catholicism is hanging by a thread, and that their only remaining hope is that a trad pope would end the (perceived) persecution of the traditional Latin Mass (which was the Mass celebrated until 1962, when what is now called the "ordinary form" and its allowance for Mass in the vernacular became standard).

Talking of betrayal, both within the Magisterial Church and in society at large, the tweets craft a sort of gritty noir image of an irreverent but deeply pious cowboy, made an outlaw by society's lack of scruples and the Church's inability to see the truth. Only the few, the true remnant, now remain, though on the margins. These narratives of persecution are quite common, especially in and around discussion of the pope. Some users use terms like "despicable," "demonic," "Masonic," and "Antichrist" to describe Pope Francis, who they say has made the Vatican nothing more than a homosexual cabal. One user argues that the swamp in the Church must be drained, and the Church should become much smaller and offer only the Latin Mass. Twitter users also perceive certain rad trads as being drawn to the "extremes" or to the margins of the margins. One user remarks that they are always weirded out by the people online who have gone from "Muslim extremist" to "trans anarcho-communist" to "radtrad sedevacantist."[23] The tweeter jokingly urges readers to stick to one single extremist ideology "like the rest of us." The joke, of course, was meant to highlight how this attraction to fringe communities is due precisely to the edginess and boundary-pushing rebelliousness itself. Political scientist Michael Barkun argues that those with "fringe" notions are drawn to the fringe precisely because of what he calls "stigmatized knowledge," or ideas that are rejected by authorities and institutions.[24] Similarly, Donovan Schaefer has pointed out that much of the appeal of this fringe is how exciting it feels to have insider information, highlighting the role of emotion in shaping beliefs.[25] By continuously discussing rad trads as an embattled few on the margins, it seems, more and more users who like the image of the "orthodox outlaws" are drawn to the thrilling and stigmatized idea of #RadTrad.

At the same time, because the term is humorous and playful, some fear that too many are now identifying as rad trad who really do not deserve the term. Indeed, a Redditor recently expressed their misunderstanding of the term, explaining that they had been using it because it sounded like a fun meme word for Catholics who like rosaries. Others do not seem to be drawn to the orthodox outlaw image, as they combine some mainstream Catholic ideas under the "rad trad" moniker. For example, there is a very interesting combination of identifying terms in one bio I came across, including pro-life, pro-distributism, pro–Pope Francis, and pro–rad trad Catholic. As the term continues to be used and adopted, the policing of authenticity continues, with some users painting with a broader brush, making #RadTrad feel more mainstream, while others continue to define it more narrowly, attempting to make #RadTrad refer only to sedevacantists or political extremists (however defined).

Another hot topic in #RadTrad Twitter that is not discussed as much by the academic discourse or media coverage (both the church media and news media) has to do with women. In fact, some Twitter users suggest that young men are pulled into #RadTrad Twitter precisely because of "the manosphere," or online communities of "incels" (involuntary celibates), "PUAs" (pickup artists), and "MGTOWs" (Men Going Their Own Way). Feminist Catholics who prefer traditional liturgy argue that these men are drawn to this side of Catholic Twitter because it is inherently and explicitly patriarchal, emphasizes masculinity, and strongly opposes feminism. One trad describes how she wandered too far into #CatholicTwitter and discovered the "rad trads." She expressed surprise that there seemed to be such a large contingent of "anti-19th amendment folks" using Catholicism to authorize their takes. Indeed, there are many opinions on what women should do (work in the home, have many children) and how they should dress (long dresses, veiled at Mass). One Twitter user with a Crusader knight as his avatar exclaimed that he would love to take his cousin, a Christian feminist, to a Latin Mass and "watch her throw a fit" over women wearing the veil. This aspect of #Radtrad Twitter heavily overlaps with the adjacent "tradwife" or "trad girl" "Wojak" memes on social media. "Tradwife," internet culture's term for a traditional wife, usually denotes a woman who has a feminine appearance, stays at home to clean house and raise children, and (most important) submits to her husband. The memified version of this (in addition to the female variation of the Wojak cartoon with blond hair and a blue floral sundress) almost always features a 1950s white woman in a kitchen with an apron. Trad girl/tradwife is a much larger internet trend that extends well beyond Catholic Twitter, but these images loom large among some self-identified rad trads. There is much to unpack in this trend, from a disillusionment with modernity and longing for a past era of abundance to its explicit connection to a white nationalist project (for instance, the "white baby challenge"), but for present purposes it demonstrates just the centrality of the discourses of gender and sexuality in certain corners of #RadTrad Twitter.[26] Traditionalists online appeal to many moments from the past, including classical Greece and Rome, medieval and Renaissance Europe, and sometimes nineteenth-century Britain. But the most common images (at least in my dataset) were those of the 1950s United States, all featuring white women performing domestic labor. Machine learning reveals that, for many self-identified rad trads, gender and the roles of women are central topics that often fall off the radar of journalists, who focus more on issues of race and ethnicity (antisemitism, Islamophobia, and white supremacy). Of course, discourses on gender cannot be separated from discourses on race, and #RadTrad often makes these connections explicit, but the awkward relationship between mainstream ideas of gender equality and the Church's teachings about gender and sexuality can make the focus on gender feel more confrontational. Twitter users have no such qualms.

PERHAPS A TAD RAD?

The most common hashtag used in conjunction with #radtrad is #traditionalcatholic and #catholictwitter. Much of the conversation, then, revolves around the overlap of, and debate about the line between, radical traditionalist and traditional Catholic, and includes discussion of the Catholic Twitter subculture itself (who is part of it, what the main discussions are or ought to be, and so on). A majority of the conversations explicitly center on the identifications, classifications, and authenticity of the group itself.

Catholics who now consider themselves "mainstream traditionalists" (on Twitter they call themselves "trad not rad") were indeed once considered radical or may still be considered radical by some. The distinction between the extreme Catholic reactionaries and mainstream "traditionalists" is contested among Twitter users. For example, I analyzed Twitter bios for "rad trad," or "#radtrad" to see how people were using the term in their profiles. Of the eighty-five accounts that had the Catholic meaning of "rad trad" in their bio, seven were some version of "trad not rad," drawing the line between themselves as "moderate" traditionalist and the radicals. Eight bios expressed uncertainty regarding the line between regular "trad" and "rad," with bios like "Tad of a Trad, and a tiny bit rad"; "Trad, but trying not to be rad"; and "Mostly trad with shades of rad." One user expressed their use of traditionalist devotional objects while also remaining loyal to Church leadership—for instance, they wore a scapular while also remaining loyal to the Magisterium. While the very term "rad trad" to some means sedevacantism (or, at the very least, an extreme dislike for Pope Francis), that is certainly not the only interpretation, as several bios and tweets expressed explicit support for Pope Francis and criticized those who seek to "tear him down." A few bios highlighted the nonstatic nature of their identities by describing themselves as "Traddening" or "Trad, more Rad by the day." One bio contained the joke "Socially Rad, Fiscally Trad," a play on the "socially liberal, fiscally conservative" trope many moderate Republicans like to use to try to carve out a subgroup within a larger community. Just a quick glance at trads "rad" enough to include the moniker in their bio (a rather intentional act of identification) shows that the term is fluid and contested, even among core users.

A good portion of the tweets containing "#radtrad" or "rad trad" were actually evaluating the term itself, attempting to decide exactly what it means and whom to include (or exclude). One user noted that "rad trad" is overused by people without proper understanding. Other tweets lamented the meaninglessness of the term, judging such labels as "leftcath," "tradcath," and "radtrad" to be obsolete. Another applied this to other imagined Twitter cultures, explaining that #RadTrad Twitter is like Atheist Twitter in that everyone pretends to have the same values, but actually do not. Several tweets (like those using the term "traddening") recognized the fluid, changeable nature of the name; one user explained that receiving Communion on the tongue is enough for one to be a rad trad in 2020. The meme "You Keep Using That Word, I Do Not Think It Means What You Think It Means," featuring the fictional character Inigo Montoya from the romantic comedy film *The Princess Bride* (1987), is very often employed in discussions about the definition and description of "#radtrad." Who is rad enough to be a rad trad is an oft-debated topic, with users perceiving that standards had shifted even since Twitter (and other social media) had helped create the identity.

Along those same lines, Twitter users discussed the role of the algorithm, too, in the construction of "#radtrad." One user complained that they watched a Latin Mass, and now "the machine" "thinks I'm a Republican." Twitter users certainly noticed (to their chagrin) the ways in which the machine recommends accounts based on certain keywords used in a tweet, and how often users engage with tweets that use similar keywords. They expressed an upsetting awareness of how the algorithm connected them with right-wing figures, regardless of where they fell on the political, theological, or liturgical spectrum. For some leftcaths, it felt disjointed. One user explained that they are just a socialist who happens to think Vatican II was a mistake. They simply want to watch a Latin Mass, not donate money to current Senate minority leader Mitch McConnell. Still others commented on the "trending" topics Twitter recommends, noting how the more they seemed to follow Catholic Twitter personalities, the more right-wing political topics or personalities would show up in their "trending" section. Likewise, some on the right found that the figures considered "right wing" were not far-right enough, chuckling at the idea that someone would consider YouTube personality Taylor Marshall "radical." This user recognized that repeatedly calling Marshall "radical" (and Marshall using the term "rad" self-referentially) constructed him as such, especially in the corners of #RadTrad Twitter that are particularly personality driven. The user mocked Twitter's algorithm for continuously showing Marshall on his "Who to Follow" list. From the Explore tab to recommended accounts, this example provides an interesting look into how media shape conceptions of communities online, and it highlights the relationship between algorithmic targeting and identity formation. After all, it is not only algorithms and computation, but especially the way people imagine and perceive them, that shape the way we think about ourselves and our communities.[27] In this way, many Twitter users point to how the machine learning continuously shapes and reshapes rad trads.

RAD TRAD RELIGIOUS STUDIES SCHOLARS

Twitter users often employ the same method as religious studies scholars when trying to describe "religion in America" (what groups exist, who are they, how many are there, and so on). Social media have provided language to theorize the relationships between and within groups, the relationship of online to in-person communities, and the relationships between the various identities people perform every day. Many users offer breakdowns and explanations of the groups within Catholic Twitter ("rad trad," "leftcath," "trad cath," "normie"), each of which differs slightly from the next. This practice makes many Catholics feel like their larger community is more divided and polarized than it had previously been. One user notes that although there have long been divisions among American Catholics between the sociopolitical "left" and "right," roughly corresponding to their theological worldviews, recent years have deeply fractured the group of "conservative" Catholics. Comparisons to other communities, such as the larger American political landscape or other "religious" traditions, usually follow. In response to lamentations about the fractured landscape of US Catholicism, one user noted that this analysis of the Catholic landscape could easily be applied to the Protestant context, regardless of denomination. Discussing the term "rad trad" specifically, Fr. Stephen Vrazel explained that "having returned to Twitter just a few months ago, I found [the term] thrown around by all sorts of people, always as a mix of joking but serious. That's what it looks like from my outsider's perspective, anyway."[28] Several tweets highlighted the fluid nature between "joke" names and the terms being taken more seriously, indicating how this demarcation of groups really is a playful, layered story of exchange and circulation.

In addition to more generally perceived divisions, Twitter sometimes draws together some seemingly odd couples. For example, while it was thought to be common knowledge that traditionalist Catholics generally did not like the charismatic renewal in the Church, "#trentecostal" has shown the affinity between Tridentine (preconciliar or traditional) Catholicism and Catholics who practice forms of Pentecostalism.[29] In this way, Twitter users debate terms, create new groups, and provide humorous descriptions that constantly create, reflect, and rework the Catholic Twitter landscape. Their method actually mirrors that of religious studies scholars, who have attempted to draw "family resemblances" between a variety of traditions and have continuously argued that each tradition was more militant and fractured than the period before it.[30]

Twitter users recognize that "rad trad" is a brand invented online and not easily explained by the "the spirit of Vatican II" or Twitter users' beefs with American bishops; just as one need not run an urban homestead to be "#cottagecore," one need not attend a bunch of Latin Masses to be "#RadTrad." Indeed, sometimes it is something they lament. One user bemoaned what they called the sad world of online trads who have (in the user's estimation) never been to the Latin Mass and "preach literal heresies." Another user explained their annoyance with current "trad types" for being authenticity fetishists; the user equated trad's love of apocalyptic, sanguine Catholic imagery and embrace of the Latin Mass with the fetishization of vintage records and horror films. Catholic influencer Tommy Tighe explains it like this: "catholic twitter is seeing 'wearing anything other than white briefs underwear to mass is a mortal sin' and then being like 'oh shit, really?!' but I click their profile and it's a 19 year old sedevacantist with a pinned tweet showing a woman in the kitchen wearing just an apron."[31] Packed into that tweet are assumptions about information, authority, and authenticity, implicitly highlighting the centrality of digital media and the relationship between multiple digital rhetorics and memes in shaping conceptions of rad trads. For Twitter, "#radtrad" is understood as a very online aesthetic. In fact, Twitter language offers several interesting terms that critique the idea of static identities and highlight continuous "acts of identification."

Terms like "LARPing" (an acronym for "live action role playing") provide a language to discuss the (more or less) self-conscious performance of identities. Oftentimes the term is used solely to police authenticity. For example, when someone accuses someone of being a "rad trad LARPer," they mean that the person is not "real," whether genuine or correct, in their traditionalist Catholicism. But other times the term is used ironically or is humorously applied to oneself. One user explained that their own take was too "sane" to be radtrad but too "LARPy" to be considered mainstream. Admitting that one is role playing, even if humorously or ironically, provides accessible language for the ways in which we perform fluid and varied acts of identification rather than embody a static identity. The idea of role playing, especially when it is not used to contrast the "really real," allows people to discuss the ways in which we perform identity, play with ideas, and utilize rhetoric that does not directly result in in-person action. Users also discuss "e-trads" (or "e trads") and "e-Catholics," which uses the language of "e-person" (or the more commonly discussed "e-girl," popularized on the video-sharing app TikTok) to discuss the way people live online. Like "LARP," the term is often used to police authenticity, but unlike "LARP," this term emphasizes the idea that the e-trad does not necessarily practice traditionalist Catholicism in person but rather gravitates to the community online. Rather than questioning the "reality" of this type of trad, this can offer language to discuss what people do only online, which is where people spend a lot of "real" time, even more so during the COVID-19 pandemic. Rather than accuse users of not being real or genuine, this term emphasizes the fact that #RadTrad Twitter is not a mirror image of those attending Latin Mass or those arguing over Vatican II in church lobbies. It is also a recognition that much of the language, topics, and ideas largely live only on Twitter: "it's a weird place to be in, having one foot in Catholic Twitter where this is all we can think/talk about and another foot in the real world at work where absolutely no one is talking about it or probably gives it as much as a thought."[32]

Still, for many #RadTrad Twitter users, online activity is not divorced from in-person practice, as many users report attending Latin Mass and engaging with traditionalist communities on the ground. Indeed, a large portion of the debates on Twitter try to deal with this question of how to think about the relationship between the "online" world and the "in-person" world, realizing that both are "real" and socially consequential, but expressing uncertainty about the relationship between them. Catholic journalist J. D. Flynn attempted to work this out: "I used to think this was just a phenomenon among the very online, but it's not. I hear from a lot of practicing Catholic families who have been seriously fractured over Trump, [Bishop Carlo Maria] Viganò, and now vaccines, etc. I hear from campus ministers who say students are confused by that."[33] Terms like "LARPer" and "e-trad" give users language to theorize with—to articulate the ways in which not all acts of identification are performed in person or with a body, and how an online aesthetic does not necessarily translate into "beliefs" or even "worldviews." One can be, as some Twitter users put it, "just e-traddening," while the in-person communities of others are reflected in their online content.

Similarly, rather than define rad trads by their affinity for the traditional Latin Mass (TLM), Twitter users analyze rad trads' love for TLM as a claim made by social actors in particular social situations. Many Twitter users consider rad trad uses of Latin as an artifact—the *idea* of the language as a socially formative device. They group together rad trad devotion to the Latin language, Gothic architecture, and ornate vestments, alongside the images of knights and fivefold crosses that serve as profile pictures for many trads and call it out as white-Western-civilization fetish. The idea of Latin (rather than actually speaking, hearing, praying, or using the language itself), they notice, is part of rad trad branding and marketing rather than merely a description of liturgical practices. Despite claims to universality and timelessness, the TLM, of course, has a particular history. One user notes that her SSPX (Society of Saint Pius X) parents used to call the Latin Mass "timeless" when it was and is a historical product. Twitter users explicitly recognize that rad trads draw upon different items from the archive of Catholicism's past—different events and actors, often held together in tension with one another, some of which are authorized by the Magisterium and others marginalized. Their narratives of the medieval or early modern Church sometimes explicitly conflict with one another, given that they are in the service of contesting positions in the present, despite supposedly narrating the same past.

A good portion of #RadTrad Twitter, then, actually problematizes and criticizes the term as well as the idea of a coherent rad trad culture. The users recognize and articulate just how manufactured and malleable the term can be. From Groyper alt-right memes and men's rights groups to debates over socialism, narrative, and memory, #RadTrad Twitter is extremely varied—which, as some users argue, renders the term rather meaningless. But by continuously using, debating, and comparing it, they reify the very communities they are calling into question.

CONCLUSION

Is this about Vatican II, or are rad trads just an angry Twitter mob? Is it a political movement, or merely "religious"? Do we include lefty trads and "church militants"? How seriously does one have to center TLM to be "rad" in their traditionalism? Figures that are often lumped together by journalists, academics, and clerics alike feel very differently about the liturgy as well as doctrine. While many rad trads identify as Republicans, or at least as Trump supporters, many reject those labels as well. Some go further into the world of the new right, where even former White House official Steve Bannon is too "neocon," while others embrace socialist policies and figures. Many of these questions echo the very conversations that happen around other problematic terms in the study of religion in America, most recently "fundamentalist" and "evangelical." It is not enough to simply recognize the diversity—to put an "s" on the end of each of these imagined identities; rather, we can read these descriptions and evaluations as an intersection of discursive practices that define these identities from a particular point of view, which leads us to a more interesting set of questions.

How is rad trad culture actually brought into existence, managed, and transformed? The act of cultural defining and describing creates the space for identities to be constructed around and in service to various forms of ideology.[34] In other words, the more people speak it into existence, the more the "identity" is differentiated. This, in turn, leads to efforts by some to reconcile these differences—to moderate these "othering" strategies by drawing a wider center and a smaller periphery. In this way, the journalists, academics, and Twitter users who discuss these groups become more like composers than prophets. Radtradism, like identity in general, operates along a fluid and changing spectrum and will continue to be measured against other "others."[35] Indeed, all of these discourses represent rad trads as reacting against modernity (however construed). In other words, their descriptions depend on their different conceptions of modernity. For those who see Vatican II and the work that is currently being carried out by Pope Francis as "progress," these are positive aspects of the modern Church. For others in the United States, modernity is nothing but political polarization, economic uncertainty, and a failing state. Still others see modernity as interreligious dialogue, toleration, and friendship. Some Twitter users see the antifeminist message behind some rad trad content as antimodern, but still enjoy liturgical traditionalism. In constructing #RadTrad identity (as in constructions of fundamentalism and evangelicalism before it), modernity itself is manufactured in its reverse image. The digital rhetoric shaping #RadTrad thus reveals the variety of ways in which people construct themselves as premodern, modern, or postmodern subjects.

This essay expresses skepticism around questions of culture and identity through the example of #RadTrad, which offers up a bundle of contradictions. There is no simple narrative to explain #RadTrad or the larger history of radical traditionalism in the American Catholic Church. Its meaning has shifted, even over the last few years, and it changes depending on whom you ask. The perceived rise of the rad trads is not an objective measure of their number or their political power, but rather a production of the imagination of those manufacturing the culture.[36] In examining the conversations about these questions, I have highlighted variations in theology, liturgy, views on gender, political affiliation, and political ideology. This case study on various discourses surrounding rad trads shows how shifts in media technology have shaped the concept of "culture" to become shorthand for a number of more complex political, social, and cultural configurations.[37] Just as Harding suggested of fundamentalist Protestants, we can conjure more situated, complex, and local accounts of traditionalist groups or individuals, which would make evaluations and even condemnations of certain positions espoused therein more effective.[38] Moreover, this case study serves as a specific instance of how internet technologies (particularly social media) have transformed how we communicate and how we imagine our communities. From its inception, “rad trad” has served as a flexible and dynamic term that communicates a relative authenticity. In some usages, the term does indeed communicate a strong restorationist impulse for the pre–Vatican II Church, but by and large this essay highlights the contested nature of the term, particularly in the last few years as “trad” rhetoric online has become more recognizable. By demonstrating the ways in which #RadTrad is constituted through digital rhetoric and algorithmic culture, I argue that while a particular Catholic's adherence to an imagined tradition is not an invention of these discourses, a RadTrad identity is.

The point, then, is not that “rad trad” cannot be defined or used (it is used, as I have shown, in many different ways). I am interested, rather, in how “trad” and “rad trad” are quickly becoming scholarly and media images that attempt to explain (and thus construct) a singular right-wing Catholic culture, especially for those interested in what they have termed white Christian nationalism and the politics of the new right. “Rad trad” is as much (if not more) a product of internet culture, mediatization, and late capitalism as it is of Catholic tradition—not to mention the ways in which discourses on Catholicism are inseparable from discourses on gender, race, and class. As I have shown, some people use “rad trad” (and even the less fraught “trad”) to wrap a variety of social phenomena into one neat package, while for others the term functions to separate “religion” and treat it as an independent variable or agent itself.

A quick glance at the uses and discussions of “trad” and “rad trad” on Twitter highlight how, though not unconnected to the traditionalist reaction to Vatican II, this is not a simple story of a singular movement over time. Taking Twitter data seriously will lead scholars to look beyond Vatican II as the catalyzing event, helping us recognize how “rad trad” is in many ways an invention of internet culture. Born of the blogs and forums of early Web 2.0 and developed as #RadTrad on social media, the media image continues to morph and expand. There are no r rad trads, in this sense, without the internet. This is not to say that there is no relationship between, say, priests like Marcel Lefebvre who were excommunicated after Vatican II and someone who has #RadTrad in their Twitter bio—indeed, many trads explicitly invoke these figures. However, if we want to understand what is going on with the wide variety of folks who attract the label, as well as those who use the term self-referentially, we will not figure it out by attempting to draw a straight line from some priests in the 1960s to a teenager in 2022 who has a fivefold cross as his Twitter avatar and has never attended a Latin Mass. We cannot understand the latter without understanding (of course) the socio-political realities and material conditions of the United States in the twenty-first century—but we must also understand key aspects of digital media and algorithmic culture. If religious studies scholars want to contribute to explaining the new right, we must think in terms of media processes as opposed to fixed categories in which religion operates as an unmediated, irreducible agent.

NOTES

1. See Mark Noll, George Marsden, and David Bebbington, eds., *Evangelicals: Who They Have Been, Are Now, and Could Be* (Grand Rapids, MI: William B. Eerdmans Publishing Co., 2019).

2. See, for example, Kristin Kobes Du Mez, *Jesus and John Wayne: How White Evangelicals Corrupted a Faith and Fractured a Nation* (New York: Liveright Publishing, 2020).

3. See, for example, Michael J. Altman, "'Religion, Religions, Religious' in America: Toward a Smithian Account of 'Evangelicalism,'" *Method and Theory in the Study of Religion* 31, no. 1 (2019): 71–82.

4. See, for example, Tish Durkin, "The Catholics Who Hate Joe Biden—and Pope Francis," *The Atlantic*, October 21, 2020.

5. Tom Gjelten, "For Trump, Conservative Catholics Are the New Evangelicals," NPR, October 26, 2020.

6. The term "radical traditionalism" is also used to refer to a school of traditionalist ideology that includes thinkers like Julius Evola and René Guénon, and it is also sometimes used to refer to traditional conservativism as a political philosophy. These are not necessarily unrelated to some of those who self-identify as traditionalist and radical traditionalist Catholics, but for the purposes of this essay I focus on the idea that traditionalist and radical traditionalist Catholics are most often talked about in terms of their reaction to or full rejection of the liturgical and social outcomes of the Second Vatical Council.

7. "Radical Traditional Catholicism," Southern Poverty Law Center.

8. Carl E. Olson, "Father Dwight Longenecker Let's 'Er Rip!" blog post, Insight Scoop, The Ignatius Press Blog, April 16, 2008.

9. Jean Francios Bayart, *The Illusion of Cultural Identity*, trans. Steven Rendall, Janet Roitman, Cynthia Schoch, and Jonathan Derrick (Chicago: University of Chicago Press, 2005).

10. Susan Harding, "Representing Fundamentalism: The Problem of the Repugnant Cultural Other," *Social Research* 58, no. 2 (1991): 373–93.

11. Many recent studies set out to explain "white Christian nationalism," for example, Sam Perry and Andrew Whitehead, *Taking America Back for God* (Oxford: Oxford University Press, 2020).

12. Tara Isabella Burton, "Christianity Gets Weird: Modern Life Is Ugly, Brutal and Barren, Maybe You Should Try a Latin Mass," *New York Times*, May 8, 2020.

13. "Radtrad" also describes a Brooklyn-based rock band as well as a genre of tattoos, so those usages were filtered out and not included in this number. Additionally, I am not using deleted tweets or tweets from accounts that have been deactivated; the removal of many accounts following the invasion of the US Capitol building on January 6, 2021, resulted in a small but noted loss of data.

14. Following the guidelines laid out by Amber M. Buck and Devon F. Ralston in "I

Didn't Sign Up for Your Research Study: The Ethics of Using "Public" Data," *Computers and Composition* 61 (2020), I do not cite or directly quote tweets from unverified users. Instead, I have paraphrased those tweets in this essay in order to protect the users.

15. See Ted Striphas, "Algorithmic Culture," *European Journal of Cultural Studies* 18, nos. 4–5 (2015): 395–412.

16. See Michael Buckland, *Information and Society* (Cambridge, MA: MIT Press, 2017). Though there are heated discussions, particularly in sociology, about how to characterize contemporary society and what balance of continuity and change one should strike in creating concepts and definitions, the role of technologies, information, and communication in shaping current society is central.

17. "Kpoppers" are fans of Korean pop music; "e-girls" refers to a TikTok subculture that draws on emo, goth, and anime images; "ancap" is a shortened term for the libertarian philosophy of anarcho-capitalism; and "MGTOW" stands for "Men Going Their Own Way."

18. The international movement called TFP (Tradition, Family, and Property, or Tradição, Família e Propriedade in Portuguese), founded by the Brazilian Plinio Corrêa de Oliveira, figures very prominently in the Portuguese "rad trad" tweets, but not at all in the tweets in English.

19. The sentiment analysis was conducted by means of VADER (Valence Aware Dictionary and Sentiment Reasoner), a lexicon and rule-based tool.

20. SSPX refers to the Society of Saint Pius X, a fraternity of traditionalist Catholic priests who offer Latin Mass. Knights of the Republic is a traditionalist Catholic men's group (it refers to itself as a "Sacred Military Order"). Steven Bannon is a former White House official who worked closely with President Trump.

21. See Kathryn Joyce, "Deep State, Deep Church: How Qanon and Trumpism Have Infected the Catholic Church," *Vanity Fair*, October 30, 2020; and Jason Horowitz, "Steve Bannon Carries Battles to Another Influential Hub: The Vatican," *New York Times*, February 7, 2017.

22. See, for example, James Martin, "Steve Bannon vs. the Pope," *AM Joy*, MSNBC, February 12, 2017.

23. "Sedevacantists" are separatists who deny the validity of the current pope and view the papal seat as empty (i.e., the "vacant seat" of the Holy See).

24. Michael Barkun. "Conspiracy Theories as Stigmatized Knowledge," *Diogenes* 62, nos. 3–4 (2015): 114–20.

25. Donovan Schaefer, *Wild Experiment: Feeling Science and Secularism after Darwin* (Durham, NC: Duke University Press, 2022).

26. For more on the "tradwife" social media trend, see Alexandra Minna Stern, *Proud Boys and the White Ethnostate: How the Alt-Right is Warping the American Imagination* (Boston: Beacon Press, 2019); and Annie Kelly, "The Housewives of White Supremacy," *New York Times*, June 1, 2018.

27. William Uricchio, "Recommended for You: Prediction, Creation and the Cultural Work of Algorithms," *Berlin Journal* 28 (2015): 6–9; and Blake Hallinan and Ted Striphas, "Recommended for You: The Netflix Prize and the Production of Algorithmic Culture," *New Media and Society* (2014).

28. Fr. Steven Vrazel, Twitter post, December 2, 2020.

29. The "Trent" in "#trentecostal" refers to the Council of Trent (1545–63), which authorized the Tridentine form of the Latin Mass that was practiced up until Vatican II. The traditional Latin Mass is often called the Tridentine Mass. For more on the conflict between traditionalist and charismatic Catholics, see Stephen Hunt, *Christian Millenarianism: From the Early Church to Waco* (Bloomington: Indiana University Press, 2001), 164.

30. For example, see R. Scott Appleby and Martin E. Marty, *Fundamentalisms Observed* (Chicago: University of Chicago Press, 2004). For a critique of the "family resemblance" method in religious studies, see Tim Fitzgerald, "Religion, Philosophy, and Family Resemblances," *Religion* 26 (1996):215–36.

31. Tommy Tighe, Twitter post, September 1, 2022.

32. Tommy Tighe, Twitter post, August 27, 2019.

33. J. D. Flynn, Twitter post, February 13, 2021.

34. See Bayart, *The Illusion of Cultural Identity*.

35. On the role of comparison, specifically on how scholars' positioning of their objects of study actually constructs them by predetermining how they relate to each other, see Jonathan Z. Smith, *Drudgery Divine: On the Comparison of Early Christianities and the Religions of Late Antiquity* (Chicago: University of Chicago Press, 1990).

36. Burton, in her *New York Times* article, mentions that Weird Catholic Twitter only contains a few hundred people. I assume this estimate comes from a look at the influential accounts and the amounts of likes or retweets or replies. But of course, the vast majority of social media users are lurkers, or people who don't create or often engage with the content. While we might question whether the old 90–9–1 rule (90 percent lurk, 9 percent contribute, and 1 percent create most of the content) is accurate for current social media communities, it is safe to say that a majority of social media users mostly lurk. The point is that many more people consume the content and might consider themselves "insiders" in a particular imagined subculture without actively creating any content or even interacting (i.e., liking, replying, or retweeting) at all. There is no way to measure this on Twitter.

37. See Bayart, *The Illusion of Cultural Identity*.

38. Harding, *Representing Fundamentalism*, 393.

Tomorrow's Past Today

The Prefigurative Construction of Christian Right Belonging

CHELSEA EBIN

INTRODUCTION: MEET THE DUGGARS

Hollywood and the entertainment industry writ large are often thought to be purveyors of progressive culture. Put in the language of the religiously and politically conservative Christian right movement, the mainstream culture industry peddles "secular humanism."[1] Diverse representations of race, religious faith, sexual orientation, and women's empowerment are cast as the visual illustration of a politically correct "war on Christmas," a homosexual "war on family values," and, in the most totalizing narratives, an all-out liberal "culture war."

Beneath the hyperbole, there is some truth to the charge that the entertainment industry skews left.[2] And yet, a cursory flip through broadcast and cable television channels quickly shows that the liberal bias of mainstream television and film is far from monolithic, as evidenced by the steady stream of more conservative-leaning reality television shows such as *Cops* or *Live PD*, and police procedurals like *NCIS*.[3] The discourse that Americans are unfairly subjected to liberal brainwashing through entertainment serves a number of purposes, chief among them the promotion of a false sense of victimhood among the country's white Christian majority.[4] But this narrative has a secondary function, which is of central concern here: it helps to obscure the meaning and impact of entertainment that promotes a Christian nationalist worldview through the production of right-wing Christian social relations. It also serves to actively remake collective understandings of the "traditional," as new beliefs and practices are justified as representative of old ways of being. In this way, the new is sanctified by the old even as it comes to replace it.

Take, for example, the reality television show *19 Kids and Counting*, originally titled *17 Kids and Counting* and then *18 Kids and Counting*, which ran on TLC from 2008 until its cancellation in 2015.[5] The show followed the lives of Jim Bob Duggar, his wife Michelle, and their growing family of children. On its surface, the show aimed to provide a peek into the daily lived experience of raising a wholesome, Christian, all-American family.

In the pilot episode of the show, viewers are introduced to Jim Bob and Michelle, and their (at the time) seventeen children, and made aware that Michelle is pregnant with child number eighteen. As the family embarks on a trip to New York City (to appear on the *Today Show*), we are instructed in the minutiae of what it takes to pack for nineteen (roughly forty pairs of shoes and more than one hundred shirts) and the difficulties of transporting nineteen related bodies through an airport and into New York City taxis. Once in New York, we are treated to the shocked responses of a worldly and diverse cast of everyday New Yorkers, many of whom appear to already recognize the family from media appearances, and who ogle and gawk at the family's size.[6] In this reading, the Duggars captivate our interest by virtue of the size of their family. We view the intimacy of their lives as voyeurs simultaneously enthralled and repulsed by a nuclear family that somehow represents an ideal of heterosexual reproduction but is rendered grotesque by its size. But this reading is, at best, a shallow one, and it omits a secondary script that structures the world of *19 Kids and Counting*.

The presentation of the Duggars as an everyday American family works to interpellate the viewing audience and, by extension, the American public as white, heterosexual, and Christian. But this representation is both misleading and exclusionary. In twenty-first-century pluralist America, the Duggars are not the average family. They are religious fundamentalists. There are hints to this effect in the pilot, such as Jim Bob's voice-over stating, "We have very conservative values," and Michelle explaining that the children do not watch television, have limited internet access, and are homeschooled. Patriarchal roles are clearly observed within the family, with Jim Bob embodying male headship and Michelle submitting to his leadership.[7] This is evidenced in the opening scene, when Michelle defers to Jim Bob on how and when they will tell their other children that she is pregnant again. In later scenes, we see the female children perform duties that are traditionally associated with the domestic sphere (such as packing), while the camera omits shots of male children engaging in any similar labor. Throughout, the ways in which the Duggar family dress, with the long hair and below-the-knee skirts of Michelle and her daughters, strongly suggest that the family may be fundamentalist in their beliefs.[8] In the pilot, and throughout the show's ten seasons, the Duggar family embodies a particular set of Christian social relations. And yet, the dominant narrative of the pilot (and the show as a whole) is arguably that the Duggars are *just like us only supersized*: they travel on planes, they eat pizza, they go sightseeing in New York's Central Park.

Media and scholarly analysis has pointed out that the Duggar family appears representative of, and may be affiliated with, an opaque Christian movement that goes by the moniker Quiverfull.[9] While the Duggars have denied membership in Quiverfull, instead self-identifying as "Bible-believing Christians," their family nonetheless bears the hallmarks of many of the movement's prevailing beliefs and provides a "reality" television representation of life governed by the doctrines of male headship, wifely submission, and reproduction in accordance with God's plan, which is to say, the repudiation of all forms of family planning and birth control.[10]

For some self-identified Bible-believing Christians, the social norms and practices modeled by the Duggars reflect an embrace of "traditional" familial and gender roles. But the Duggars are reality television stars who have chosen to forego the privacy and sanctity of the domestic sphere. As such, they also embody an identity and a way of being that is anything but representative of a bygone era. Taking on faith that the Duggars seek to emulate "traditional" social relations begs the question of what we mean by "tradition." Rather than assume that Christian conservatives ascribe to a singular or static conception of "tradition," we should ask how the meanings ascribed to the "traditional" are produced.

Querying the relationship between tradition and the social relations embodied on *19 Kids and Counting* gives rise to a more far-reaching question: what kind of sociopolitical world do right-wing Christians want to live in, and how does one locate that sociopolitical world temporally? If we draw on a stock definition, as an ideology that opposes social and political change, it will follow that to make America Christian again would be to return the nation to its traditional values and practices. The aim would, in effect, be to *conserve*.[11] But to make such an assumption requires us to willfully overlook the constitutive practices and policies that characterize Christian right sociopolitical practices and activism.

The following examination of right-wing Christian movements and practices seeks to demonstrate how some conservative Christian groups have sought to initiate sociopolitical change by enacting new forms of social relations that are premised on faulty, if not outright revisionist, conceptions of the past in order to portend, or *prefigure*, the world they wish to create. The practice of prefiguration serves two important purposes: First, prefiguration offers important affective benefits for members of these conservative Christian communities as it provides a framework for social inclusion and belonging. Second, in laying claim to the "traditional," the Christian right is able to obscure the radicality of its political agenda, which contributes to the broader perception that it is a backlash-driven movement. The adoption of a reactionary and self-defensive posture, in turn, feeds the narrative of victimization and persecution that has become central to Christian right discourse.

Running counter to the Christian right's narrative, this essay proposes that, beginning with the activists of the New Right in the early 1970s, we should understand the movement's politics as fundamentally modern and future-oriented. Rather than return us to the past, the Christian right seeks to manifest transformative social and political change.[12] The movement uses the *idea* of the past as a justification for implementing its vision of the appropriate form American social relations and political institutions should take. The future envisioned by the Christian right is not modeled on the past so much as it is predicated on a presentist manifestation of *new* understandings of the traditional. The Duggar family represents just one manifestation of this process, but the Duggars are far from alone. This essay focuses on three case studies, including Christian Identity, Quiverfull, and Purity Balls, to make the case that the Christian right does not seek to return to the past any more than the Duggars—as a thoroughly modern family that relies on high-speed internet access, vacations in New York, and profits from reality television—want to return to the past.

PREFIGURATIVE POLITICS AND THE LEFT

The Marxist scholar Carl Boggs coined the term "prefigurative" in his writing on workers' councils, explaining, "By 'prefigurative' I mean the embodiment, within the ongoing political practice of a movement, of those forms of social relations, decision-making, culture, and human experience that are the ultimate goal."[13] Put another way, prefiguration is the practice of preemptively living out the social changes that would necessarily follow from a large-scale political transformation that is sought but has not yet taken place. Taking inspiration from Boggs, I argue that the political success of conservative Christians has hinged in no small part on the production of a politics that can best be termed *prefigurative traditionalism*.

The strategy of prefiguration is most commonly, if not exclusively, associated with leftist political organizing. There is good reason for this. On one hand, prefigurative politics is deeply tied to a Marxist understanding of praxis, insofar as it demands that actors embody and put into practice their political ideologies. On the other hand, prefiguration necessarily conjures the utopian, insofar as it demands a belief that activists can effectively change the world through individual participation in collective action.

In the 1960s, the New Left, particularly Students for a Democratic Society (SDS), adopted prefigurative politics as a principal logic of the movement. As the political theorist and cultural critic James Miller has detailed, SDS drew much of its intellectual foundations from the work of sociologist C. Wright Mills. Mills had argued that feelings of personal frustration and powerlessness ought to be connected to public issues—and that the way to change the public was through face-to-face interaction.[14] Mills's ideas were reiterated and developed by Tom Hayden, a principal author of the Port Huron Statement and architect of the SDS, and other members of SDS as they became a foundational basis for the characteristic assertion by the new left (and later, by second-wave feminists) that "the personal is political." Drawing on the work of Arnold Kaufman as well, Hayden proposed that an answer to the political alienation and subjugation of the people could be found in the individual and active practice of politics via the form of participatory democracy.[15]

The new left, which emerged alongside rights-based movements and the broader counterculture of the 1960s, signaled a break from the past. The old left's Marxist aim of capital redistribution gave way to a new aim: political recognition—the intrinsic value and respect of individuals as political subjects and agents—accompanied by a commitment to democratic participation as the foundation for equality. The means of bringing about political revolution were also reconceptualized. In place of vanguardism and hierarchical organization, and related to the belief that personal participation in collective action could transform society, prefigurative action emerged as a new mode of political organization.

As Wini Breines explains in *Community and Organization in the New Left*, "the term *prefigurative politics* is used to designate an essentially anti-organizational politics characteristic of the movement, as well as parts of new left leadership, and may be recognized in counter institutions, demonstrations and the attempt to embody personal and anti-hierarchical values in politics . . . The crux of prefigurative politics imposed substantial tasks, the central one being to create and sustain within the live practice of the movement, relationship and political forms that 'prefigured' and embodied the desired society."[16] Prefigurative politics within the new left was tied up in the creation of new forms of community and the practice of participatory democracy. Moreover, the relationship between prefiguration, community building, and anticapitalism within the movement should not be understated: within the new left, prefiguration meant the creation of a community—a set of social relations—that existed outside the system of economic, racial, and gender exploitation demanded by capitalism.[17]

Breines asserts the relationship emphatically: "the search for and/or struggle to defend community, both the 'sense' of community and actual community institutions, becomes political in the context of the changes that capitalism has brought in the everyday life of the individual . . . The desire for connectedness, meaningful personal relationships and direct participation and control over economic, political and social institutions on the basis of the needs of the individual and community, takes on radical meaning in a period such as ours."[18] In a similar vein, recent scholarship on prefiguration, which has tended to focus on movements like Occupy Wall Street and workers' cooperatives, asserts the integral link between democratic norms, anticapitalism, and prefiguration. Prefiguration has largely been defined in such a way as to necessarily exclude conservative movements.[19]

Nonetheless, while democratic practice and anticapitalism were integral to the new left's formation and mobilization, it is not immediately evident that these are necessary and defining, or substantive, attributes of all prefigurative politics. Returning to Boggs's original definition of prefiguration as "the embodiment, within the ongoing political practice of a movement, of those forms of social relations, decision-making, culture, and human experience that are the ultimate goal," a more generalizable theory can be operationalized. Doing so opens the door to a reconsideration of prefiguration as a set of political practices that can be adopted by and adapted to a spectrum of political ideologies.

PREFIGURATIVE POLITICS AND THE NEW RIGHT

On its face, conservativism necessarily runs counter to prefiguration as it looks back in time to hew to the traditional. Understood in this way by activists and scholars alike, conservative movements are viewed as reactionary, while progressive or leftist movements are credited with being generative and proactive. But superimposing this dichotomous understanding of right and left onto conservative movements only serves to obscure the radicality of the right and has contributed to a misrecognition of the capacities and capabilities of right-wing movements since the 1970s.

In the early and mid-1970s, an insurgent right-wing movement, termed the "New Right" by Republican strategist Kevin Phillips, began to take shape.[20] Ostensibly a secular movement, the New Right sought to advance true "conservatism" in electoral and legislative politics by building new institutions and supporting the candidacies of right-leaning candidates.[21] Over the course of the decade, the movement actively redefined what conservatism meant as it fused a plurality of socially conservative single issues with anticommunist, procapitalist, and pseudo-populist lunch-pail politics (characterized by economically protectionist overtures to the white working class).[22]

By the close of the 1970s, Catholic New Right (CNR) activists recruited and were joined by a movement of evangelical and fundamentalist Protestants, commonly referred to as the religious right, and social conservatives who identified as "profamily" activists. Despite having overlapping leadership, these movements strategically sought to remain discrete from one another. Nonetheless, and despite the particularities of each movement, it is fair to say that they collectively formed a new, broad-based social movement that successfully mobilized conservative Christians on the basis of their Christian identity.

Belying the New Right's secular and anti-elitist rhetoric, the leadership was largely composed of conservative Catholics who were Washington insiders. Savvy and well-connected, these activists can best be characterized as political entrepreneurs who possessed expert political knowledge and skills.[23] Notably, a key architect of the movement, Paul Weyrich, claimed to have learned how to organize politically from watching new left activists lobby their representatives, in his capacity as an aide to Republican Senator Gordon Allott. Weyrich recounted his epiphany in an interview on C-SPAN: "And I'm looking at this. And I said, that's how they do it . . . All of a sudden, I was granted the opportunity to see the mechanics. And from that day . . . That was 1969. And from that day forward, I was insufferable. Wherever I went I said, we've got to do something about this. We've got to have our own organizations. We've got to have our own meeting, and you know, so on."[24] Richard Viguerie, another New Right political entrepreneur, would make a similar claim about learning from their opposition, but would aim it at the Democratic Party more generally: "we soon realized there was a better way for conservatives to win power than by forming their own party. We didn't have to look far for models: The Democrats had known it all along."[25]

Historians and political scientists have been eager to repeat Paul Weyrich's and Richard Viguerie's adage that they learned from their enemies, often citing Viguerie's line that "all the New Right has done is copy the success of the old left."[26] In his book about Weyrich and Viguerie, Alf Tomas Tønnessen uncritically accepts this New Right narrative, examining "Weyrich's tireless effort in the early 1970s to help create a right-wing mirror image of the Left, starting with his groundbreaking involvement in the planning of the research center that became known as the Heritage Foundation."[27] That Weyrich sought to develop new institutions, such as the Heritage Foundation, to mirror the left-leaning Brookings Institution has been widely accepted. And while Weyrich explicitly referenced the left's embrace of coalition politics and its development of think tanks as inspiration for the New Right, it is not difficult to see how the New Right, along with the religious right and profamily affiliates, may have borrowed another political strategy from the New Left: prefigurative politics.

Given our longstanding association of prefigurative politics with participatory democracy on the left, it is difficult conjure an image of suit-and-tie-clad, right-wing, Washington Beltway political insiders enacting a utopian set of social relations. And, by and large, CNR political entrepreneurs at best only ever partially embodied the social relations they promoted. Rather, they articulated a set of ideas about "traditional" gender roles, the family, and parental rights that were expressed through the introduction of social policy, aimed at forcing others to realize these relations, and embodied by grassroots members at the community level. A brief example, drawn from family policy advocacy, helps illustrate the ways in which CNR political entrepreneurs helped to promulgate the practice of prefigurative politics within the Christian right.

PREFIGURATIVE POLICY

In remarks prepared for the Republican Platform Committee in 1976, Paul Weyrich articulated the demands of "profamily" politics: "The Republican Party should draw the lines very clearly here, in its defense of the family and family values. That means that it should defend the right to life, oppose the Equal Rights Amendment, expel the Federal government from its role in the design of elementary and secondary school curricula intended to undermine the family and the Judaeo-Christian ethic on which our society is based, stop forced busing, eradicate child development legislation, and so forth. The Republican Party must defend the family structure, and the right of the individual to live his own life."[28] Five years prior to Weyrich's testimony, a CNR activist, Connaught (Connie) Marshner, had already undertaken action to make "profamily" politics a reality.

Over the course of the 1970s, Marshner would become a protégé of Paul Weyrich, first at the Heritage Foundation and later at the Committee for the Survival of a Free Congress. While she was a skilled political organizer and legislative and policy advocate, Marshner was also a mother of several children, and both she and her husband, William H. Marshner, a theologian, were conservative Catholics who viewed politics—and the family—through the prism of religious orthodoxy. While William Marshner dedicated his time to writing religious treatises and building Christendom College,[29] Connie Marshner worked tirelessly in Washington politics to advance policy and legislative positions that reflected her religiously conservative worldview.

An early example of Marshner's "profamily" advocacy work dates to 1971, shortly before she began working with Weyrich, when she mobilized a letter-writing campaign in opposition to the Comprehensive Child Development Bill on the grounds that it represented government intrusion into the home.[30] The historian Leo P. Ribuffo explains that Marshner targeted "local church women" and was surprised to find that evangelical and fundamentalist women constituted a readily mobilized army who submitted "hundreds of thousands of letters" in opposition to the legislation.[31]

On December 9, 1971, President Nixon vetoed the Economic Opportunity Amendments Act, singling out for special censure Title V (the Child Development Bill), which would have created government-subsidized universal day care. Nixon justified his veto on the grounds of support for small government, fiscal conservatism, states' rights, and, in a nod to Marshner's social conservatives, parental rights. In the veto, Nixon explained, "For the Federal Government to plunge headlong financially into supporting child development would commit the vast moral authority of the National Government to the side of communal approaches to child rearing over against the family-centered approach."[32] Nixon's veto did not keep the government from taking an active role in child policy; rather, it mandated that the government's actions would actively work to maintain the nuclear family and constrain women from seeking employment outside of the home.

Marshner would make "profamily" advocacy central to her political work, providing support for conservative Christian parents waging war on public school textbooks[33] and writing the "Family Protection Report," a newsletter with updates on the profamily agenda, throughout the 1970s and 1980s. Marshner's role in the movement highlights a seeming contradiction: as social conservatives within the New Right avowed the primacy of the family and traditional gender roles, women occupied central leadership and organizing roles within—and parallel to—the movement.

In addition to Marshner, Phyllis Schlafly was central to the development of the "profamily" movement.[34] While Schlafly and Marshner were both successful career political activists, they also projected—or embodied—the image of what Marshner referred to as the "new traditional woman" (religiously devout wives and mothers).[35] Rather than giving the lie to the myth of traditionalism they espoused, the social deviance of their political activism was simply deemed necessary to secure a future for the past. Using their identity as women to insulate themselves from the charge of misogyny, conservative female activists, such as Schlafly and Marshner, were able to push for socially conservative politics and policies premised on a perceived need to protect women from victimization at the hands of progressives and "secular humanists"—an all-encompassing and expansive term that could easily encompass the perceived threat of liberals, progressives, feminists, homosexuals, and communists in equal measure.

It mattered little that the "traditional" institution of the family that Weyrich and his fellow CNR activists fought so dearly to protect had not always been a *cause célèbre* of conservative Christians.[36] Nor did it matter that the idealized housewife and nuclear family, in reality, had never existed in the manner the CNR defended. As a host of feminist and labor scholars have made clear, there has not been a time in US history when women have been so dutifully and faithfully supported by husbands as to effect their complete absence from the wage-labor market.[37] And so, in order to make "profamily" politics a reality, the conditions for the creation and maintenance of an idealized family structure needed to be implemented concretely through legislative reform. Put another way, family policy initiatives held the potential to enforce the embodiment of a set of social relations that CNR activists simultaneously asserted were representative of the nation's past and necessary for its future survival.

PREFIGURATIVE COMMUNITIES AND PRACTICES FROM THE 1970S TO THE PRESENT

A central question remains: by whom and how were prefigurative social relations, premised on the operationalization of tradition, manifested? The long decade stretching from the late 1970s through the early 1990s was, in many respects, the movement's heyday. Formal religious right organizations, such as the Moral Majority and the Christian Coalition, flourished, and the "culture wars" defined political discourse.[38] At the same time, Christian right beliefs and attitudes informed grassroots activism and shaped the daily lives of individuals. At the most radical end of this spectrum lies Christian Identity. A racist movement that blossomed in the 1970s and continues to spawn offshoot communities, Christian Identity sought to prefigure the creation of a white Christian ethnostate. The patriarchal traditionalism of the Quiverfull movement falls somewhere around the middle of the spectrum, with religious beliefs that are stringently conservative but political attitudes that are not necessarily inconsistent with a democratic republic. Continuing along the spectrum, and providing a bridge to the mainstream, we find groups like the Promise Keepers and their antecedents, which reflect the embodiment of what might be termed "patriarchal traditionalism lite."

Throughout this period, Christian groups from across the right-wing political spectrum created communities and enacted social practices that sought to both represent and realize a future Christian world through the enactment of "traditional" social relations. An examination of these groups shows how the practice of living out a new set of sociopolitical relations not only provided members of these groups with a sense of belonging, but also reinforced narratives of victimhood that helped obscure the proactive and radical transformations sought by the Christian right. The following discussion briefly spotlights how each of these movements, along with its contemporary analogues, represents a proactive right-wing politics and reflects the embrace of participatory and prefigurative social relations.

Christian Identity and Other White Ethnonationalist Christian Groups

Christian Identity is an umbrella label used by scholars to describe a constellation of beliefs that ground white supremacism in Christianity. Three tenets are central to the Christian Identity belief system: "white 'Aryans' are descendants of the biblical tribes of Israel and thus are on earth to do God's work"; "Jews are not only wholly unconnected to the Israelites, but are the very children of the Devil"; "the world is on the verge of the final, apocalyptic struggle between good and evil, in which the Aryans must do battle with the Jewish conspiracy and its allies so that the world can be redeemed."[39] Overall, the movement can be characterized as virulently antisemitic, white supremacist, and fixated on both a mythical narrative of the past (constructing "Aryans" as the "true" tribes of Israel) and the future (insofar as all political organizing is geared toward the creation of an Aryan kingdom in the aftermath of the apocalypse). Central to white supremacist belief systems is a preoccupation with control of white women's sexuality and the exercise of patriarchal authority over the white family in order to maintain racial purity and propagate the white race.[40]

Offshoot movements are frequently characterized not only by their adherence to these three core beliefs, but also by their attempts to create "Aryan" communities. For example, in the early 1970s, Richard Butler established the Church of Jesus Christ-Christian and "built a survivalist compound and training facility in Hayden Lake [Idaho] to promote the idea of creating a racially pure country composed solely of people from the various historic and genetic 'Aryan Nations.'"[41] Other splinter groups include the Aryan Nations, Fellowship of God's Covenant People, and Marble Community Fellowship. Recently, the secretive Marble Community Fellowship compound, in Marble Country, Washington, has been tied to the Christian Patriot movement and the antigovernment protests led by the Bundy family in 2014 and 2016.[42]

As scholar of right-wing movements Chip Berlet explained, Christian Identity movements aim to create an "integralist totalitarian society." In other words, the Christian Identity belief system seeks to bring about "armed revolution" in order to eradicate Jews and "parasites" from the nation.[43] The necessity of the revolution is justified by reference to theological "tradition" and the construction of a mythical Aryan past. In the interregnum, as Christian Identity communities await the revolution/ apocalypse they believe is imminent, they model the white ethnostate through the construction of communities like those at Hayden Lake and Marble Country. In doing so, they call on the past to manifest in the present the Aryan community they believe the future will bring.

Quiverfull

As sociologist of religion Steven M. Tipton has shown, the 1970s were characterized for many by the repudiation of the loss of norms associated with the counterculture, and a turn toward authoritarian and hierarchical, faith-based communal living instead.[44] By the late 1970s, the antifeminist and profamily message propounded by Marshner and Schlafly had found an expressly evangelical complement in Nancy Campbell and her *Above Rubies* Christian women's magazine, which promoted a "return" to patriarchal traditional modes of domestic life. In *Quiverfull: Inside the Christian Patriarchy Movement*, journalist Kathryn Joyce explains: "When Campbell started printing the magazine in 1977, she says she was seeking to fill a void in encouragement to women who resisted the lures of feminism and careers . . . she felt bereft of guidance and encouragement in her stay-at-home life and determined to provide it herself for other young mothers living a homemaker's life. She started from scratch and eventually went on to mentor thousands, leading women back to hearth, home, and the proper honor of their husbands."[45] In the pages of *Above Rubies*, Campbell articulated for her readers a belief that can be summarized by the term "biblical womanhood." The doctrine of biblical womanhood holds, in part, that women are the keepers of the home and should serve as their husband's "helpmate." A woman's power is seen to come from her ability to enforce religious observance and codes of conducts that are necessarily dictated to her by the Bible, the Church, and her husband.[46]

In some ways, biblical womanhood can be understood as a continuation of the ideology attendant to the nineteenth-century cult of domesticity, which held women should be judged by their "piety, purity, submissiveness, and domesticity."47 In seeking to maintain the distinction between public (coded male) and private (coded female) spheres, the doctrine does seem to recall the historical experience of some white women in the nineteenthcentury. But, as sociologist John Bartkowski reminds us, "spousal authority" and "gendered domestic relations" are not synonymous. As such, he explains, "patriarchy—which literally means 'rule of the father'—may be defined rather narrowly as the concentration of power (e.g., decision-making authority) in the hands of a family's husband/father. According to this definition, then, patriarchy should not be conflated with "traditional' dichotomized household responsibilities (e.g., husband-providership and wifely domesticity), although these two gender role orientations may be closely aligned in practice."48 Beyond drawing an important distinction between historical gender roles within the domestic sphere, there is another reason that it would be a mistake to understand the late twentieth-century concepts of patriarchal traditionalism and biblical womanhood that Quiverfull is built on as merely a backward-looking embrace of the cult of domesticity. The family, and the place ordained for women in it, imagined by Quiverfull has never existed in America's past.

In 1985, echoing Campbell's arguments against feminism and in favor of wifely submission, the evangelical activist Mary Pride[49] published *The Way Home: Beyond Feminism, Back to Reality*, which became a "founding text" for Quiverfull. The advice given in *The Way Home* went further than Campbell's, however, in that Pride advocated a rejection of all family-planning methods and a complete disavowal of women's bodily autonomy.[50] Four years after the publication of *The Way Home*, the Quiverfull movement was launched. Again, Joyce details the origins of the movement: "Quiverfull, as a contemporary movement, began with the publication of Rick and Jan Hess's 1989 book, *A Full Quiver: Family Planning and the Lordship of Christ*, in which the Hesses, a Nebraska couple encouraged to write by Mary Pride, argue that God, as the 'Great Physician' and sole 'Birth Controller,' is in charge of opening and closing the womb on a case-by-case basis. Women's attempts to control their own bodies—the Lord's temple—are a seizure of divine power."[51] Put simply, within the Quiverfull movement, women are commanded to act as vessels and are expected to dutifully and obediently fulfill their God-given role as mothers and wives. The rejection of family planning is supported by the belief that "Christians are to have lots of children, in order to bring more sound Christian voters into this world and thus combat non-Christian influences in society."[52] In other words, Quiverfull women are meant to go forth and produce—quite literally—a new army of Christian soldiers.[53]

Since the publication of the Hesses' book, the Quiverfull movement, which is largely decentralized and characterized by members' adherence to a common set of fundamentalist Protestant beliefs and attitudes concerning hierarchical gender and familial roles, has grown online and been popularized through reality television shows such as *19 Kids and Counting*. At first blush, Quiverfull might seem to be a straightforwardly backlash-driven movement, with adherents aggressively rejecting the advances of second-wave feminism and the changes wrought by modernity. In this reading, the movement seeks to return women to their traditional Christian roles. But to which "traditional" role are they being returned?

Once again, the obvious answer, suggested by the movement's frequent criticisms of modern society, would be that of the nineteenth-century "true woman." And yet, this assumption quickly falls apart: the cult of domesticity was soundly rejected by fundamentalist Protestants because it venerated women as repositories of moral virtue. While men were expected to serve as the public head of the household, women were understood to be the spiritual head The cult of domesticity served to challenge patriarchal norms and facilitated the rise of first-wave feminism;[54] it did not advance the form of male headship Quiverfull avows. This is to say little of the historical anachronisms that color the movement's rejection of family planning. Christian teachings on family planning have not been consistent across time,[55] and family planning, in one form or another, has been practiced by women throughout the history of the United States.[56] The Quiverfull family—composed of a dominant patriarch, a submissive and subservient housewife (who contributes neither economically nor spiritually), upward of six children who survive into adulthood, and a household high-speed internet connection for surfing mommy blogs and streaming reality television—simply has never existed in the American past.

Put in terms of prefigurative traditionalism, the Quiverfull movement realizes a set of social relations that are predicated on a fictionalized past in order to obscure the radicality of the movement's demands for the creation of a new future. As Laura Harrison and Sarah B. Rowley have argued, "Quiverfull members rearticulate what it means to be a modern American by emphasizing the relevancy of female submission, male headship, and subservience to God in contemporary society. Quiverfull members, particularly by engaging with mainstream media and technology, demonstrate their wish to engage with modern American culture and to spread their particular Christian worldview to the society at large. Far from wishing to retreat to some mythical past, the movement advocates reforming our current society to fit the movement's ideals."[57] Neither the Duggars nor the Quiverfull movement seeks to return the nation to the way it was before the women's liberation movement transformed gender roles; rather, they aim to create a future Christian society predicated on an entrenched gender hierarchy unlike any the nation has historically lived under.

The Patriarchal Traditionalism of Promise Keepers and Purity Balls

The year after the Hesses published *A Full Quiver*, in 1990, coach Bill McCartney launched Promise Keepers. Conceived of as a national revival, throughout the 1990s, Promise Keepers mobilized tens of thousands of men to converge in large stadiums where they would hear sermons on how to be Godly men and leaders.[58] A softer, gentler patriarchal movement, Promise Keepers trained its eye on reforming the behavior of men. Never mind that men's behavior was understood as being in need of reformation because men were failing in their God-given role as provider and shepherd. As right-wing movement analyst Jean Hardisty explains, "Promise Keepers offers hope to conservative Christian women that it will make their husbands better family men. In return, Promise Keepers men require that their wives adhere to the traditional female role of helpmate."[59] After a "million man" march held in Washington, DC, called "Stand the Gap," bankrupted the organization in 1997, the movement has since shown signs of resurgence.[60] In 2021, the group hosted an in-person Men's Conference in Arlington, TX, alongside a host of virtual events such as the "Men's Marriage" and "Fatherhood" summits.[61]

The Promise Keepers was one manifestation of a large-scale movement seeking to create a society organized around the principle of biblical manhood through the manifestation of a particular set of social relations in the 1990s. A smaller, but more pronounced, manifestation of prefiguration traditionalism can be found in the father-daughter Purity Ball movement. Started in 1998, just as Promise Keepers began to wind down, the Purity Ball movement is, in effect, a spectacular representation of prefiguration in action.

In practice, Purity Balls look much more like intergenerational weddings than they do typical father-daughter dances.[62] At the formal event, according to the founder's website, "the fathers sign a pledge that they will be the example of purity and model integrity for their daughter's lives. The daughters silently commit to live pure lives before God through the symbol of laying down a white rose at the cross." The pledge, quoted here in full, reads: "I, (daughter's name)'s father, choose before God to cover my daughter as her authority and protection in the area of purity. I will be pure in my own life as a man, husband and father. I will be a man of integrity and accountab[i]lity as I lead, guide and pray over my daughter and my family as the high priest in my home. This covering will be used by God to influence generations to come."[63] Dressed as child-brides, daughters are symbolically wed to their fathers who, in turn, take "ownership" over their child's virginity until it will be transferred to the man who becomes her husband. The ceremony is an attempt not only to manifest traditional gender roles, but also to project those roles into the future by denying the female child any period of time in which she may have ownership over her own body and sexuality.

Despite high-profile criticism of the Purity movement (of which Purity Balls are a part) from within the evangelical community,[64] the balls remain common. And in the thirty years since it was first launched, Promise Keepers has been joined by new groups that host conferences aimed at instructing men and women on how to properly embody their appropriate gender roles and relations.

CONCLUSION: WHAT WILL THE FUTURE HOLD?

Less explicitly Christian, but by no means less patriarchal, events like the 22Convention promise to "Make Women Great Again." Borrowing antifeminist and gender-essentialist language from the Christian right and the hypermasculine bravado of the men's rights movement,[65] the 22Convention's website represents a synthesis of the two movements. Advertising for the convention boldly proclaims: "Women today are being taught to act more like men. Where has that led us? Skyrocketing rates of broken families, a documented decline in female happiness since the 1970s, endless social and dating dysfunction, and America at the #1 spot in the world for single motherhood. No longer will you have to give in to toxic bullying feminist dogma and go against your ancient, biological nature as a woman, the men have arrived to help #MWGA. Experience a miraculous three day (and night) event with iconic 100% pure male speakers gathered from the worldwide manosphere community to help you dramatically improve your life as a woman and total femininity."[66] By offering to teach women how to reclaim their "ancient, biological nature," the 22Convention insinuates that it is merely trying to revert to a simpler time, prior to the 1970s, when things were better. But the hypercontemporary rhetoric, exemplified by the #MWGA, signals not a return to the past, but rather an embrace of a new political world. In this future, social relations are stamped by the internet and marked by the convergence of right-wing fundamentalist Christianity and secular men's rights and male supremacist activism.

Returning to the other side of the same spectrum, we find a similar message promoted by the ostensibly feel-good television reality of *19 Kids and Counting*. The Duggars model one way for women to embrace their "ancient, biological nature" and live a simultaneously pre-1970s and postmodern life. In this way, the Duggars package white, Christian, and male supremacism in a kinder, gentler, hokier fashion. But it is white, Christian, male supremacism nonetheless. The movements analyzed in this essay span the spectrum of right-wing Christian social practices. What unifies them is a vision of a future America that is hierarchical and ordered around patriarchal authority. It is a future defined by the supremacy of husbands over wives, men over women, Christianity over all other beliefs and ideologies. It is a mistake to understand contemporary right-wing Christian politics as either retrograde or wedded to static conceptions of "tradition." By adopting a reactionary posture and occupying the position of aggrieved victimhood, the Christian right has successfully deflected attention from the real dangers posed by political and social movements that seek to fundamentally transform the nation's political and social relations. Read as parts of a whole, these movements underscore the productive capacity and future-oriented vision of the Christian right.

NOTES

1. A note on key terms used in this essay: Scholars frequently use the term "Religious Right" or "Christian Right" for the behemoth sociopolitical movement of conservative Judeo-Christian religious believers in the United States, which began in the late 1970s, flourished in the 1980s, and continues to operate in American politics. In this essay, I have intentionally adopted the term "Christian Right" (alternately, "right-wing Christians") to refer to formally mobilized political actors, groups, and grassroots as well as to individuals who identify as being on the Christian Right of the political spectrum. All of the groups under analysis are expressly Christian even as they run the denominational gamut from traditionalist Catholicism to fundamentalist Mormonism. "Secular humanism," a term popularized in part by the fundamentalist Protestant theologian Francis Schaeffer, is an umbrella term for the cultural displacement of God from the center of social and political relations wrought by modernity. While the term is used less frequently in popular discourse now, in the 1970s and 1980s, it served as a catchall for describing what was perceived as a coordinated liberal attack on Christian values, norms, and practices. Secular humanism was pitted against Christianity as an oppositional religious worldview. See, for example, John W. Whitehead and John Conlon, "The Establishment of the Religion of Secular Humanism and Its First Amendment Implications," *Texas Technical Law Review* 10, no. 1 (1978–79), 1: "Secularism, or what is commonly referred to as 'Secular Humanism,' poses a serious constitutional quandary because its purpose is to eliminate traditional theism as a significant aspect of reality by forcing traditional theism from the arena of public discourse and American institutional life." For a discussion of secular humanism, see Carol Mason, *Reading Appalachia from Left to Right: Conservatives and the 1974 Kanawha County Textbook Controversy* (Ithaca: Cornell University Press, 2009), chap. 3.

2. See, for example, Andy Kiersz and Hunter Walker, "These Three Charts Confirm Conservatives' Worst Fears about American Culture," *Business Insider,* November 3, 2014.

3. For an examination of *Cops* and *Live PD*, see Dan Taberski, *Running from Cops*, podcast, April–May 2019. See also Johanna Blakely, "Liberals and Conservatives Have Wildly Different TV-Viewing Habits—But These Five Shows Bring Everyone Together," *The Conversation*, July 1, 2019.

4. For an examination of how "victim claims" are constructed and operationalized, see Mitch Berbrier, "The Victim Ideology of White Supremacists and White Nationalists in the United States," *Sociological Focus* 33, no. 2 (2000): 175–91.

5. The show was canceled shortly after InTouch broke the story that the eldest Duggar child, Joshua, had molested several young girls when he was a teenager and that the Duggar patriarch, Jim Bob, had helped to bury the allegations. "Bombshell Duggar Police Report," *InTouch*, September 22, 2016.

6. "Big Family Meets Big Apple," *Seventeen Kids and Counting*, E01S01, September 28, 2008, TLC.

7. John Bartowski explains, "Commentators who embrace a patriarchal family structure construe several key biblical passages as advocating 'husband headship' and 'wifely submission' in the home. Most popular among these is a series of verses from the Bible's book of Ephesians (ch. 5: 22–24) . . . 'Wives, submit to your husbands as to the Lord. For the husband is the head of the wife as Christ is the head of the Church, his body, of which he is the Savior. Now as the church submits to Christ, so also wives should submit to their husbands in everything.' Focusing upon the first of these passages (i.e., Ephesians 5: 22), many of these commentators frequently remind wives that submission to their husbands serves as an indicator of their commitment to Jesus Christ, for whom their husbands are serving as a divinely appointed proxy." "Debating Patriarchy: Discursive Disputes over Spousal Authority among Evangelical Family Commentators," *Journal for the Scientific Study of Religion* 36, no. 3 (1997): 402.

8. For a discussion of the religious significance of the Duggars' dress code, see Sasha Aborn, "The Truth about the Duggars Dresscode," *The List*, n.d.

9. The Quiverfull movement is discussed in more detail later in this essay. For a reading of the Duggar family as representative of the Quiverfull movement, see Christy Ellen Mesaro-Winckles, "Christian Patriarchy Lite: TLC's 19 Kids and Counting," in *Media Depictions of Brides, Wives, and Mothers*, ed. Alana Amato Ruggerio (Lanham, MD: Lexington Books, 2012).

10. See Antonia Blumberg, "What You Need to Know about the 'Quiverfull' Movement," *HuffPost*, May 26, 2015.

11. Edmund Burke, *Reflections on the Revolution in France* (London, 1790), 18.

12. Didi Herman, "'Then I Saw a New Heaven and a New Earth': Thoughts on the Christian Right and the Problem of 'Backlash,'" in *Dangerous Territories*, ed. Leslie G. Roman and Linda Eyre (New York: Routledge, 1997).

13. Carl Boggs, "Marxism, Prefigurative Communism, and the Problem of Workers' Control," *Radical America* 6 (Winter 1977).

14. C. Wright Mills, *The Power Elite* (Oxford: Oxford University Press, 2000).

15. James Miller, *Democracy Is in the Streets: From Port Huron to the Siege of Chicago* (New York: Simon and Schuster, 1987) chap. 5.

16. Wini Breines, *Community and Organization in the New Left, 1962–1968: The Great Refusal* (New Brunswick, NJ: Rutgers University Press, 1989), 6.

17. This is not the place to detail the breakdown of the new left, or to engage in a debate about how to judge the relative successes or failures of the movement. Rather, suffice it to say that the desire to embody equitable social relations and to bring forth new institutions

through the active practice of democracy was not sustained—on the left—through the 1970s.

18. Breines, *Community and Organization in the New Left*, 7.

19. F. Cornish, J. Haaken, L. Moskovitz, and S. Jackson, "Rethinking Prefigurative Politics: Introduction to the Special Thematic Section," *Journal of Social and Political Psychology* 4, no. 1 (2016): 114–27.

20. Another note on terminology: The new right can briefly be described as a self-identified insurgent and radical political movement that formed in the early 1970s with the intent of advancing "true" conservatism. Composed of a network of overlapping political brokers and conservative institutions, the new right sought to force the Republican Party to adopt more right-wing positions while also disrupting the two-party system through the creation of a broad-based conservative coalition that would cleave across traditional Republican and Democrat party lines. The religious right emerged with the help of new right political entrepreneurs in the late 1970s and early 1980s, and explicitly sought to inject Judeo-Christian values into American politics and public discourse. While largely composed of white evangelical and fundamentalist Protestants, the religious right did attempt to incorporate conservative Jewish groups.

21. The first incarnation of new right institutions, Analysis and Research Associates and the Heritage Foundation, focused on producing policies and setting legislative agendas, but changes in the political climate coupled with campaign finance reform created an opening in the political opportunity structure that new right activists rushed to fill via the creation of conservative fund-raising institutions. Between 1971 and 1975, new right activists launched more than a dozen political organizations, including the Heritage Foundation; Center for the Public Interest; American Conservative Union; Americans for Constitutional Action; Committee for the Survival of a Free Congress; Free Congress Research and Education Foundation; National Conservative Political Action Committee; Conservative Caucus; Conservative Caucus Research, Analysis, and Education Foundation; and Committee for Responsible Youth Politics.

22. William J. Lanouette, "The New Right—'Revolutionaries' Out after the 'Lunch-Pail' Vote," *National Journal*, January 21, 1978; Paul M. Weyrich, Scrapbooks, Library of Congress (hereafter WS), 1978, box 6, folder 7, vol. 22.

23. Adam D. Sheingate, "Political Entrepreneurship, Institutional Change, and American Political Development," *Studies in American Political Development* 17, no. 2 (2003): 185–203.

24. C-SPAN, "Q and A with Paul Weyrich," March 22, 2005.

25. Richard Viguerie, "Ends and Means," in *The New Right Papers*, ed. Robert Whitaker (New York: St Martins Press, 1982), 29.

26. Daniel Schlozman, *When Movements Anchor Parties: Electoral Alignments in American History* (Princeton: Princeton University Press, 2015).

27. Alf Tomas Tønnessen, *How Two Political Entrepreneurs Helped Create the Conservative Movement, 1973–1981* (Lampeter, Wales, UK: Edwin Mellen Press, 2009), 54.

28. "CSFC Statement before the Republican Platform Committee," August 10, 1976, WS, 1976, box 6, folder 1, vol. 19.

29. Misc. Christendom College documents, including correspondence and grant application, American Heritage Center, University of Wyoming, Laramie (hereafter AHC), Paul M. Weyrich Papers, 10138, box 15 (1977–78).

30. Annelise Orlick, *Rethinking American Women's Activism* (New York: Routledge, 2015).

31. Leo P. Ribuffo, "Family Policy Past as Prologue: Jimmy Carter, the White House Conference on Families, and the Mobilization of the New Christian Right," *Review of Policy Research* 23 (April 2006): 325.

32. Richard Nixon, Veto of the Economic Opportunity Amendments of 1971, December 9, 1971, The American Presidency Project, University of California, Santa Barbara.

33. Mason, *Reading Appalachia*, chap. 3.

34. See, for example, Donald T. Critchlow, *Phyllis Schlafly and Grassroots Conservatism: A Woman's Crusade* (Princeton: Princeton University Press, 2008); David Farber, *The Rise and Fall of Modern American Conservatism: A Short History* (Princeton: Princeton University Press, 2012); Lisa McGirr, *Suburban Warriors: The Origins of the New American Right* (Princeton: Princeton University Press, 2015).

35. Connie Marshner, "Who Is the New Traditional Woman," AHC, 10138, folder 18, box 82 (undated).

36. Margaret Lamberts Bendroth, "Fundamentalism and the Family: Gender, Culture, and the American Pro-family Movement." *Journal of Women's History* 10, no. 4 (1999): 35–54.

37. See especially Amy Dru Stanley, "Conjugal Bonds and Wage Labor: Rights of Contract in the Age of Emancipation," *Journal of American History* 75, no. 2 (1988).

38. See, for example, James Davison Hunter, *Culture Wars: The Struggle to Define America* (New York: Basic Books, 1991), writing about the pervasiveness of culture war discourse in American politics during the 1980s.

39. Michael Barkun, *Religion and the Racist Right: The Origins of the Christian Identity Movement* (Chapel Hill: University of North Carolina Press, 1997), x–xi.

40. For an examination of the relationship between white supremacy and sexuality, see Abb L. Ferber, *White Man Falling: Race, Gender, and White Supremacy* (Lanham, MD: Rowman and Littlefield, 1998), especially chap. 6.

41. Chip Berlet, "Christian Identity: The Apocalyptic Style, Political Religion, Palingenesis and Neo-fascism," *Totalitarian Movements and Political Religions* 5, no. 3 (2004): 471.

42. Leah Sottile, *Bundyville: The Remnant*, podcast series, Longreads and Oregon Public Broadcasting, July 2019.

43. Berlet, "Christian Identity," 473.

44. Steven M. Tipton, *Getting Saved from the Sixties: The Transformation of Moral Meaning in American Culture* (Berkeley: University of California Press, 1982).

45. Katherine Joyce, *Quiverfull: Inside the Christian Patriarchy Movement* (Boston: Beacon Press, 2009), 47.

46. John P. Bartkowski, "Debating Patriarchy: Discursive Disputes over Spousal Authority among Evangelical Family Commentators," *Journal for the Scientific Study of Religion* 36, no. 3 (1997): 393–410, at 398.

47. Barbara Welter, "The Cult of True Womanhood: 1820–1860," *American Quarterly* 18, no. 2 (1966): 152.

48. Bartkowski, "Debating Patriarchy," 408n2.

49. Joyce, *Quiverfull*, 135.

50. Joyce, *Quiverfull*, 134.

51. Suzanne van Geuns, "Mothers for a Christian Nation," *Exchange* 43, no. 2 (2014): 195.

52. Laura Harrison and Sarah B. Rowley, "Babies by the Bundle: Gender, Backlash, and the Quiverfull Movement," *Feminist Formations* 23, no. 1 (Spring 2011): 55.

53. Paula Baker, "The Domestication of Politics: Women and American Political Society, 1780–1920," *American Historical Review* 89, no. 3 (1984): 620–47.

54. Leslie Woodcock Tentler, *Catholics and Contraception: An American History* (Ithaca: Cornell University Press, 2009).

55. Linda Gordon, *The Moral Property of Women: A History of Birth Control Politics in America* (Chicago: University of Chicago Press, 2007).

56. Harrison and Rowley, "Babies by the Bundle," 51.

57. C-SPAN, "Roundtable with Bill McCartney," September 30, 1997.

58. Jean Hardisty, *Mobilizing Resentment: Conservative Resurgence from the John Birch Society to the Promise Keepers* (Boston: Beacon Press, 1999), 94.

59. John P. Bartkowski, *The Promise Keepers: Servants, Soldiers, and Godly Men* (New Brunswick, NJ: Rutgers University Press, 2003.

60. Promise Keepers website, January 2021.

61. Priscilla Frank, "Welcome to the Bizarre and Beautiful World of Purity Balls," *Huff-Post,* December 6, 2017.

62. Generations of Light website, January 2021.

63. See, for example, Sarah McCammon, "Evangelical Writer Who Influenced Purity Culture Announces Separation from Wife," NPR, July 21, 2019.

64. Alex DiBranco, "Before the Alt-Right: Anita Hill and the Growth of Misogynist Ideology," Institute for Research on Male Supremacism, August 13, 2018.

65. 22Convention website, May 2020.

Becoming Hindu in the Greater Caribbean

Making Racial Religious Difference and Experimental Kinship between Panama and Trinidad

Alexander Rocklin

In 1926, the Republic of Panama passed laws restricting immigration into the country, including that of "East Indians, Indo-Aryans, and Dravidians."[1] In response, South Asian merchants in Panama identifying themselves as racially Hindu, led by Sindhi merchant firms, petitioned the government to be exempted from these restrictions. Besides the economic hardship, they objected to being designated as racially "degenerate" under Panamanian law. Rather, they claimed, as high caste and religiously devout, to be racially superior and pure. At the same time, they differentiated themselves from the other "Hindus" in Panama and the Greater Caribbean, specifically Indo-Caribbean and other so-called coolie laborers. They severed relational ties with them by portraying them as morally, economically, and racially questionable. These self-described Hindu merchants were making an intervention in a particular racial regime that the Panamanian state partly defined by anti-Blackness and also anti-West Indianness or anti-Caribbeanness.[2] In denying any kinship with South Asian manual laborers in the Americas, the Hindu merchants in Panama were separating themselves from their own internal others who were also categorized as Hindu but who were entangled with the categories "Black" and "West Indian" (Caribbean) in Central America.

Around the same time, though, in contrast to the racially, religiously, and economically exclusivist kincraft of the elite racial Hindu identifications created by the Sindhi merchants in Panama,[3] Afro- and Indo-Caribbean subalterns in places like Trinidad were using the category "Hindu" and related nomenclature to authorize their own nonnormative modes of social formation. They were engaging in experiments in kin-making through a science of occult powers and spiritual entities resulting in relational connections across lines of racial religious difference. They did this in the face of the violence of colonial racial and religious norms.

In this essay, I use these two contrasting examples of the making and unmaking of relatedness in the Greater Caribbean, one from Panama and one from Trinidad, in order to analyze differing co-productions of racial religious identifications performed across ethnoracial lines connecting the Afro-Atlantic and Indian Ocean worlds, between India, Latin America, and the Caribbean. These are differing modes of becoming Hindu, Hindu identifications that different groups took up as tactics in different social contexts in the Greater Caribbean. Taken together, these examples shine a light on the ways in which the categories "religion" and "race" have been ineluctably entangled and disentangled through modes of creating relations. At the same time, they allow us to analyze the ways in which the engagements of Hindu-identified practices have been performatively enacted in ways that challenged the taken-as-given understandings of race and religion in the Americas, creating intimacies across reified ethnoracial religious lines.

In the Americas, various actors have given the category "Hindu" simultaneous, at times clashing, racial, ethnic, regional, class, occupation, and religious meanings. Around the Caribbean world, in English and Spanish usage, people conflated the categories "Hindustani" and "Hindu," terms indicating geography and race, respectively. The latter term could be given religious connotations, suggesting a practitioner of the Hindu religion (with the emergence of the idea of a so-called world religion, Hinduism). Yet, people also used the word "Hindu" in a vaguer way, to connote magic, mystery, and the spiritual more exclusively. These connotations were variously (dis)articulated from colonial race theories and a specific world religions discourse connected with emergent Hindu nationalisms.[4]

In this essay, I am not concerned with Hinduism, who is or is not truly Hindu, or what "Hindu" really ought to mean. The term "Hindu" does not have necessary contents or essential meanings.[5] In the following examples, I examine the ways in which different groups in different contexts with different audiences and different stakes used the category "Hindu" as part of differing sets of contested practices of racial religious identity- and community-making. Following Stuart Hall, I hold that we should see identity not as "an already accomplished fact," but as always already in process.[6] Hall calls identities "unstable points of identification or suture, which are made, within the discourses of history and culture. Not an essence but a *positioning*."[7] With Hall I see identification, unlike a stable or essentialized identity, as an unfinished and unfinishable set of procedures, never complete, and always unsettled, shifting and negotiated.[8] And with Hall I argue that processes of identification must be understood within their particular and changing historical contexts and within their particular relations of power, keeping in view their role in the confection of difference and sameness, inclusion and exclusion.[9] In line with this, and following Jasbir Puar, the Feminist Critical Hindu Studies Collective has also urged scholars not to take Hindu identities as stable, which is sometimes suggested by analyses of intersectionality. Rather than suggesting an intersection of already-made identities, the collective adapts assemblage theory to intersectionality, arguing that scholars can see Hindu subject positions as always in motion, shifting as contexts are shifting within relations of power.[10] In this way, I see the category of "Hindu" as a context-specific identification that has been continually co-produced with other intersecting social categories. Therefore, religion- and race-making have never been static and have always been done together.

Like identity, kinship is contingent and social, not inevitable and natural.[11] Taking kinship as a basic collective unit for the nation-state and its heteronormative reproduction, states, including colonial regimes, have used kin-making to institute racialized heteronormativity and naturalize the reproduction of the national formation.[12] Kinship, though, has also been highly contestable and partially outside of state control. Colonial regimes in the Pacific and Latin America were wary of the possibility that unchecked claims of kinship connections across racial lines and outside of state-defined and state-sanctioned racial mixings could undermine the integrity of colonial racial regimes and white supremacy.[13] Looking beyond kinship as heteronormative biological reproduction, Elizabeth Freeman takes up queer theory and kinship studies to think of kinship as human relations that involve dependency, nurture, and renewal (including the renewal or re-creation of cultural forms).[14] While still in line with this, I am using the term "kinship" at its broadest, as making and unmaking forms of relatedness. Adapting anthropologist J. Brent Crosson's scholarship on Caribbean spiritual work (what is often called obeah or witchcraft) as "experiments with power," I use the phrase "experimental kinship" to refer to the complex investments in living together in multiply entangled social relations across difference that, in my example of the obeah court case (below), Caribbean subalterns authorized under the category "Hindu."[15] Experimental kin-making is not rooted in biology. It does not lead to stable conflations of religion, race, and nation, unlike regnant nationalist ideologies of kinship in Latin

America and the Caribbean, such as mestizaje, or the racial religious kincraft of the Hindu merchants I also examine in what follows.[16]

This essay is organized into four sections. The first looks at the history of anti-immigration laws and immigration in Panama, focusing on the movements of Sindhi merchants. The second surveys the clashing and competing ethnoracial religious hierarchies of the Panama Canal Zone and the Republic of Panama. The third examines the petition of the Hindu merchants in depth, looking at the fractures and breaks in the Hindu identities they constructed. This section takes a closer look at the complexities of social formation and Hindu identification in colonial Sindh and the Sindhi diaspora and how those complicated the Hindu merchants' claims. In contrast to some of those claims, Sindhis in the colonial period were viewed as religiously questionable by other Hindu-identified groups, in part because Sindhis' ritual practices have involved the coming together of practitioners and the incorporation of practices and objects from across reified religious lines. The fourth section presents modes of becoming Hindu otherwise, analyzing the case of four men, including one Charles Bartholomew, on trial for obeah in Trinidad, who called their ritual work of healing and restoration "Hindu magic." In contradistinction to the stereotype of obeah as antisocial magic, Charles Bartholomew and his associates used Hindu-identified practices involving spirits of the dead to create and maintain relational ties across difference, engaging in activities of experimental kin-making.

ANTI-IMMIGRATION LAW AND IMMIGRATION IN PANAMA

In the wake of the US Chinese exclusion act of 1882, governments around the world began enacting anti-immigration laws excluding immigrants from Asia.[17] This included countries in Latin America, such as Argentina or Panama, attempting to define their populations as primarily European/white or as a continuum of European and Indigenous, with idealized ethnoracial hierarchies that erased or marginalized peoples of African descent. South Asians were variously situated within these social orders.[18] Elites in early twentieth-century Panama saw independence from Colombia in 1903 and the US government's building of the canal as opportunities to "modernize" as well as to make more Hispanic and whiter an otherwise cosmopolitan and ethnoracially diverse country. This diversity included peoples of African descent (the descendants of enslaved peoples and migrants from the Caribbean who came to work on the railroad and canal), as well as people from China, India, and the Middle East. Anti-immigrant policies against such groups became baked into the institutional structures of the new nation.[19] Laws passed beginning in the

1920s barred reentry of immigrants who left the country and made Hispanicization a requirement for citizenship.[20] The rising anti-immigrant sentiment in the 1920s was directed to a significant degree at Afro-Caribbean Panamanians (former canal workers and their descendants), but included noteworthy anti-Asian elements as well, even though Asians made up only a small percentage of the overall population.[21]

On October 23, 1926, the Panamanian National Assembly passed a sweeping anti-immigration law, the first article of which prohibited the immigration of "Chinese, Japanese, Syrians, Turks, East Indians, Indo-Aryans, Dravidians," as well as "Blacks of the West Indies and Guianas whose language of origin is not Spanish."[22] In 1927 the government began to implement the law with a census of immigrant populations, posting notices on billboards throughout the city declaring: "All persons of prohibited immigration resident within the territory of the Republic must present themselves to the offices of the Governor of the respective province of their domicile, during the usual office hours, to be inscribed in the census ordered by law 13 of 1926." The prohibited ethnoracial groups and nationalities were all listed on the announcements.[23] The law led to racist attacks and intimidations. After the passage of the anti-immigration law, the English-language, Afro-Caribbean newspaper *The Workman* reported that "native" Panamanians were insulting and abusive to West Indian residents in Colón, and the paper published a story in circulation about rewards being offered for turning in banned immigrants.[24] Panamanians and residents of the US–controlled Canal Zone (or Zonians) also protested against "Hindu" or South Asian merchant shops.[25] Sindhi merchants saw the law as specifically targeting them, the motivation behind the law being "to drive out the Indian traders altogether from the Panama territory."[26]

Sindh, in what is now Pakistan, has long been an important juncture point in the web of trade in the Indian Ocean world and beyond, with Sindhi merchant networks extending all over the globe over the course of the second half of the nineteenth century.[27] In the mid-nineteenth century, merchant peddlers from Hyderabad, Sindh, began selling Sindhi handicrafts to Europeans in Bombay. These goods became known as "Sindwork," and the Sindhi merchants selling them were called "Sindworkis." In the second half of the nineteenth century, with the rise in global travel, these Hyderabadi merchants expanded their sales of "oriental" goods acquired from across India, as well as China and Japan, around the world. Following the new routes of steamships, Sindworkis sold souvenirs to European and North American travelers who were cultivating new tastes for exotic Asian goods globally.[28] Two of the largest global firms were Pohoomull Bros., founded in 1858 by the Khiani family, and D. Chellaram, founded two years later.[29] In Panama, the first Sindhi shops were established in 1905, and by 1927 there were ten firms in Colón with a monopoly on the tourist trade selling "oriental" souvenirs to travelers going through the Panama Canal.[30]

Sindhi and other merchants were not the only class of South Asian migrants in Panama. "East Indian" laborers, pejoratively referred to as "coolies," had been working there as early as the mid-nineteenth century, since the first French rail project across the Isthmus to connect the Atlantic and Pacific. They continued to arrive as former indentured laborers from the Caribbean with the large influx of Afro-Caribbean workers, who came mainly from Jamaica and Barbados, but also from other islands, such as St. Lucia, Grenada, and Trinidad.[31] In 1912, during US canal construction, a little more than one percent of laborers working in the Canal Zone were born in India.[32] Historian Lara Putnam points out that there were likely more than that living outside the Canal Zone in Panama.[33] As we will see, there were significant social gaps between South Asian migrant laborers and the merchant class in Panama.

Indian goods stores catered largely to American tourists who were hungry for something exotic while traveling. For instance, the Eastern Bazaar, owned by Verhomal and Khubchand, sold shawls, linen, silk, and "oriental goods" at two stores, one in Panama City and one in Colón.[34] Sindhi merchants were economically more well off than other Indian immigrant groups.[35] As we will see below, with the petition to the National Assembly regarding the anti-immigration law, they were very vocal, claiming to speak for the whole of the community, as part of their attempts to navigate the ethnoracial religious hierarchies of the Isthmus.

ETHNORACIAL RELIGIOUS HIERARCHIES IN PANAMA

The Republic of Panama and the US Canal Zone had unequal competing and contradictory claims to sovereignty and regnant social hierarchies on the Isthmus that immigrant groups had to navigate as they moved back and forth across borders and lines of control. The Canal Zone's founders hierarchized the races: those identified as white Anglo-Saxon (and we should add Protestant) were at the top, then Southern and Eastern Europeans, Mestizos, Asians, Indigenous, and at the bottom Black Caribbeans. The majority of canal workers came from the Caribbean. The Canal Zone's social divisions were institutionalized in the Zone through the US government's segregation of living quarters, hospitals, leisure facilities, and train cars by what they called "gold" and "silver" pay grades. The US American gold elite were paid in US gold currency, and the mostly unskilled silver workers were paid in Panamanian silver.

Those non-American workers who were nonwhite, non–Anglo-Saxon, and/or non-Protestant were usually placed on the "silver roll" and put in "silver" housing. The differently identified races and nationalities on the silver roll were then separated out.[36]

The majority of US officials and workers were Protestant, and Protestantism played an important role in Canal Zone or Zonian identity. Canal Zone officials consigned European Catholic migrant worker groups to the silver roll. Though it was not policy to designate them based on religion (the basis was, rather, national origin), Catholic workers were suspicious that this was the basis for the discrimination.[37] National and religious identifications inflected how European workers were categorized in terms of whiteness. Catholic Spaniard and Italian workers were considered "semi-white" by the Canal Zone regime. They could be identified as either white or not-white depending on the context.[38] Though most Afro-Caribbean workers were Protestant, their perceived Blackness was the primary criterion the US regime used to categorize them, placing them at the lowest rung of the social hierarchy. Because of segregation, West Indians had their own fraternal organizations and religious institutions.[39] White American Zonians stereotyped them as excessively religious, "superstitious," and "childish."[40] This categorization as lacking true or appropriate religion was part of white Zonian positioning of Afro-Caribbeans as racially inferior. Indo-Caribbean and South Asian laborers would not have fit easily into the racial religious hierarchy in the Zone, though most Zonian elites would likely have been largely oblivious of their ritual communities of whatever formation.

Panamanians were shocked by the stark racial hierarchies and overt segregation in the Canal Zone.[41] Yet the group in power in Panama primarily identified as being of European, largely Spanish, descent,[42] and Latin Panamanians had their own complex taxonomy of race and color.[43] Outside the Zone, Afro-Caribbean immigrants faced significant discrimination from Panamanians as well (though it was subtler than the extreme segregation in the Zone). Spanish language and Catholicism were important markers for Panamanian identity construction.[44] Panamanian society defined Blackness in large part by language, region of origin, and religion. To be designated as "*negro*" in Panama involved being English-speaking, from the Anglophone Caribbean, and Protestant. Afro-Panamanians who spoke Spanish and practiced Catholicism and who had Hispanicized names were identified not as *negro* but instead as *mulatto, moreno,* or even *mestizo.*[45] Immigrants to Panama, such as South Asian merchants, were quick to learn Spanish and to adapt to Panamanian culture.[46]

In 1926, at the same time that the immigration law was being debated and passed, Panamanian intellectuals were defining a nationalist ideology of race and culture mixture as the coming together of Christians of European/Spanish descent with Indigenous (or "Indian") peoples. Theorists of Panamanian race and nation in this period excluded peoples of African descent (and, we might add, any other descent) from their formulations of this "Indo-Hispanic nucleus."[47] Part of these formulations included arguments against Asian immigration to Panama. In one column published in August 1926, Demetrio Fábrega wrote in the *Star and Herald (La Estrella de Panama)* of a "dangerous enemy" coming over Panama's borders, the "constant invasion of a certain class of Orientals that came from far off lands like a formidable army": "Chinese, Japanese, Hindus, Syrians, Turks, all of the legendary Orient with its customs and its vices" arriving "like a great tentacle threatening to absorb us [*como un gran tentaculo amenaza absorbernos*]."[48] In Fábrega's racist screed the relatively small number of Asian immigrants to the republic became an amorphous tentacular monster, a penetrating appendage that could eliminate the distinctness of the Panamanian nation. It also reproduced the idea of Asia as "legendary" or fabled, somehow fantastic, alluring, and ancient, but also dangerous in its difference, defined in terms of its blind fidelity to its longstanding "customs" and "vices." The "Oriental" tentacle threatened to absorb Panamanian purity into itself, its vices and customs making it ill suited to adapt to Panamanian civilization.[49]

Peoples of South Asian descent did not easily fit into the racial religious norms of the hierarchies of either the Canal Zone or the republic, just as they did not fit easily into the race/color/class hierarchies of the Caribbean.[50] Other groups across borders saw them as religiously other, neither Protestant nor Catholic. They were understood to not share cultural mores with Euro-Americans or Latin Panamanians. They could not convincingly identify as white in the hierarchies across Panama's interior borders. However, this did not stop them from trying to make a place for themselves within those hierarchies.

THE AMBIGUITY OF BEING HINDU

In September 1926, the Panamanian National Assembly received a petition, sent on behalf of the "members of the Hindu colony" and signed by P. P. D. Chellaram, U. Roopchand, P. P. Pohoomul Bros., and M. S. Kotai. These self-identified Hindu merchants, led by Sindhi merchant firms, wrote to express their surprise and disappointment that the Panamanian government had designated them as "undesirables," and as part of "a degenerate race." They wrote, regarding the "racial aspect" of the law, that Hindus could not be considered a "degenerate race" because they were "absolutely free from physiological and moral characteristics pertaining to such a race." To support this argument, the memorialists pointed to the social system in India, which was regulated by the "Caste Regime" and which "excludes all others who do not belong to that particular Caste" and prohibited "sexual intercourse between members of different Castes." They wrote that they considered such "adulteration of different blood" to be "a very grievous fault." They proudly declared that they were, as "a high Caste of East Indians," a virtual aristocracy in India, and so were uncontaminated by "foreign blood" because their "religious beliefs as contained in our Holy Texts and the sacred pride of our race" prohibited such mixing. They were a pure race of Hindus.

At the same time, these Hindu merchants acknowledged that there was another South Asian group, the "coolie" class, "a type of poor labourer," who, if he emigrated, "does not take with him any capital, and wherever he lands becomes in time, a menace to the unemployed problem." Though the merchants identified such men as "Hindu," they denied relations with them. They wrote that this "type of Hindu" had been a more frequent immigrant during the construction of the canal at the beginning of the century, but were not seen coming to Panama much any longer. If the government excluded "this type of Hindu," they admitted, this would be justifiable. They wanted to come to the defense of these "coolie" Hindus by saying they were not "degenerates in the strictest sense of the word," though many of them were still "undesirable" owing to "their personal habits, customs and manners of living." The self-identified, high-caste Hindu merchants, by contrast, were wealthy and brought in their own employees from India to work at their stores to vend their merchandise shipped in especially from India to sell to wealthy tourists. Their businesses needed to be staffed by Indians, they argued, not because of a sense of superiority but because of the "oriental" nature of what they sold, "its conditions naturally and logically give us the prerogative we claim."

Regarding the "moral aspect," their behavior in Panama had only been that befitting their "inborn pride of the Caste System, a Caste which is moderate in living principles, but without vices." They wrote that not "a single Hindu" had ever gotten in trouble with the law or caused any trouble for the authorities. They concluded by imploring the National Assembly to clarify the immigration law so that only the "Indian Coolie" would be excluded and not "those Hindus already established in Panama, their employees, the new employees whom they might bring down here under contract and to ship them back at the expiration of their services, and every other Hindu who may arrive on the Isthmus, and who according to the Panama Consul in Calcutta has filled the requirements of good conduct and personal merit."[51]

The South Asian merchants petitioning the Assembly in September 1926 were mobilizing a Hindu identity that was primarily racial. This was in line with widespread Panamanian understandings of this category in both Spanish and English. Panamanians used "Hindustani" and "Hindu" (*indostano* and *hindu*) interchangeably to mean either a person from Hindustan (India) or a member of the ethnoracial groups of that region. A 1932 Panamanian decree, for instance, that made more lenient the rules restricting South Asians entering and leaving the country for business referred to them as both "*indostanos*" and "*hindues*."[52] Panamanians' usage of "Hindu" in these fashions was even noted in the legislature in India, during the period of debates over Panamanian anti-immigration laws, and this further makes evident the varied and contested translocal uses of this term. A Sindhi representative in the Legislative Assembly in Bombay, Lalchand Navalrai, asked, regarding the contributions of Indians in Panama and possible legal restrictions on their engagement in commerce: "Are Government aware that these Hindus and Mahomedans who are called 'Hindus' in that country are put to great hardship and inconvenien[ce] by the 'Panama Government'?"[53] This usage here, distinguishing Hindu and Muslim (or "Mahomedan"), and noting the conflation of the two in Panama, points us to the emergence, after the turn of the twentieth century, of a more exclusively religious definition of the category "Hindu" that was becoming ascendant globally (which would have excluded Muslims or Christians from the term). This was "Hindu" as a member of a so-called world religion named Hinduism.[54]

The proliferation of ethnoracial terminology for people from the Subcontinent used in the anti-immigration law of 1926—East Indians, Indo-Aryans, Dravidians (*indio-orientales*, *indo-arios*, and *dravidianos*)—suggests the government's particular concern to keep people from this region out of Panama. But it also suggests the complexity or ethnoracial ambiguity of the populations under state regulation and the ambiguity of becoming Hindu in the Americas. Within this Panamanian threefold matrix, Sindwork merchants counted themselves among the Indo-Aryans or, as they translated it, "Hindu Aryans." In doing so they made a claim to whiteness, expressed religious fidelity, and professed an elite caste status that, if convincing, would have made them compatible with the European-descended elites in Panama.[55] Identifying as Hindu in this way, the merchants were engaging in a tactic to more freely navigate Panama and the Canal Zone's already contested borders with their personnel and money. However, the religious and caste identities of Sindhis in this period, what they claimed were the guarantors of their racial purity, were much more multifaceted and contested than the merchants suggested in their petition. Ritual communities and dominant modes of devotion in Sindh were not "religious" in the way many people understand that today, in that practitioners would have been from what today we would call different religions.

For the merchants in Panama, the "purity" of their racial identification was dependent on their religious and caste identifications (however vague those were). They argued that their religion guaranteed their caste fidelity, which guaranteed their racial purity. They made their Hindu religion pure and purity-creating. They were true and pure Hindus because of the "religious beliefs" of their "Holy Texts." As self-identified, high-caste Hindus (and so not Christian), the merchants would have had difficulty situating themselves in Panama's racial religious hierarchies. However, their focus on belief and texts in their explanation of their racial Hindu-ness helped to situate them in relationship and make them intelligible to elite normative Christianities in the country. Yet, in contrast to the discrete and pure religion postulated by the Hindu merchants, becoming Hindu has always been complex and variegated.

The ways in which many Sindhis have historically performed their Hindu identities challenge the rigid boundaries and exclusivism suggested by the Hindu merchants. Sociologist U. T. Thakur has written that "there is very little religion among Sindhis that would be taken as Hinduism in the rest of India."[56] In the late nineteenth and early twentieth centuries, groups identified today as Sindhi Muslims, Hindus, and Sikhs shared overlapping and variegated ritual communities and sociality. Hindu Sindworkis abroad have shared worship spaces with Khalsa Sikhs. This included Hindu Sindworkis helping to fund Sikh religious temples (gurdwaras).[57] Sindhi Hindu practice included, then, what colonial officials and exclusivist Hindus would have seen as a mix of Sikh and Sufi Muslim discourse, practice, and iconography.[58] Sindhis had "Holy Texts," but these included Sufi devotional poetry and the Sikh-identified Guru Granth Sahib, writings that were not concerned with fortifying race or caste distinctions, but challenged them.[59] Only gradually, beginning at the turn of the twentieth century, as the colonial regime in India successfully imposed its regnant categories like religion and race on colonized populations, did middle-class Sindhis begin to identify with a particular and discrete religion as colonial officials and Indian religious nationalists would recognize that.[60] However, still today Sindhis' Hindu identifications have been contested by other Hindus over issues of what could be defined as religious purity.[61]

The Hindu merchants also argued that the "Caste Regime" and their high-caste pride kept castes strictly exclusive and racially pure, preventing the "adulteration of different blood." Their claim to racial purity relied in part on the rigidity and surety of caste discrimination and endogamy, and the absolute distinction between the races. However, U. T. Thakur has described caste among Sindhis as "not rigid"[62] but "highly flexible"[63] and purity/impurity restrictions as "mild" or "almost absent."[64] Hyderabadi merchants typically identified their caste as Lohana when filling out official forms.[65] Most of the merchants who went abroad were Bhaibands.[66] The Lohana jatis, which include the Bhaibands, were considered Vaishyas, not the highest caste "aristocracy," as the merchants seemed to imply.[67] With most workers coming from the Bhaiband community, the division of workers in the firm was based not on caste but on economic status.[68]

South Asian merchants constructed a racialized and exclusivist Hinduness, a Hindu identity that they wanted to use to intervene in, to make themselves a place in, but ultimately to reinforce the ethnoracial hierarchy in Panama that put European and mestizo at the top and Black at the bottom. Through their Hindu identifications they attempted to create borders of blood, fortified by caste and religion. However, we can see here some of the ways in which South Asian merchants' Hindu racial identifications were fractured by and highly contested across lines of power, formulated in terms of religion, caste, and class. But theirs was not the only racialized Hindu identity they were constructing. Hindu merchants racialized Indo-Caribbean laborers and in so doing severed relations with them, making them a Black(ened) West Indian(ized) foil meant to help their case for the privilege of mobility across Panama's borders.

The Indian merchant petitioners suggested that the working-class Hindus were the true "undesirables," even if they were not, strictly speaking, racial "degenerates." Yet the merchants were still racializing the laborers. According to the Hindu merchants, degenerate races were defined by their inferior physiology and morality. If the Hindu merchants were openly designating the laborers' habits, customs, and way of life as undesirable and so morally questionable, this made them racially questionable, if not "degenerate," and so, according to the merchants, a better class of Hindus to be excluded. Their attempt to position these workers as racially inferior was in line with their racial positioning in Central America. In parts of Central America in the late nineteenth and early twentieth centuries, Indo-Caribbean laborers were sometimes identified as Black, and so could be situated toward the bottom of social hierarchies. Putnam gives an example of a Costa Rican journalist referring to a South Asian laborer as "*el negrito de las Indias Orientales*."[69] We can speculate that their positioning as working class, their labor status as "coolie" manual laborers, and their association with the Anglophone Caribbean all contributed to Indo-Caribbeans' racial positioning as in some sense Black in this region. Given these associations and the government's racist exclusions of Afro-Caribbeans in Panama, it is perhaps unsurprising that Hindu merchants attempted to reinforce this racialization by bringing South Asian laborers' race into question. They denied them as kith and kin, offering them up to the government in their own stead. This was an element of the merchants' larger negotiations of the social hierarchies defining and variously dividing up the Isthmus.

In the circum-Caribbean migratory sphere, Indo- and Afro-Caribbean laborers did not always get along.[70] However, Afro- and Indo-Caribbeans often worked and lived together amicably.[71] Older Caribbean Panamanians described a time when the forms of exclusionary nationalism and racism driving the anti-immigration laws in that country did not exist or were not so influential, a time when no "absurd ideas about nationality or race had as yet seized the mind of the people of the country; but instead everybody lived in the bond of friendly relations and expressed good will."[72] This tells us that the racializing hierarchies being contested in this period were not eternal or inevitable, and that there existed other ways for groups to be in relation in the circum-Caribbean world. There were other ways to become Hindu, not as race or world religion, but through often delegitimized practices working with spirits.

BECOMING HINDU OTHERWISE

The Hindu merchants in Panama claimed that their stores had to be staffed by Hindus because of the "oriental" nature of their merchandise, saying that "its conditions naturally and logically give us the prerogative we claim."[73] They used their ethnoracial identifications to claim expertise and exemptions from the law because, they appealed, non-Hindus could not do what they did. However, their merchandise further troubled the pure and clearly delineable Hindu identity they constructed. Like Panamanian lawmakers, the Hindu merchants operated under an Orientalist logic. In their store offerings they blurred the lines dividing up "the Orient," selling Indian, Japanese, and Chinese curios all together. The objects they sold, such as art, clothing, and silk cloth, could become the basis for self-cultivation among a variety of ethnoracially identified groups around the globe. In the Americas, these kinds of objects could become stepping stones for customers to cultivate curiosity, fascination, appreciation, and claimed expertise.[74] With their customers dressing in Hindu attire and decorating their homes with Hindu images, Hindu merchants through their own products helped to create their doubles, undermining their assumption of privileged entitlements. Having Hindu-identified items for sale in their own stores opened up other possibilities for becoming Hindu in a way that stretched and challenged the Hindu merchants' own special claims to an exclusive Hindu-ness. But though they claimed exclusive proprietorship of these kinds of "oriental" items, Hindu merchants and Euro-American tourists were joined by people from a variety of class, ethnoracial, and religious social positionings from around the Greater Caribbean, in accessing the power of Hindu identities in order to sell and buy esoteric and spiritual products.[75]

Connecting Asia and the Americas, the Sindhi merchants and their customers were nodes in a series of interconnected networks of circulating people, goods, and ideas from around the world. Sindhi merchants and their Asian goods traveled out of Sindh; American and European Zonians and tourists moved to and through the Panama Canal purchasing such goods; Indo-Caribbean and Afro-Caribbean workers and ritual specialists traveled the Caribbean and migrated to Central America; and "spiritual" entrepreneurs marketed Indian-identified goods through the mails from Chicago, Harlem, and Paris around the globe, allowing consumers to become virtual Hindus by mail anywhere. Various organizations used the medium of the mail to distribute and gain access to products such as Hindu- and Indian-identified books, correspondence courses, herbs, unguents, and astrological readings.[76] Among these was the Chicago wizard and publisher of esotericism, Lauron W. de Laurence, who boasted that among the places across the globe where he had shipped his mail-order books on Hindu magic were Bocas Del Toro and Colón on Panama's Caribbean coast, as well as Jamaica and Trinidad.[77] Becoming Hindu in this manner included the use of that category to authorize experimental self and social formation, including what I am calling an experimental kinship that countered regnant definitions of Hindu we have seen above. But, in the Caribbean world, this was, if not an illicit mode of becoming Hindu, one that made practitioners more vulnerable to obeah prosecution, in part because it challenged colonial norms of religion and race.

In 1917, Charles Bartholomew, Anthony Bartholomew, and Hubert Alexander, all Afro-Caribbean, and Airic Achaitar, Indo-Caribbean, were in court together in San Fernando, in the south of Trinidad. The police accused them of obtaining $5.50 from Henry T. Warner "with intent to 'cheat' and 'defraud' through the practice of obeah," African-identified witchcraft or the pretended assumption of supernatural power. They had supposedly done so after promising to heal Warner's wife and help him to get back his job. Sargent Major Richard Everley had received a warrant to search Charles Bartholomew's house at Vista Bella Village, Naparima, where Charles Bartholomew and the young men (who were in their early to late teens) appear to have lived, for objects related to practicing obeah. There he found the four defendants working together on a session of healing and restoration. He testified that Charles Bartholomew was "making motions," contorting his body and "muttering aloud in a language that I [Everley] do not understand." Anthony Bartholomew lay on the couch "muttering out something." There was a banknote marked by the police near him, evidence of the work of a police agent provocateur. Airic Achaitar (whom the police called "the Indian boy") was sitting in a chair with a book open next to him, which Everley produced in the court as evidence of obeah. The police found a variety of objects that they identified as being used in obeah, including a crucifix with eggs and lighted candles around it, books on esotericism and religion, a Bible, other "printed matter" such as prayers and handwritten papers with "writing against lightning, thunder and other dangers," as well as boxes and bottles.

Instead of an "obeahman," Charles Bartholomew's lawyer told the court that Bartholomew was a "Christian Scientist." However, Bartholomew himself testified: "I am a disciple of Professor De Laurence [described in cross-examination as "the great Hindu Magician Dr. De Laurence"] and I have studied the science taught by him. I have been practicing my profession since 1912 and I have been doing so quite openly all over the Island. I have put up my sign-board and have never been molested by the police. All my work is conducted by prayer." Rather than touting obeah, outside the house Bartholomew had a signboard advertising: "The School of Natural Science by Prof. Chas Bartholomew. Guarantees to cure all long standing diseases. Having many years experience of Hindu Magic, he is prepared to cure all internal and external diseases of those sufferings."[78]

Colonial officials and other elites separated Indo-Caribbean and Afro-Caribbean in Trinidad.[79] With their arrival from South Asia in the mid-nineteenth century, there was a widespread perception in Trinidad that Indian indentured laborers were separate from and unmixed with the rest of Trinidadian society.[80] In particular, many people held an opposition between "Creole/African" and "Indian" that still persists today.[81] This enduring perception has been in the face of a long history of complex social entanglements between the various groups living in Trinidad, particularly Indo- and Afro-Trinidadian, including exchanges and social formation through the authorizing powers of superhuman beings.[82]

Charles Bartholomew and his associates were clearly drawing on a variety of translocal movements in their ritual work (the details of which are not entirely clear), including forms of Christianity, Hindu spiritism from de Laurence and other global esotericisms, and other Caribbean ritual modes of healing and restoration. Anglophone Caribbean ritual and spirit worlds are highly diverse and complex.[83] The exchange of spiritual work and knowledge brought peoples from diverse backgrounds together as people, objects, and ideas traveled and engaged with one another.[84]

What was called obeah in the Caribbean was often about healing, restoration from loss, and preventing harm and creating accountability when formal avenues for redress of harm were not available or accessible.[85] Both in colonial discourse and in scholarly literature, what has been called obeah, like "magic," has been assumed to be antirelational, to not be able to create community or even to actively destroy community, in contradistinction to religion.[86] Counter to this, as Crosson has argued, what gets called obeah has also been a technique for creating communities of various sorts, including what he has called "altered solidarities," forms of relation across and through racial and religious difference, bringing together African and Indian Trinidadians, Christians, Muslims, and Hindus.[87] In the colonial Caribbean, as today, people sought out "occult expertise from afar"[88] to solve a variety of problems. People sought help from outside their own community because of distrust or embarrassment, but also because of the power of alterity.[89] The connections individuals created through what some call obeah, those between spiritual workers and their clients who often come from other parts of a region, an island, another island, or the mainland, though, appear to have been temporary.[90]

When thinking about the relations between the Afro- and Indo-Trinidadian men on trial in 1917, who appear to have been both working and living together, I would use the term "experimental kinship" to describe these more sustained forms of being in relation created through what has been called obeah. This experimental kin-making involved the creation of intimacies between reified racial others,[91] with an emphasis on the usages of "intimacy" as expertise and knowledge transmission, such as "having intimate knowledge of." The men on trial were working their "Hindu magic" together out of a space they called a "School of Natural Science." In the contemporary Caribbean, the word "science" is a synonym for what gets called "obeah," though the two words have been connected since at least the mid-eighteenth century.[92] "Natural science" here likely referred, at least in part, to mesmerism or animal magnetism and also to the esoteric knowledge of the variety de Laurence discussed in his works on Hindu spiritism, but science may also have borne some resemblance to Crosson's interlocutors' understanding of science as experiments with occult powers and to Katherine McKittrick's idea of science as "scientia" or knowledge more broadly, the interdisciplinary methods used by Black scholars, broadly conceived, "to explain, explore, and story the world."[93] The purported universality of "science" defies the conflation of race and religion,[94] while, as we have seen, the term "Hindu" often operated as a particular racial identity in this context. In contradistinction to the particularism of the Panamanian Hindu merchants and their racial religious Hindu kincraft, by bringing these two terms, "science" and "Hindu," together on the sign outside the house to describe their practice, Bartholomew and his colleagues were perhaps attempting to remake the category "Hindu" as universal and so allow the diverse practitioners at the "School of Natural Science" to come together to do their work of healing.

In her book *Kincraft*, Todne Thomas discusses forms of "spiritual" kinship among Black evangelicals in the contemporary United States that traverse barriers of ethnicity between Caribbean Americans and African Americans. She connects this to modes of social formation within and also constitutive of the African diaspora.[95] I echo Thomas's emphasis, in her idea of "kincraft," of kinship as an ongoing, negotiated, and contested set of practices and not simply a biologically or culturally predetermined set of relationships. However, the example of what I call experimental kin-making, done through practices colonial officials called obeah, went beyond a spiritual kinship as racial/religious solidarity of Black diasporic or Christian identities and challenged regnant colonial regimes of religion and race.[96] The experimental kinship Bartholomew and company were creating under the authority of the category "Hindu" does not seem to be based on simple claims of sameness, of ethnoracial or diasporic identity. They were not creating connections with one another as a collectively identified community, becoming Hindu in the way that the Panamanian Hindu merchants sought to; rather, their experimentation in relation-making defied colonial norms for racial and religious social formation.[97]

Bartholomew and colleagues experimented with kin-making through shared ritual practice that created relations with spirits of the dead. Elizabeth Freeman defines a person's desire for belonging, through kinship, as also a longing to be temporally bigger, to "touch the dead or those not born yet, to offer oneself beyond one's own time."[98] Charles and Anthony Bartholomew, Hubert Alexander, and Airic Achaitar made connections with one another through their practices of touching the dead, of working with the dead through Hindu spiritism to help make community, creating connections rather than racial hierarchy between what were assumed at the time to be disparate groups, "Creole" and "East Indian." Lauron W. de Laurence's Hindu spiritism did provide a model of esoteric and experimental kinship from which Bartholomew and company to some degree may have been drawing. In *The Great Book of Magical Art, Hindu Magic and East Indian Occultism*, first published in 1902, de Laurence signed his "Epistle to the Disciple" as "Thy Friend and Brother in

Magic,"[99] and in his *The Sacred Book of Death, Hindu Spiritism, Soul Transition and Soul Reincarnation,* he referred to "the Fraternity of Hindu Spiritism."[100] Being disciples of de Laurence and doing his Hindu magic together may have meant for the group on trial that they were part of a global and secret brotherhood with the powerful magician and scientist from Chicago and the legions of benevolent spirits upon whom they could draw for help. We cannot know for certain whether Charles and Anthony Bartholomew, Hubert Alexander, and Airic Achaitar saw their work in this way. This can only ever be "critical fabulation."[101] But if I might move further into speculation, in their experiments in kin-making we might see "eclipsed and alternative futures,"[102] intimacies through ritual and knowledge pushing against modern liberal social logics of race, labor value, and commodity,[103] alternative ways of creating social relations that countered colonial, and later postcolonial, nationalist knowledges.

The practices of what gets called obeah and the relationships they helped to create are frequently difficult to see in the colonial archive, and as is evident here, they were legally targeted by the colonial state.[104] To be a practitioner of Hindu magic did not require Bartholomew and his associates to convert or to claim Hindu racial origins, either. It involved the summoning and embodiment of spirits through ritual for healing and restoration. Bartholomew and his experimental kin were using the practice of Hindu magic to create connections across what were assumed to be inviolable ethnoracial religious lines. The creation of connections through life and work between Airic Achaitar and his Afro-Caribbean colleagues is something that colonial officials would have found suspicious and troubling. In court, Bartholomew and his fellow spiritual workers were unlikely to authoritatively make the argument that they had any claim to Hindu-ness. Judges and police in colonial Trinidad did not recognize the practices forwarded by de Laurence and adopted and adapted by those like Bartholomew. The colonial regime's understanding was that for all these men to claim India, the East, and a Hindu identity of some kind was fraudulent unless they were all racially Hindu. Hindu magic, unlike Hindu race or Hindu religion, was not seen as acceptable practice. The police and the court denied the connections and intimacies between Afro- and Indo-Caribbeans enacted through Bartholomew's science of Hindu spiritism. Yet Afro- and Indo-Caribbeans in places like Trinidad, Guyana, Jamaica, and Panama adopted, adapted, and reimagined South Asian and Indo-Caribbean Hindu identificatory modes, ritual forms, and cultural materials across community lines. Bartholomew and his associates' embodiment of spirits short-circuited the kinds of racial kincraft that the Hindu merchants in Panama were attempting to mobilize in 1926. His community's experiments in Hindu-identified practices authorized the creating of relatedness between Afro- and Indo-Caribbean spiritual workers. In so doing they opened up other possibilities for becoming Hindu beyond those formulated and performed by groups like the translocal Hindu merchants who petitioned the Panamanian National Assembly.

CONCLUSION

In the 1920s, elites in Panama sought to maintain the purported racial, religious, and civilizational purity of their republic by passing laws limiting immigration from Asia, the Middle East, and the Caribbean. Hindu merchants in Panama and India sought to intervene in those restrictions, to limit Hindus' crossings of Panama's borders to only the racially pure, civilized, and wealthy. Across the Caribbean, Charles Bartholomew's itinerant community of Hindu scientists and healers defied regnant colonial definitions of racial belonging and religious and civilizational divisions. In this essay, I have been working through the politics of negotiated borders between Asian, Latin American, and African in the Americas, the ways in which social actors contested the category of "Hindu" across lines of race, nationality, magic, science, and religion.

In debates across borders geographical, racial, and religious, Indian merchants and Panamanian elites defined Hindu and Panamanian racial, ethnic, and religious identities in tandem. In this context, both groups understood "Hindu" to be an exclusive ethnoracial category the purity or danger of which was guaranteed by Indian religion and custom. This Hindu identificatory logic was rooted, a mode through which actors attempted to fortify and limit the crossing of lines of racial religious difference. At the same time, Afro- and Indo-Caribbeans were using the category "Hindu" as part of Caribbean esoteric science to authorize the crossing of borders and the formation of complex, multiply entangled social relations through spirit practices that helped to create experimental kin, making connections through and across difference. This experimental Hindu identificatory logic was mobile, used to help facilitate the crossing of borders and the creation of solidarities between reified groups. In the face of colonial violence, these students of Hindu magic were creating bonds across reified ethnoracial religious lines, doing experiments in kinship in violation of colonial norms.

What is true for the intersectional complexities of Hindu identification is true for other modes of identity construction more broadly. Racial, ethnic, religious, gendered, national, and other co-constituted identifications intersect not as ready-made and settled but as shifting dynamics within fields of power. Stuart Hall has called identities "the necessary fiction of action."[105] Identities are performative processes, ongoing becomings, but their fictions as settled facts are useful for social actors navigating other purportedly settled facts and their potentially dangerous power dynamics, such as police sting operations, court hearings, or national border crossings. In such contexts, social actors' strategic redeployment of state-recognized identities can be advantageous but is not necessary or the only strategy available. As we have seen, groups assigned certain ethnoracial religious identities by state power have experimented with, reimagined, and redeployed those modes of identification, creating other solidarities not outside of but around or at the margins of state power. These forms of experimental kinship can challenge official reified identities, pulling at the ragged edges of those fictions, but without some other source of authorization the possibilities for their range of action become highly limited. The significance of these experiments with identity and relationality is not in their success at evading state violence, but their ability to make kin in the face of that violence.

NOTES

1. "Ley 13 de 1926 (de 23 de Octubre) sobre inmigración," Republic of Panama, *Gaceta Oficial*, No. 4977, October 28, 1916.

2. The Spanish and English words used for people of Afro-Caribbean origin in Panama are *antillano* and West Indian, respectively.

3. On "kincraft" see Todne Thomas, *Kincraft: The Making of Black Evangelical Sociality* (Durham, NC: Duke University Press, 2021).

4. Michael J. Altman, *Heathen, Hindoo, Hindu: American Representations of India, 1721–1893* (Oxford: Oxford University Press, 2017); Gyanendra Pandey, "Which of Us Are Hindus?" in *Hindus and Others: The Question of Identity in India Today*, ed. Gyanendra Pandey (New Delhi: Viking, 1993), 238–72; Alexander Rocklin, *The Regulation of Religion and the Making of Hinduism in Colonial Trinidad* (Chapel Hill: University of North Carolina Press, 2019).

5. Altman, *Heathen, Hindoo, Hindu*, xvi–xvii; Rocklin, *The Regulation of Religion*, 7–8.

6. Stuart Hall, "Cultural Identity and Diaspora," in *Identity: Community, Culture, Difference*, ed. Jonathan Rutherford (London: Lawrence and Wishant, 1990), 222.

7. Hall, "Cultural Identity and Diaspora," 226, emphasis in original.

8. Stuart Hall, "Introduction: Who Needs 'Identity'?" in *Questions of Cultural Identity*, ed. Stuart Hall and Paul Du Gay (London: Sage Publications, 1996), 2.

9. Hall, "Introduction," 4.

10. Feminist Critical Hindu Studies Collective, "Feminist Critical Hindu Studies in Formation," *Religion Compass* (2021): e12392.

11. Elizabeth Freeman, "Queer Belongings: Kinship Theory and Queer Theory," in *A Companion to Lesbian, Gay, Bisexual, Transgender, and Queer Studies*, ed. George E. Haggerty and Molly McGarry (Malden, MA: Blackwell, 2007), 299; David M. Schneider, *American Kinship: A Cultural Account* (Chicago: University of Chicago Press, 1980); Thomas, *Kincraft*.

12. Freeman, "Queer Belongings," 295; Denise Youngblood, "Rainbow Family, Rainbow

Nation: Reflections on Relatives and Relational Dynamics in Trinidad," in *The Ethics of Kinship: Ethnographic Inquiries*, ed. James D. Faubion (Lanham, MD: Rowman and Littlefield, 2001), 62, 65.

13. Ann Laura Stoler, *Race and the Education of Desire: Foucault's History of Sexuality and the Colonial Order of Things* (Durham, NC: Duke University Press, 1995), 48–49.

14. Freeman, "Queer Belongings," 298.

15. J. Brent Crosson, *Experiments with Power: Obeah and the Remaking of Religion in Trinidad* (Chicago: University of Chicago Press, 2020), 185.

16. On nationalism and ideologies of mixing in Panama, see Luis Pulido Ritter, "Armando Fortune y la identidad cultural Panameña," *Tareas* 140 (January–April 2012): 83–106.

17. Claude Markovits, *The Global World of Indian Merchants, 1750–1947: Traders of Sind from Bukhara to Panama* (Cambridge: Cambridge University Press, 2000), 214.

18. David Scott FitzGerald and David Cook-Martín, *Culling the Masses: The Democratic Origins of Racist Immigration Policy in the Americas* (Cambridge, MA: Harvard University Press, 2014), 42. For the case of Argentina, see Benjamin Bryce, "Undesirable Britons: South Asian Migration and the Making of a White Argentina," *Hispanic American Historical Review* 99, no. 2 (2019).

19. Robin Elizabeth Zenger, "West Indians in Panama: Diversity and Activism, 1910s–1940s," PhD diss., University of Arizona, 2015, 44–45.

20. Zenger, *West Indians in Panama*, 46.

21. See, for example, "Señalando un Peligro," *Star and Herald*, August 9, 1926, 13.

22. Katherine A. Zien, *Sovereign Acts: Performing Race, Space, and Belonging in Panama and the Canal Zone* (New Brunswick, NJ: Rutgers University Press, 2017), 89; "Ley 13 de 1926 (de 23 de Octubre) sobre inmigración," Republic of Panama, *Gaceta Oficial*, No. 4977, October 28, 1916.

23. "First Move in the New Immigration Law," *The Workman*, September 17, 1927, 4.

24. "Rumour, West Indians at Colón Subject to Abuse," *The Workman*, November 13, 1926, 1; "New Immigration Law Affects Foreigners Here," *The Workman*, September 25, 1926, 1.

25. "Protest against Hindu Venders on Sidewalk," *Star and Herald*, April 12, 1928, 5.

26. From the District Magistrate's Office, Hyderabad, Sind, May 26–31, 1927, IOR/L/PJ/8/278: January 1925–December 1938.

27. Mark-Anthony Falzon, *Cosmopolitan Connections: The Sindhi Diaspora* (Brill: Leiden, 2004), 108; Markovits, *The Global World of Indian Merchants*.

28. Markovits, *The Global World of Indian Merchants*, 116–18, 124–25.

29. Markovits, *The Global World of Indian Merchants*, 132–33.

30. Markovits, *The Global World of Indian Merchants*, 240–41.

31. Velam Newton, *The Silver Men: West Indian Labour Migration to Panama 1850–1914* (Kingston, Jamaica: Ian Randle Publishers, 2004), 80–88.

32. "British Subjects in the Canal Zone," IOR/L/PJ/6/1125, File 4559: 18 October 1911–21 August 1912.

33. Lara Putnam, "Undone by Desire: Migration, Sex across Boundaries, and Collective Destinies in the Greater Caribbean, 1840–1940," in *Connecting Seas and Connected Ocean Rims: Indian, Atlantic, and Pacific Oceans and China Seas Migrations from the 1830s to the*

1930s, ed. Donna R. Gabaccia and Dirk Hoerder (Leiden: Brill, 2011), 312.

34. Advertisement, *Star and Herald*, December 3, 1926, 7.

35. Markovits, *The Global World of Indian Merchants*, 226.

36. Donoghue, *Borderland on the Isthmus*, 28; Newton, *The Silver Men*, 122–23.

37. Donoghue, *Borderland on the Isthmus*, 54.

38. Julie Greene, "Spaniards on the Silver Roll: Labor Troubles and Liminality in the Panama Canal Zone, 1904–1914," *International Labor and Working-Class History* 66 (Fall 2004): 81.

39. Zien, *Sovereign Acts*, 62–65.

40. Donoghue, *Borderland on the Isthmus*, 52–53.

41. Donoghue, *Borderland on the Isthmus*, 53.

42. Zenger, *West Indians in Panama*, 12.

43. Donoghue, *Borderland on the Isthmus*, 105.

44. Donoghue, *Borderland on the Isthmus*, 94.

45. Donoghue, *Borderland on the Isthmus*, 106.

46. Donoghue, *Borderland on the Isthmus*, 100.

47. Ritter, "Armando Fortune y la identidad cultural Panameña," 84, 88. An example of this was the diplomat colonel Olmedo Alfaro; see his *El peligro antiallano en la America Central: La defensa de la Raza*, 2d ed. (Panama: Imprenta Nacional, 1925).

48. "Señalando un Peligro," *Star and Herald*, August 9, 1926, 13.

49. On the stereotype of Asian "invasion" depicted as an octopus or tentacled monster, see John Kuo Wei Tchen and Dylan Yeats, "Introduction: Yellow Peril Incarnate" in *Yellow Peril! An Archive of Anti-Asian Fear*, ed. John Kuo Wei Tchen and Dylan Yeats (London: Verso, 2014).

50. Aisha Khan, "Caucasian, Coolie, Black, or White? Color and Race in the Indo-Caribbean Diaspora," in *Shades of Difference: Why Skin Color Matters*, ed. Evelyn Nakano Glenn (Stanford: Stanford University Press, 2009).

51. "Memorial Submitted to the National Assembly by the Members of the Hindu Colony," Enclosure No. 3 in Panama dispatch No. 102 of July 20, 1927, IOR/L/PJ/8/278: January 1925–December 1938.

52. "Se Adiciona el Decreto N. 43 de 27 de Mayo de 1931 Sobre Inmigracion de Hindues" (Decree No. 16 of 1932, *Official Gazette*, No. 6251, March 15, 1932). Also see a letter from J. E. Lefevre, secretary of exterior relations, to K. A. Mahtani, Manghanmal Detaram, Issarsing Premsing, and Dharm Singh, dated July 9, 1937, representing the "Asociacion de Comerciantes Indostanos" (IOR/L/PJ/8/278: January 1925–December 1938); and a letter from K. A. Mahtani, Issarsing Premsing, Manghanmal Detaram, and Dharamsing to the secretary of exterior relations of Panama, dated June 22, 1937, called "Associacion de Comerciantes Hindues" (IOR/L/PJ/8/278: January 1925–December 1938). It seems to be the same organization, but given different names in Spanish.

53. "Starred Question and Answer in the Legislative Assembly for the Meeting on the 8th February 1933," IOR/L/PJ/8/278: January 1925–December 1938.

54. On the emergence of the "world religions" discourse, see Tomoko Masuzawa, *The Invention of World Religions Or, How European Universalism Was Preserved in the Language of Pluralism* (Chicago: University of Chicago Press, 2005). On the exclusivistic religious con-

structions of "Hindu" and "Hinduism" in the Caribbean, see Rocklin, *Regulation of Religion.*

55. From the District Magistrate's Office, Hyderabad, Sind, 26–31 May 1927, IOR/L/PJ/8/278: January 1925–December 1938.

56. U. T. Thakur, *Sindhi Culture* (Bombay: University of Bombay, n.d.), 71.

57. Markovits, *The Global World of Indian Merchants,* 255.

58. Steven W. Ramey, *Hindu, Sufi, or Sikh: Contested Practices and Identifications of Sindhi Hindus in India and Beyond* (New York: Palgrave Macmillan, 2008), 4.

59. See Michel Boivin, *The Hindu Sufis of South Asia: Partition, Shrine Culture and Sindhis in India* (London: I. B. Tauris, 2019); and Ramey, *Hindu, Sufi, or Sikh.*

60. Boivin, *The Hindu Sufis of South Asia,* 38.

61. Ramey, *Hindu, Sufi, or Sikh,* 2.

62. Thakur, *Sindhi Culture,* 68.

63. Thakur, *Sindhi Culture,* 71.

64. Thakur, *Sindhi Culture,* 70, 71.

65. Markovits, *The Global World of Indian Merchants,* 252.

66. Markovits, *The Global World of Indian Merchants,* 130.

67. Falzon, *Cosmopolitan Connections,* 33; Thakur, *Sindhi Culture,* 56.

68. Markovits, *The Global World of Indian Merchants,* 170.

69. Putnam, "Undone by Desire," 324.

70. In one example, "East Indians" in Panama working on the canal objected to being housed with Barbadian laborers and had to be rehoused (Greene, "Spaniards on the Silver Roll," 87).

71. Putnam, "Undone by Desire," 325.

72. "Why West Indians Are Misunderstood," *The Workman,* March 5, 1927, 4.

73. "Memorial Submitted to the National Assembly by the Members of the Hindu Colony," Enclosure No. 3 in Panama dispatch No. 102 of July 20, 1927, IOR/L/PJ/8/278: January 1925–December 1938.

74. Altman, *Heathen, Hindoo, Hindu,* 4–8; Vivek Bald, *Bengali Harlem and the Lost Histories of South Asian America* (Cambridge, MA: Harvard University Press, 2013), 18–21. Lauron W. De Laurence's whole self-presentation in the front matter of his books is a very telling example of this from both the consumption and production sides of this phenomenon; see, e.g., L. W. de Laurence, *The Great Book of Magical Art, Hindu Magic and East Indian Occultism* (Chicago: de Laurence Co., 1915).

75. On mail-order "spiritual" goods, see Carolyn Morrow Long, *Spiritual Merchants: Religion, Magic, and Commerce* (Knoxville: University of Tennessee Press, 2001).

76. For example, the Wilson Finley Company of Chicago advertised "magnetic sand, gazing crystals, roots, herbs, incense, occult and spiritual books" along with "Hindu Psychology Courses" in Panama's *Workman* newspaper (advertisement, *The Workman,* November 8, 1924, 8). The De-la-Herb Agency, at 2802 Cottage Grove Ave., Chicago, also advertised esoteric books on "East Indian spirit healing, 50c; the secret of Hindu visualization, 50c; [. . .] the priesthood of India, 50c; [. . .] Manta Yoga, 50c," as well as "Mantram's words of power $2; the master key book" . . . "lesser key of Solomon" . . . "the great book of magical art, $15; the sixth and seven[th] books of Moses, 75c," and "de-la-sphinx Hindu temple incense" (advertisement, *The Workman,* June 13, 1925, 4).

77. See the advertisement at the back of Henry Cornelius Agrippa and L. W. de Laurence, *The Philosophy of Natural Magic* (Chicago: de Laurence Co., 1913), 315.

78. "San Fernando News," *Port of Spain Gazette*, January 18, 1917.

79. Khan, "Caucasian, Coolie, Black, or White"; see also Bald, *Bengali Harlem*.

80. Youngblood, "Rainbow Family, Rainbow Nation," 55; Kevin Birth, "Most of Us Are Family Some of the Time: Interracial Unions and Transracial Kinship in Eastern Trinidad," *American Ethnologist* 24, no. 3 (1997): 587.

81. Birth, "Most of Us Are Family," 589–90.

82. J. Brent Crosson, "What Obeah Does Do: Healing, Harm, and the Limits of Religion," *Journal of Africana Religions* 3, no. 2 (2015); Rocklin, *Regulation of Religion*.

83. Jean Besson, *Martha Brae's Two Histories: European Expansion and Caribbean Culture-Building in Jamaica* (Chapel Hill: University of North Carolina Press, 2002); Diana Paton, *The Cultural Politics of Obeah: Religion, Colonialism and Modernity in the Caribbean World* (Cambridge: Cambridge University Press, 2015); Lara Putnam, "Rites of Power and Rumors of Race: The Circulation of Supernatural Knowledge in the Greater Caribbean, 1890–1940," in *Obeah and Other Powers: The Politics of Caribbean Religion and Healing*, ed. Diana Paton and Maarit Forde (Durham, NC: Duke University Press 2012); and *Radical Moves: Caribbean Migrants and the Politics of Race in the Jazz Age* (Chapel Hill: University of North Carolina Press, 2013); Sylvia Wynter, "Jonkonnu in Jamaica: Towards the Interpretation of Folk Dance as a Cultural Process," *Jamaica Journal*, June 1970, 34–48.

84. Putnam, *Radical Moves*, 59–61.

85. Paton *The Cultural Politics of Obeah*; Crosson, *Experiments with Power*.

86. Aisha Khan, "Dark Arts and Diaspora," *Diaspora: A Journal of Transnational Studies* 17, no. 1 (Spring 2008): 40–63.

87. Crosson, "What Obeah Does Do," 167–69. On "altered solidarities" in rural cosmopolitan Trinidad, see J. Brent Crosson, "Own People: Race, 'Altered Solidarities,' and the Limits of Culture in Trinidad," *Small Axe* 45 (November 2014).

88. Putnam, "Rites of Power," 249.

89. Sinah Theres Kloß, "Manifesting Kali's Power: Guyanese Hinduism and the Revitalisation of the 'Madras Tradition,'" *Journal of Eastern Caribbean Studies* 41, no. 1 (April 2016): 95; Crosson, *Experiments with Power*.

90. Putnam, "Rites of Power."

91. Lisa Lowe, *The Intimacies of Four Continents* (Durham, NC: Duke University Press, 2015).

92. See Crosson, *Experiments with Power*; Paton, *The Cultural Politics of Obeah*.

93. Katherine McKittrick, *Dear Science and Other Stories* (Durham, NC: Duke University Press, 2021), 3n4, 3–4.

94. Crosson, *Experiments with Power*.

95. Thomas, *Kincraft*, 46–47.

96. I am conceptualizing these forms of relationality as kin-making in the face of racializing colonial structures of group separation (the colonial constructions of the separateness and separability of reified ethnoracial groups based on biocultural difference).

97. "Experimental," then, operates here also in similar fashion to experimentation in the arts, creating contingency and inverting regnant norms (Crosson, *Experiments with Power*, 17).

98. Freeman, "Queer Belongings," 299.

99. De Laurence, *Great Book of Magical Art*, 55.

100. L. W. de Laurence, *The Sacred Book of Death, Hindu Spiritism, Soul Transition and Soul Reincarnation* (Chicago: de Laurence, Scott and Co., 1905), 16.

101. Saidiya Hartman, "Venus in Two Acts," *Small Axe* 26 (June 2008): 11.

102. Stephen Best and Saidiya Hartman, "Fugitive Justice," *Representations* 92, no. 1 (Fall 2005): 11.

103. Lowe, *The Intimacies of Four Continents.*

104. Rocklin, *Regulation of Religion.*

105. Stuart Hall, "Fantasy, Identity, Politics," in *Cultural Remix: Theories of Politics and the Popular*, ed. Erica Carter, James Donald, and Judith Squires (London: Lawrence and Wishart, 1995), 66.

The Rhythms of Ritual

HINASAHAR MUNEERUDDIN

Performing poetry instills a form of musicality into the body—a form of movement and rhythm. Together, the words, movements, rhythms, and melodies illustrate the truth of the performer. From spoken word and hip-hop to *qawwalis*[1] and *dhikr*[2], poetry and musicality are inextricably tied not only to the truth of one's identity, but also to the act of ritual.

Scholarship has shown how artistic forms such as poetry, hip-hop, and qawwalis have been linked to identity-making and truth-telling. In *Being Muslim,* Chan-Malik writes about the poetry of Sonia Sanchez, a poet and activist who joined the Nation of Islam (NOI) in 1972. During her time in the NOI, Sanchez wrote a series of poems expressing her experiences as a Black Muslim woman. One poem in particular, "We Are Muslim Women" (1973), articulates Black Muslim womanhood (through its affect, practices, and desires), and also expresses a type of "againstness" and "insurgency" in contrast to the realities of white supremacy. Chan-Malik argues that for Sonia Sanchez, the poem articulated a way of being Muslim "in which the embodiment of Muslim womanhood itself is a form of unruly and rebellious expression against social, cultural, and political norms of race, gender, and religion."[3] In fact, poetry offers a way for the poets to express their identities, desires, and emotions as an act of transgression against the status quo. Sanchez's poem "We Are Muslim Women" is reminiscent of Kishwar Naheed's poem "We Sinful Women." Naheed (b. 1940) is a feminist Urdu poet and activist from Pakistan. Her poem also offers an "againstness" in that it transgresses social gender norms, the military rule of the nation-state, and the traditional *ghazal* form of Urdu poetry (which requires a particular rhyme scheme).[4] Although Naheed's poem reflects an intense affect, often expressed in ghazals or in qawwalis[5] (the musical performance of a ghazal), this emotion is not reflected toward the divine or an object of love. Naheed instead expresses intense frustration against patriarchal social norms and also issues a proclamation—of being a strong Muslim woman, sinful and rebellious. In this way, poetry operates as a poweful mechanism for performing and expressing queer affect, including a way of instantiating the truth of the self.

Amiri Baraka (LeRoi Jones, 1934–2014), a Black Muslim poet and writer, has written that art allows one to express that which cannot be explained through the use of language, rhythm, and syntax.[6] His poem "Black Art" (published in 1966 after the assassination of Malcolm X) sparked the Black Arts movement, which cultivated a culture of Black empowerment through art and activism in the 1960s and 1970s. Along with Sufi poets who have long understood that poetry is what allows one to approach the ineffable—where language may approach the experience of the real[7]—James Baldwin has expressed similar sentiments about the connections of poetry and truth:

> "The poets (by which I mean all artists) are finally the only people who know the truth about us. Soldiers don't. Statesmen don't. Priests don't. Union leaders don't. Only poets . . . [This is] a time . . . when something awful is happening to a civilization, when it ceases to produce poets, and, what is even more crucial, when it ceases in any way whatever to believe in the report that only the poets can make."[8]

For Baldwin, poets are tasked with the responsibility to communicate the realities of our experiences, and their poems and words bear witness to the consciousness of the human experience—where the poetry is intimately linked to the realities of being human. Audre Lorde further elucidates the role of poetry in the structuring and restructuring of lives, identities, and behaviors:

> Poetry is not a luxury. It is a vital necessity of our existence. It forms the quality of the light within which we predicate our hopes and dreams toward survival and change, first made into language, then into idea, then into more tangible action. Poetry is the way we help give name to the nameless so it can be thought. The farthest horizons of our hopes and fears are cobbled by our poems, carved from the rock experiences of our daily lives . . .
>
> Right now, I could name at least ten ideas I would have once found intolerable or incomprehensible and frightening, except as they came after dreams and poems. This is not idle fantasy, but the true meaning of "it feels right to me." We can train ourselves to respect our feelings, and to discipline (transpose) them into a language that matches those feelings so they can be

> shared. And where that language does not yet exist, it is our poetry which helps to fashion it. Poetry is not only dream or vision, it is the skeleton architecture of our lives . . .
>
> Our poems formulate the implications of ourselves, what we feel within and dare make real (or bring action into accordance with), our fears, our hopes, our most cherished terrors.[9]

In this passage, Lorde describes the power of poetry—or more so, the role of poetry in *becoming*. With poetry, the poet is able to weave impossibilities into possibilities, envision futures, express affects, and transform realities. Here, Lorde comes close to describing the queering power of poetry. Poetry *queers* and *is queering* because it not only engenders subversive expressions of identity, religion, politics, thoughts, and feelings through words (written or performed), but also gives rise to a continuous *process* of subversion as practice that is embodied and transformative.

In the United States especially, poetry and truth-telling hold a close connection to hip-hop and a Black consciousness.[10] Historically, hip-hop offers a mode of artistic expression that constitutes a way of being and becoming that resists and contradicts societal norms. In particular, in *Muslim Cool*,[11] Su'ad Abdul Khabeer credits hip-hop with playing an important role in "Muslim cool," which she defines as a way of being Muslim that resists and reconfigures US racial hierarchies. In addition, rap music performance emerges as a platform in which Black female rappers (Muslim or other) are able to "refute, deconstruct, and reconstruct alternative visions of their identity" as a mechanism by which to "seek empowerment, make choices, and create spaces for themselves and other sistas [sisters]."[12] Performance of rap or any other poetry contributes to a *becoming*—a shifting of identities by which the performer can manifest their desires and envision various versions of their self. Along with Khabeer, scholars such as Hisham Aidi, Mark Anthony Neal, and June Jordan have illustrated the use of hip-hop, poetry, and music as expressive forms of Black liberation and truth-telling in the United States. Moreover, in *Rebel Music* Aidi contends that music functions as a "powerful lens through which to view the identities and movements emerging in Muslim communities. Music has long been used by youth to protest, proclaim identity, build community, and interpret the world."[13] The arts are and have been embedded in long histories of protest and affective transformation for marginalized peoples. In *Yearning*, bell hooks further illustrates the ways art has been seen as intrinsically serving a political function where Black art overtly challenged racist thinking that dehumanized Black people and deemed them as uncivilized.[14]

This affective forming of self through poetic truth-telling reads similarly to the performances of self-expression that occur during ritual performance. In this way, poetry becomes ritual. Even when considering the repeating sounds, words, beats, rhythms, and vibrations in the performance of the spoken word, poetry invokes ritual. Just as repeated actions in ritual prayer elicit a continuous process of reorienting the self,[15] the repetition in poetry offers the same transformation for the participant—an alternate reality that exists outside of mainstream norms. Khabeer illustrates this connection between repetition and transformation in hip-hop music in her *Muslim Cool*. She utilizes the term "loop" from hip-hop sampling techniques in which a piece of music is played over and over in order to create a new piece of music. Khabeer maintains that the "loop extends and returns, not in a closure but in a cypher, the communal and competitive space in which hip hop culture regenerates and develops."[16] In this way, while for Khabeer the sonic repetition of a looped musical sample poses a metaphor for a site of both continuity and change, in this essay, repetition of sound, beats, words, and gestures in a performance can all signal a transformation of the self, of affective environments, and of political empowerment.

Using the ethnographic fieldwork I conducted from 2016 to 2021 at various open mic performance spaces in the United States, this essay focuses on the ways "scenes" of spoken-word poetry performance formulate the continuous process of *becoming* Muslim and *becoming* gendered through moments of self-definition. Through interviews with participants and real-time observation of their poetry performances, I collected field notes modeled as "thick descriptions"—detailed narratives of events, conversations, and interactions that reveal how meaning and identity are constructed in the daily activities of participants.[17] In a move influenced by Sara Ahmed, I was able to sense and note the ways emotions (such as grief, joy, trauma, hopelessness, anxiety, and so on) permeated the performance space to shape the body language of both the participants and the audience members.[18] Further, through open-ended interviews with participants, I gained insight into the ways their performances affected them and their identities. This essay seeks to find out how certain Muslims negotiate the binary of masculinity and femininity through spoken word and Islamic prayer performances. I am interested in exploring what is happening in these spaces: what role does spoken-word performance play in *gender-becoming*, and how is gendered self-naming (with terms such as queer, genderqueer, nonbinary, trans*, and so on) a part of this negotiation or becoming? Further, this essay explores whether spoken-word performances can be analyzed as religious rituals, especially since both are embodied practices that, in Muslim contexts and understandings, aare lready gender-specific and work to transform and temporarily stabilize identity. Central to this analysis is exploring the ways race and sexuality affect this Muslim *gender-becoming.*

I pause here to define three key terms and concepts I use throughout this essay. The first is "gender-*becoming,*" a term I employ to capture the fluid nature of the process of gendered self-definition for some Muslims. I focus on those who negotiate the boundary of the gender binary—constantly moving on and around this border of masculinity and femininity. They may choose to identify as trans*,[19] genderqueer, nonbinary, women, or men. By using the word "becoming," I seek to highlight the perpetual instability of gender identification in my participants. It indicates a journey that may never come to a final destination and where what the body does (its performance) in a particular moment tells us how identities are constantly shifting. Second, I utilize the words "space" and "scene" interchangeably to capture the physical and/or virtual space of performance, and also all that is encompassed within that, including, but not limited to, discourses, temporalities, affect, bodies, and various material objects. Together, for my purposes, these aspects make up the geography of a "space" or "scene." Lastly, I use the word "queer," as well as its verb form, "queer(ing)," not only to highlight nonnormative gender and sexual identities, but also to capture the ruptures, disruptions, and overall "againstness" with respect to normative time, space, and constructions of gender, sexuality, and Muslim-ness. In other words, for my purposes, "to queer" is *to subvert* normativity.

With respect to theory, this essay contends with the methodological and theoretical framework of affect and emotion in a variety of ways. For example, I build on Charles Hirschkind's work in his book *The Ethical Soundscape: Cassette Sermons and Islamic Counterpublics* by proposing that to study religion and emotion in relation to each other means to contemplate what exists beyond language, signification, and normative regulation; in essence, emotion becomes a decolonial tool for studying religion. Hirschkind's book looks at the effects of the audio of a cassette sermon through Brian Massumi's notion of affect (which implies that religious feeling may be garnered not necessarily through doctrine or cognition, but instead through affect, sense, and feeling) to talk about the level on which the effects of listening to the cassette sermon resounded within the body and how these effects on bodies functioned to shape ethical practices for the participants. In this way, sensory conditions formulate the possibility for shaping a form of Islamic ethics for the participant. Affect operates here as a way to privilege religious feeling and the role it plays in shaping subjectivity without resorting to theories of universal religious feeling along the lines of Schleiermacher or William James. This essay argues that affect operates in a similar way in the gender-becoming of my participants.

Sara Ahmed's *The Cultural Politics of Emotion* helps me think about emotion as a decolonial approach to the ethnographic study of my participants. Ahmed proposes that emotions shape the very surfaces of bodies, which in turn take shape through the repetition of actions over time. Thinking about the ways in which emotions circulate through bodies and how they *stick* to these bodies, as well as considering how they move, would approach a decolonial, feeling-forward method in studying performance and the way my participants are affected by such emotion—how they are made and unmade by them. Privileging emotions as opposed to mere discourse reveals the way emotions can connect bodies to other bodies—illuminating modes of attachment through movement and how such circulation of objects of emotions can lead to the transformation of others into objects of feeling. In this way, an analysis of feeling advances emotion as a means of cultural politics or world-making. Ahmed also proposes that emotions can open up futures, as they can include a variety of orientations to others, thus offering a means of considering the decoloniality or queerness of time. In this way, considering emotions enables me to approach my participants in an embodied, sensory way that can allow for stories that are accessed through decolonial means.

I also consider "The Event and the Everyday" by Veena Das[20] and Kathleen Stewart's *Ordinary Affects*.[21] These two scholars offer everyday or ordinary affects as a decolonial way of looking at ethnographic research. Das aims to describe, in the context of violence against Muslims in Gujrat, Pakistan, in March 2002, how feelings of skepticism become immersed in everyday life, such that promises of belonging by the state cannot undo the violence that is experienced by Muslims within their daily lives. Das writes this as a decolonial move to excavate the marginalized voices explicitly marked by a biopolitical state that produces killable bodies. She also maintains that her research process involved allowing the knowledge of her participants to color the story she herself tells. Similarly, Kathleen Stewart aims to highlight how outwardly "ordinary" events can comment upon the social stresses, ills, and vulnerabilities of the ordinary person who is marked by structural disenfranchisement. Much like Sara Ahmed's "emotions," ordinary affect are public feelings that circulate and map connections and trajectories, as well as tracing flows of power. Stewart maintains that affect does not operate like knowledge (the production of which can be colonial by nature, especially within academia), but instead can be conceived as the expression of ideas or problems performed as spontaneous, yet powerful modes of learning and participation. In this way, ordinary affect is not only about people's feelings being shared with another, but also about bodies affecting other bodies. In this way, focusing on the minute, everyday or ordinary modes of feelings and affects, we can dismantle the colonial pitfalls of traditional ethnography. Instead, by focusing on the body and its sensory experiences, we can produce a type of learning and communication of ideas that is ultimately decolonial.

While ethnography can be a useful methodological tool in studying the complexity of the lived realities of our subject, this type of research is entangled with a deep history of colonial and colonizing modes of knowledge production. To combat this, decolonial methodologies of mapping affect and emotion have been theorized and utilized as a means not only to construct alternative modes of knowledge, but also to center the subjects themselves in the stories and knowledge they convey to the researcher. Thus, these decolonial methodologies provide my own research project with the frameworks needed to approach an ethical and participatory way of thinking about my project participants.

AFAQ MAHMOUD AND THE SPOKEN-WORD STAGE

The date is March 31, 2017, and the event is a collaboration between Muslim Writers Collective and Muslim Protagonist: an "annual literary symposium of Muslim and minority writers, artists, and thinkers at Columbia University, hosted by the Columbia Muslim Students Association . . . as a means of facilitating dialogue, networking, and inspirational as well as practical tools for pursuing 'literature as an agent of social, intellectual, and spiritual change.'"[22] The theme of the night is "Centering the Margin," and it aims to capture the narratives that are often relegated to the margins, frequently overshadowed by hegemonic representations, perceptions, identities, and language.

Afaq Mahmoud[23] is a Sudanese-American, who was born in Yemen and raised in Philadelphia. She is a twenty-two-year-old artist, activist, educator, poet, and photographer from a family of refugees.[24] On this evening, she performs two pieces that illustrate how she has been able to carve a subjectivity and identity for herself outside of the perceptions other entities have placed upon her. In particular, Mahmoud's spoken-word performance offers her a mechanism that reaffirm all her identities, which she lists as Muslim, Black, and femme. For example, in her first piece, Mahmoud says, "Faith is a choice unless you're Muslim, then it's conviction. Skin is skin, unless you're Black. Then it's a death sentence. And to be femme and all these things is to always die fighting and have your death ruled a suicide." Here, Mahmoud delineates the complications of being Muslim, Black, and femme in the United States. With many state-sanctioned forms of violence against Muslims and Blacks in the form of surveillance laws and police brutality, Afaq highlights the lack of futurity and eventual death of Black, Muslim femmes. In particular, oppressive systems of language ("choice" vs. "conviction") subject the visibly Black, Muslim femme toward an unjust death ("ruled a suicide"). The affect is palpable; the hurt in her voice and the unshed tears in her eyes reflect a truth about herself—what she has been through and the trauma she has undergone. In the next section of her piece, Mahmoud speaks the role her racial-religious identity plays in how she is included in particular spaces. She says, "On Saturday, I am told all the Islamis like me should jump into a river. In the same hour, another *hijabi* calls me a slave. And I ask myself, is it a leap of faith if the fall kills you. And I ask myself, when did the house of God become a broken home . . . The same man trying to ban the burka will say you're asking for it if you're not wearing one." These lines of poetry complicate her sense of belonging not only within non-Muslim spaces, but also within non-Black Muslim spaces.

In the narrative Afaq provides, both the anti-Muslim slur "Islami" and the anti-Black slur "slave" are used against her. "Islami" is not an actual term but is used as a rubbish term to refer to Muslims in a derogatory way; this indicates the exclusion she feels in non-Muslim spaces. But when a hijabi calls Afaq "slave," a word that in Arabic is used as a slur against Blacks, she constructs a parallel narrative of exclusion from non-Black Muslim spaces. The use of the word "hijabi," referring to a Muslim woman who covers her hair, indicates that this speaker should be a person who would feel a sense of community and solidarity with Afaq (especially as Afaq is a hijabi as well), but by using the slur they reveal the ignorance and racism that can be present even within the Muslim community. In this way, Mahmoud complicates the notions and perceptions of intra-Muslim relationships, as well as complicating notions of how she understands herself. In referring to the house of God as "broken," she illustrates the contradictory ways her identities as Black and Muslim are formulated through encounters with racist others (which include Muslims), through being labeled as an "Islamist" by others (even though she does not identify as such), and through overarching patriarchal structures whereby men (whether non-Muslim or Muslim) seek to police women's bodies. Afaq's piece continues: "I'm Sudanese, born in Yemen, live in the United States. I have yet to love a country that did not try to kill me. Which is to say . . . I meet death and live anyway . . . it's to be made voiceless and still sing . . . I can be all that I am and all that I've lost with me. Home is wherever I am and I'm here to stay." With these words, Mahmoud inscribes a subversive voice and narrative that is all her own as she locates herself *outside* of the narratives surrounding ethnicity and nationality. She maintains her existence and positionality on her terms.

In her second piece, Mahmoud addresses the conceptualization of her self, identity, and name. Her poem beautifully weaves together various scenes within her life that depict the journey of her *becoming*—how she has come to understand her gender, race, and religion. Her story begins during childhood: "I am five years old. The first time I am called a girl and not my name. A boy in Khartoum in Sudan tells me I remind him of a rose. This is the first time I remember being mistaken for a flower . . . since then I have been called a thousand things that are not my name." In this instance, Mahmoud attempts to carve out an identity outside of the categories that are prescribed for her. She holds a closer connection to her name than to anything else. Her name is her identity, not her gender ("called a girl") or gender expression (femininity likened to a flower). This importance placed on name and "being called by her name" in her poetry offers an insight into the ways Afaq uses her art to connect to and express feelings of belonging. She continues: "In Philadelphia, a boy says he wants to find my broken and fix me. He thinks this is charming and not snake. Girls don't break easy. We shatter—ceilings, expectations, idiot boys, sometimes ourselves in the process. And when we're told finding yourself is for White girls, we try to look anyway." Here, Mahmoud inscribes herself as a Black Muslim femme (a word she uses to describe her own gender). Her gender as femme, as girl, is reinscribed as significant to her identity, where her gendered becoming—her journey to find herself—is differentiated from that of white girls.

Mahmoud finishes:

> In Syracuse, New York, a boy tells me I'm his world!? Unlike this world, I have buried more people than I have birthed. And I still do not know what it is to be a girl, and I still do not know what it is to be a femme—a word often mistaken for womb. I'm told I must be a mother or a monster, then I was once a child too . . . I am always hungry, never welcome at the table. Unless I learn to leave the Black girl, bring just the magic. And my child would be the same . . . I will try not to forget my name.

In this final section, Mahmoud struggles with others' ideas of what it may mean to be Black and femme. She observes that gender identity is often conflated with body parts ("womb") or reproductive ability. This does not sit well with Mahmoud ("I must be a monster or a mother"), which may be the reason why she resonates more with her name than anything else. Her name is the perfect encapsulation of her identity—within it she reveals her religion, gender, race, and cultural heritage. She stresses that she will try not to forget her name—an everyday articulation of the longing she feels to perpetually define her identity as a Black Muslim femme.

Furthermore, Afaq utilizes cities and states as physical spaces that mark her own scenes of subjection—from being taken as a rose in Khartoum or broken in Philadelphia to reclaiming what it may mean to her to be femme, girl, or mother in Syracuse. Even as she is aware of the hegemonic discourses that surround all the identities she occupies, she still holds sacred her name and with it, her shifting identities, which are hers alone—in the liminal space of this performance that is unmarked by anything else in this precise moment.

Ultimately, through her spoken word, Afaq Mahmoud portrays how her body and sense of self are subjected in various ways, through a variety of discourses—such as those of gender, racism, sexism, and anti-Muslim hostility. By taking the audience through her journey of becoming in her performances at the open mic, she illustrates this becoming physically and emotionally as well. As Mahmoud locates affects such as violence, longing, and terror as well as strength and magic as sites of her identity as a visibly Black Muslim femme living in New York City, her embodied response to this truth-telling is palpable; it affects not just her, but the whole audience as well, as they hum, grunt, and surreptitiously wipe away their tears—expressing an Ahmedian "stickiness" of emotions that *adhere to* and *through* bodies.

The open mic performance stage serves as a site of becoming for Muslim femmes, and not only through affect, discourse, and their embodied performances: the material stage itself *transforms* the body into a Muslim femme. As she is able to embody who she is and narrate her stories on the stage, the affects she emanates that stem from her traumas interpellate her. Furthermore, this site serves as a decolonial space of liminality where she may be able to invoke her futurity into existence—even though her futurity may seem bleak outside of this space. Here, her stories set her free—expressing the truth of her being and her ways of knowing.

In 2020, Afaq Mahmoud was featured in a documentary directed by Stéphane de Freitas called *On Est Ensemble/We Are One*. By highlighting the stories and causes of various activists from around the world, the documentary seeks to illustrate that perhaps solidarity is the key to healing. The main narrator of the documentary is French musician Mattheiu Chedid. In an effort to cultivate global solidarity, Chedid brings together activists from around the world to participate in music video for his song, "Solidarité." Through the snippets and scenes of the documentary film, we learn about Afaq's story—the blatant anti-Muslim and anti-Black racism she has faced during her time in the United States. In the documentary, we come across a scene where Afaq is performing her spoken word. She holds the audience in rapture with her words as her emotions flow across the audience, especially affecting Chedid. The camera zooms in on his eyes as they well up when Afaq's words stream toward him. The camera also pans across the audience's faces—capturing their solemn and sobering expressions. She recites:

> To be Black and Muslim in this America,
> Is to be buried twice.
> It's to be left out of every conversation that concerns you.
> To constantly have your humanity questioned.
> To always fight to be seen as what you are.
> To only be accepted in fragments.
> They say Muslim is the new Black,
> As if I never existed,
> As if I'm just a shadow in the prayer room
> Or a crack in the Liberty Bell.
> I'm stuck between the faith I chose and the skin I didn't.
> I can't be Black and Arab,
> I can't be both and welcome here . . .
> I carry all that I am,
> And all that I've lost with me.
> So home is wherever I am.
> And I'm here to stay.[25]

MASJID AL-RABIA'S QUEER EID OPEN MIC (IN COLLABORATION WITH MASGD)

It is spring 2021, and in the past year the COVID-19 pandemic has changed the face of the world. Gathering in person, especially in crowds, feels like a distant memory—a phenomenon that has led many people to feel isolated. This time also coincides with the holy month of Ramadan for Muslims everywhere, a sacred month for many and a time to be spent in community, and the second Ramadan during the pandemic. Since many cities at this time were in lockdown in the United States, it was impossible for many Muslims to celebrate Ramadan in communal ritual. This feeling of isolation was exacerbated for queer Muslims, who are often dismissed from mainstream Muslim communities anyway.

In 2020, during the first Ramadan in the pandemic (April 5–May 14, 2020), four US-based Muslim organizations organized a month of virtual programming that culminated in a Queer Eid Open Mic: Masjid al-Rabia, Muslim Alliance on Gender and Sexual Diversity (MASGD), Muslim Justice League, and *Reconstructed Magazine*. Masjid al-Rabia and MASGD, in particular, cater to LGBTQ+ Muslims, and together they hosted the Queer Eid Open Mic. Masjid al-Rabia is based in Chicago (mostly virtually since 2020) and is a "radically accessible, BIPOC-led, and LGBTQ+ affirming Islamic community center . . . with a mission to provide spiritual support for marginalized Muslims with healing just practices in mind."[26] Masjid al-Rabia opened in 2016 through the efforts of leaders from the Transgender Muslim Support Network, Third Coast Queer Muslims, and other local groups as a way to create a pluralistic, faith/justice space rooted in principles of accessibility and radical inclusion. Its mission is to foster an Islam and a way of being Muslim that include every identity. In 2018, Masjid Al-Rabia became "the first trans-led, women-centered, and LGBTQ+ affirming mosque in North America."[27] MASGD is another LGBTQ+-affirming organization. It works "to support, empower, and connect LGBTQ+ Muslims . . . [to] celebrate gender and sexual diversity within Muslim communities and promote an understanding of Islam that is centered on inclusion, justice, and equity."[28] Interestingly, at the core of these two organizations is the promotion of an interpretation of Islam and a way of being Muslim that is radically inclusive—the resonances of which one can see in the open mic event they host.

On May 14, 2021, Masjid al-Rabia and MASGD hosted their third biannual Queer Eid Open Mic Night Celebration. Due to the pandemic circumstances, the event was held on Zoom. As the host waited for more participants to arrive, the song "Ana Dammi Falasteeni [My Blood Is Palestinian]" by Mohammed Assaf was blasting in the background. This year, Eid-ul-Fitr was celebrated with conflicted feelings as it coincided with the violent deaths of 120 people in Palestine as well as the ongoing genocide of Uyghur Muslims in China. The Zoom event had some fifty participants and wasd filled with gender, sexual, racial, and sectarian[29] diversity. Zoom is an interesting site of study, as it does operate in the virtual world, but simulates the in-person world in that every action is taking place in real time and the audience can interact with the speakers and each other in real time. It is quite different from other sites of digital ethnography in Islamic studies, where content (videos, threads, comments, interactions, and so forth) is posted on varied timelines.[30] In this way, even though Zoom operates as a different forum from an in-person venue, it still allows us to capture the affective nature of the audience and the performance itself. In some instances, we are better able to gauge participants' reactions and affect by observing participants' individualized video and through the chat function, which enables all voices and reactions to be heard. Of course, with Zoom, not everyone has their video on, which may compare to the anonymity many people experience in a crowd.

The first performer of the Queer Eid Open Mic was a queer performer on the oud (a Persian lute-type stringed instrument), who proceeded to play a tune that felt mesmerizing, relaxing, and sad all at the same time. We all seemed to sway our heads and bodies to the rhythm of the music. The chat function in Zoom started to come alive, with comments like these: "The sounds tell a story"; "So true—it's so emotive"; "It's easy to see Allah's power through the talents Allah (SWT) gives Allah (SWT)'s creations"; "This music has made me so emotional"; "Beautiful and moving." Even though no words were being used, the rhythm, tone, and pitch of the oud were able to elicit emotional responses from the audience, calling forth the truth and story of the performer. It even allowed at least one participant to feel a spiritual connection to the divine—as she calls upon the miraculous nature of Allah's power. It seems as if the the musicality of the oud cast a spell on all of us, creating an intimate bubble with all of us inside, a place where we could forget all harsh realities. Here, art not only has the power to evoke, but also to create a world unto itself—queering the future and filling it with possibility. The sound and the story the oud transmitted seemed to transform both our bodies and our space.

The next two performers were queer, Black Muslim spoken-word artists. One of them was Nyuma Waggeh (she/they),[31] a well-known and published spoken word artist. She ended up performed many of her newer works in progress, along with some of her more established works. One of their pieces is called "Exploring Queerness," and it weaves together their many identities of artist, Black, Muslim, and queer into a manifesto of their life. In the first part, she explores her artistic self:

> The idea of a "tortured" artist,
> once was a mantra.
> A way of living.
> I, a physicist formed a formula of chronic pain and anguish,
> a weathering process breaking down who I am to create a grain of art.
> I decided to live in that pain never letting go,
> It never dawned on me to separate the pain from the art,
> Or rather the person from the pain.
> Call me nobody, for I have stricken my own self blind.

The deceitful wine left me mad for years, sitting on my own
island
Accompanied by demons resembling Circe coercing me off my
journey.
I lived in my sadness allowing it to tie sandbags around my
ankles.
She deceived me to walk in the stormy sea, telling me I could
swim
unscathed if I
Never acknowledged the rocky seas crashing at the edge of my
heart.
If, I'm being honest I think I always knew.[32]

For Nyuma, their gender and sexual identity is interspersed with their art; in fact, it becomes a mechanism by which they are able to transform their pain and sadness into a manifestation of their truth as queer. On a meta level, the performance of the spoken word itself speaks truth to Nyuma's artistic self. Here, poetry and art play an integral role in Nyuma's queer gender becoming—a way for them to come to terms with their queerness. Poetry and spoken word also allow Nyuma to name her emotions, bringing them to the fore in order to connect them to her reality, her "way of living." In particular, this first stanza of Nyuma's performance offers an entryway for both the performer and the listener to *feel* and *touch* what has been hidden about Nyuma's self, inspiring our collective embodied and emotional healing by giving voice to past traumas and future possibilities. The way Nyuma's performance reaches out through the screen and touches our hearts, forcing us to reckon with our own traumas, is indicative of the transformative power of spoken-word performance. It transforms our emotions, our bodies, the performance space, and even our futures. As Nyuma's next stanza indicates, only by giving voice to past traumas can one move on to understand the present and create a future:

At the age of 13, I gathered my 3 closest childhood friends.
All wrapped in our hijabs and our melanin skin not teaching
us the harsh
life lesson
Of being black in the land of the triple K's disguised in green
robes of the
American Dream, the
view from down here has always been an embellished blessin'.
I, defiantly stand at the top of the white marble staircase

In an apartment lobby where I spent my days being a
mischievous rebel
amongst the crowd.
I say, "I'm bisexual."
I don't remember what they said.
But, I remember what I felt.
The questionable looks were all I needed to validate people of
my kind
weren't welcomed here.
Each step away from me, an imaginative barrier being put in
place, a
vaccination from
something they never wanted to contract.
A plague, an illness of sorts.
The queer was contagious, and I caught wind of it.
The young naïve black queer girl had found her welcoming
arrival into the
world.
It was judgement,
Fear,
Internalized homophobia.
The whole ordeal made me rescind my queer citizenship and
live my
teenage years with the ruling class of American citizens: the
heterosexuals.
These dead-in living puritans have crucified my sexuality.
Condemned me to a life of heteronormativity.[33]

In this portion of Nyuma's performance, she brings attention to being Black and Muslim in the "land of triple K's disguised in green robes of the American Dream"—a land that routinely marks Black Muslim bodies by state securitization, surveillance, white supremacy, and citizenship. For Nyuma, being a Black Muslim *and* queer placed them in a particular liminality, where they felt that they could not belong and speak truth to who they are. For this reason, she had to "crucify" her sexuality—suppressing parts of her identity as she became awash in fear and confusion. In this way, Nyuma has faced rejection not only from the state, but also from her young Muslim community.

Now, 21 I have arrived to a gay club in Washington D.C.
Scanning my body over to my tattoo that reads,

"I understood myself only after I destroyed myself.
And only in the process of fixing myself, did I know who I
really was."
I am in a room filled with so many people across all spectrums.
Dancing in a darkness that no longer frightens me,
she entices me closer.
I follow.
She inches me in,
Calling my name.
A sweet aroma,
A sound that has never sounded so welcoming.
I am free, in the darkness where there has always been light.
Her comfort has gracefully saved me from living a lie.
I am free,
Free,
At last *free*.[34]

In the last part of the performance, Nyuma calls forth smells and sounds that paint a picture, illuminating a scene of acceptance and belonging. Here, they highlight how they are called by their name—a time when who they are and perceived as finally aligns with how they feel inside. For Nyuma, this moment is felt viscerally in the body, where she is free from the bindings of white supremacy, misogynoir, anti-Muslim hostility, as well as normative patriarchal and queer-phobic interpretations and spaces of Muslimness. Even as Nyuma performs this over Zoom, no one remains unaffected by her words—including Nyuma herself. In fact, Nyuma's words about "dancing in the darkness . . . where there has always been light" speaks to liminal space she occupied in her marginalized identities. Although Nyuma has not completely escaped the darkness, they have managed to find light within it—ultimately, they found an alternative way of being and healing.

After Nyuma's performance, one participant writes in the chat: "Your words have a very steady, soft-spoken but unspeakable power." This reaction from the audience member speaks to the affective power of Nyuma's spoken-word performance. Nyuma's words change the mood of the space, bringing with them a vibration that reverberates throughout us all. We feel ourselves transforming, morphing into alternative versions of our selves—a self that is allowed to be free. Another participant in the chat writes, "This is a prayer!! [I am] Feeling this on a spiritual level, literally." Here, one sees the immediate connection of spoken-word performance to ritualization. For this participant, experiencing the affective and transformative power of the spoken word was akin to engaging in prayer—an experience that felt spiritual. More specifically, this experience was a testament to the queering of Islamic ritual, where nonnormative practices operate in the same manner as normative Islamic rituals, especially in how they offer a space of meditation, connection to the divine, a reclamation of space to affirm one's own truth, and the option to bare one's soul and its burdens to the One who will listen. For these participants, spoken-word performances offer a space of becoming, both gender-becoming and Muslim-becoming. It is a space where their identities are constantly formed and re-formed to align with their inner truths and inner subjectivities.

One of the groundbreaking constructions of queerness has been historically defined by Eve Sedgwick in *Tendencies*. Sedgwick defines queerness as a continuous moment and movement, stemming from the German word "quer" which means "transverse" and the Latin word that means "to twist"—ultimately conceiving "queerness" as something that operates "across" genders and sexualities, or something that is "transitive." Sedgwick also illustrates that while queerness is often invoked in regard to sexuality, it is more expansive than that—referring to possibilities, gaps, dissonances, overlaps, and lapses when applying meaning to gender and/or sexuality.[35] Furthermore, in *Queer Muslim Diasporas*, Alberto Carbajal maintains that queer Muslims seem to inhabit a space that routinely disorganizes and redefines normative, hegemonic categories and identities—thus, queerness can be seen as disorienting and as proposing alternative ways of becoming.[36] Together, this puts forward alternative interpretive possibilities and assemblages of queer Muslim gender-being and -becoming in opposition to normative categories and dominant modes of knowledge and power. In this way, the shifting characteristic of queer(ing) serves as the perfect lens to think about the ritualization of spoken-word performances by queer participants.

ARTISTIC PERFORMANCE AS RITUAL

On May 3, 2021, I attended a virtual, creative workshop called "Art as Worship." It was hosted by *Reconstructed Magazine*, which is "a creative magazine and conversation space between all Muslims, including Muslim-heritage folks, and individuals with evolving proximity to Islam, that recognizes religion to be a non-linear journey."[37] Founded by queer, Black, and Shi'a Muslims, *Reconstructed Magazine* seeks to empower those who have been most marginalized within, and outside of, the Muslim community, including Black Muslims, LGBTQ+ Muslims, disabled Muslims, Shi'a Muslims, converts, and others. This event, in particular, was intended to challenge the premise that art and

Islam are often seen as antithetical to each other, especially in conservative and/or normative Muslim perspectives. In actuality, figurative and devotional art has historically served as a mode of understanding the divine in Islam by the creation of symbols, figures, and portraits. The goal of the workshop was to reinvent what creating and beholding divine beauty meant to each of us by crafting symbolic portraits or designing prayer mats. It also explored the ways one can incorporate artmaking into religious practice and expression. The workshop was led by Nabi Haider Ali, a Tamil Shi'a Muslim artist based in California, who is well known on social media for his illustrations and handicrafts focused on Shi'i iconography. Ali considers this practice of creating art, especially Shi'i iconography, as a form of meditation and worship.

For Ali, representation of the divine can be illustrated through the abstract, such as through geometry in the sacred environment, which represents the perfection of both the divine and paradise. The divine can also be represented through symmetry, which Ali sees as a metaphor for *Tawhid*, or the oneness of God, where everything unfolds from one point or center, Allah. It also represents the one essence of supreme truth. For Ali, prayer mats convey these very ideas of the divine in the geometric/symmetrical abstract, as the art upon the mats tries to immerse the user in the sacred space of the divine and/or paradise. When considering art that is based upon symbols and iconography, Ali uses imagery of paradise (roses [Prophet Muhammad also loved roses], nature), light (sun, moon, fire, halos, stars), and prophetic symbology (ark of Noah to symbolize salvation, hands to symbolize connections to Fatima and Prophet Muhammad's family, six- or eight-pointed stars as the emblems of Prophets Solomon and Muhammad, and the Zulfiqar [sword of Ali]) to capture the divine in his art. Ali has also found that calligraphic compositions of the Qur'an also hold the beauty of the divine, as they formulate the literal word of God.

As we began the process of creating our pieces of art, the Zoom room was silent as various members started their sketching, with pens/pencils/markers going back and forth to establish their designs. The scratching of the tools on paper in the silence created a cacophony of scratches and even breathing. After a time, Nabi confided to us the meditative and spiritual qualities of creating art. Each stroke we make upon the paper is followed by another stroke, then another, and so on. This repetition, performed when creating art, or even the repetition seen in symmetrical, infinity designs, can be taken as a form of *dhikr*, or as continued remembrance of the divine. One sees God and connects with the divine in the mundane, everyday parts of our life—as in noticing the symmetry of a leaf. This connection through performing art as a form of worship or ritual is key to the ways one can connect not only to the divine, but also to oneself. This is the exact connection that Jordan Ahmed, a queer Muslim dance and performance artist, writer, educator, and organizing director of the Muslim Justice League, experiences whenever he performs.

I had the pleasure of sitting down with Jordan Jamil Ahmed (they/he) on March 29, 2022. We decided to meet at a well-known, cozy eighteenth-century residence turned Middle Eastern coffee shop in Cambridge, Massachusetts. As we sipped our cardamom-spiced tea and lentil soup, Jordan regaled me with stories about his dreams and passions. Jordan is a Shi'a Muslim of South Asian, Indonesian, and Dutch ancestry. They prefer being identified as queer and genderqueer and hold dear the idea that their queerness gestures toward nonnormativeness in all facets of their life—maintaining that they find multiplicity in many of their social identities, such as gender, sexuality, race, and religion. Jordan recently found their connection to Islam after being drawn away from it in college, where finding their connection to queerness took precedence. It was when Jordan found outlets in dance and poetry that they were able to make meaning of their identity, faith, desire, and art all in one form.

Now, as a Shi'a Muslim performance artist, Jordan maintains that they have always found art and faith/ritual to be inextricably tied together. For instance, Jordan recalls that moments when they improvised as a dancer were times when they felt closest to the divine. They maintain that since ritual is embodied, so too is artistic dance—closely aligning both modes of being and becoming. For Jordan, movement has been a way for them to access ecstatic states in direct remembrance of God and the divine. They especially feel that improvisational dance and movement feels spiritual because the best improvisation comes with surrendering oneself to the flow of movement and the same phenomenon occurs in Islamic ritual, when one attempts to submit or surrender oneself to God. It is in these moments that Jordan feels close to both the divine and the community. This moment is also queered for Jordan, because they compare feeling desire in romantic others as similar to feeling desire in the closeness of God. It is in this way that ritual and art seemed to be so closely aligned.

Often, stigma and fear of sex and sexuality in mainstream Muslim communities removes the body from ways of being and becoming Muslim. For Jordan, embodied performances can express both religion and desire in ways that are celebratory. In this way, art is inherently tied to identity, and the body is a vessel for that art. Furthermore, connection to the divine does not necessarily have to associated with a particular traditionally religious act; rather, that connection to the divine is something that is held within us, which is why any action that makes this connection known or felt can be considered a queered ritual act. Emotions live in our body and spoken-word or dance performance is the energetic vessel that releases those emotions and makes Jordan feel closely connected to the divine. In addition, they feel that this is an effective way to access the self in order to create emotional and spiritual experiences. For Jordan, making art generally feels like this.

For Jordan, being queer, genderqueer, Muslim, and a performance artist are all integral identities. For them, all of these identities seek a lack of definition at any given moment in time. The ways these identities shift and morph during ritual and artistic performances indicate the way artistic performance operates as queered ritual. As someone who is genderqueer, Jordan's gender shifts and blurs during performances—swaying between the feminine and masculine. Whenever Jordan performs traditional Islamic rituals, such as *salah*, or prayer, and *dhikr*, or chanting in remembrance of God, they can feel very expansive or somber. Their level of comfort and confidence depends on the day and is reflected in the energy they give to the performance. During this traditional ritual experience, Jordan often feels immersed in the energy of the crowd, and in that immersion they find connection to God. But it is not only during these moments that Jordan feels connection to the divine, as they explain: "honestly, there are times when I'm at the club dancing and I am lost in the closeness to God. I connect to God through light, and when I feel a light inside me radiating out, I have found a connection to God." Here, the performance of dancing in a crowd offers, at times, unexpected moments of *feeling* God.

Oftentimes, Jordan has found that anything that had to do with sex, desire, and the body carries stigma in many mainstream Muslim communities in the United States, including queerness, overt sexuality, and the bending of gender norms. For this reason, even ecstatic experiences carry shame because in the performance of a body that is enraptured by God, there is a moment when desire and spiritual connection become manifest in the body, in the movement of the body that is wholly unrestricted, in the embodied performance that is open to receiving the light of the divine. Jordan emphatically tells me, "Most mainstream Muslims love to shame art. But *dhikr* is art! They want to shame anything that feels good. Any indulgence is seen as *haram* [forbidden]." Then what does it mean when connecting to God through poetry, art, or dance feels good or that it feels like an indulgence? It often means that it gets erased as a "legitimate" means of remembering the divine. For Jordan, the impulse to dance and perform poetry/art is inherently divine. Art is the connection to the divine, so much so that it operates as a ritualistic movement. Jordan maintains that

> artists are fundamental to society since the Divine speaks through them. In fact, artists are seen as closest to God. Even prophethood can be interpreted

> as an artistic experience—there is art in relaying the message of God, engaging in various modes of reflection, and letting your body and emotions be a way to interact with God. Art is the best way to bring the self closer to God and to the community that surrounds us—because the only reason we consume art is so we can feel a connection to others.

In this way, the connection between art and ritual becomes seamless—a queering of ritual. Queerness is also an important facet to this because Jordan also sees queerness as art, especially in the ways one can express queerness in various modes of expression and performance. Ultimately, the power of art and ritual comes from the ability to use them to interrogate ourselves and to challenge (as well as change) perceptions in the world. Jordan feels that during artistic performance an aspect of transformation is always present—their sense of self, body, and identity seems to shift and adjust throughout a performance. Jordan says that "we're all (re)creating ourselves during ritual and art performance. Everything is an assertion of the self and the best moments are when I feel *transformed* by consuming and performing it." During these performances Jordan can express their insecurities and actually become new or alternate versions of themself by trying on various identities and gender-becomings throughout a performance. In either *dhikr* or art performance, Jordan enters into a state of light and connection with the divine. They arrive at a state of flow, where they become very conscious of others' energy, light, and vibrations. Jordan maintains that in this moment, they seek an emotional connection with others and God—hoping to dissolve all boundaries and restrictions. For Jordan, artistic performance is definitively a form of ritual and worship. They feel the most connected to the beloved and the divine when performing and doing art. Doing art is a reminder that there is something bigger than themself. It is for this reason that, just as queerness lacks boundaries, in the same way ritual performance and artistic performance blur together in compelling ways—offering queer Muslims a way to be and become who they desire to be while maintaining a spiritual openness and connection to the divine.

CONCLUSION: QUEERING RITUAL

In "Rehearsed Spontaneity and the Conventionality of Ritual: Disciplines of 'Salat,'" Saba Mahmood centers the role of emotions and embodiment in traditional Islamic ritual, under the rubrics of power and truth. She found that her mosque participants identified prayer as an important site for intentionally molding their intentions, emotions, and desires in agreement with Sunni "orthodox" standards of piety. The highly structured performance of prayer allowed Mahmood's participants a mode of ethical being that was not completely isolated from the ordinary, routinized tasks of everyday life. In this way, for Mahmood's participants, ritual act did not necessarily operate as a script for social action, but instead was a place where the self would acquire and express its "proper" form. Mahmood maintains that in this case, ritual prayer is transformative but not always a space of spontaneous emotion—although emotion is definitely a part of prayer ritual. In this way, ritual prayer transforms daily action that creates and reinforces the desire for worship, and thus, an experienced body is produced and an embodied subject formed. Ultimately, this repeated performance of ritual acts engaged participants in a continuous process of reorienting (or transforming) their desires, gestures, and emotions toward their norms of piety. This mode of "experiencing" and "transformation" during a ritual act, I argue, similarly occurs during spoken-word poetry performances. I have illustrated some of the myriad ways participants undergo transformative experiences—experiences of change or a fluid shifting of identities—when, during a spoken-word or artistic performance, they are able to hold onto a portion of their identity. It is a space where their truth, their identity, *becomes* and is *emoted* through their bodies—whether by movement, sound, rhythm, or vibration.

In a similar vein, Donna Auston exemplifies a productive way of expanding ritual within the study of Islam and Muslims in "Prayer, Protest, and Police Brutality: Black Muslim Spiritual Resistance in the Ferguson Era." Auston posits marching, grassroots organizing, and challenging the legal system as ritual practices (alongside more "traditional" acts of worship, such as prayer and fasting) that approach alternative modes of expressing identity and personal politics. Such acts of ritualized protest are not part of "sacred" space but operate within spaces with particular historical and sociopolitical contexts. Auston maintains that ritual acts as inscribing and acting upon the body are a way to *express* discontent, and also to *actively* reconcile and resist the restrictions of social strictures. In this way, ritualization can be expanded to include not only routinized acts of prayer, but also actions such as routinized modes of protest—or even art and poetry (as I argue in this essay). This new, expansive definition of ritualization can operate as an embodied, affective process that produces transformed or transforming ritualized subjects—and also as a process that can be utilized by Muslims as a means to *resist* oppressive norms by progressing toward an ethics of antiracist empowerment.

By thinking with both Mahmood and Auston, I argue that since ritual is an act that expresses and transforms desires, gestures, and emotions through the body as a way to *express* discontent, as well as to *actively* reconcile and resist the restrictions of social strictures, spoken-word poetry performance can rightly be articulated as a ritual. We know ritual operates in very particular ways in normative religions. Scholarship in religious studies has found that ritual is not just thoughtless action, but instead a strategic and embodied practice produced in order to transform a particular situation.[38] Such a phenomenon can also be mapped onto artistic and spoken-word performances. In this way, our notions of ritual can be expanded to include forms of art, poetry, and musicality that transform and confirm not only the truth of one's Muslim-ness, but also their gender and race. Furthermore, spoken-word performance operates as a queered ritual, as it can be characterized as a symbolic process that communicates not only one's Muslim-ness, but also queer identities. In this way, the act of spoken-word performance becomes a queering of ritual. Ultimately, this queering of ritual expresses not only queer identities, but also nonnormative mechanisms through which to seek, connect, and *feel* the divine.

This essay has considered the ritualization of spoken-word performance as a way to reclaim and reimagine the analytic category of ritual within Islamic studies to conceive of it as an expansive phenomenon that can involve the queering of time, sound, and space, while simultaneously transforming the self, bodies, emotions, spaces, and ethics. Moreover, it is significant to recognize how notions of Muslim gendered *becoming* are configured both by people individually and by various communities in specific spaces. Thus, gendered Muslim becoming is always already in opposition both to Islamophobic discourse and to Muslim communal normative, regulatory ideas of gender and sexuality. In this way, gendered Muslim self-expression can be seen as a queered space of constant negotiation where framing the self in perpetual opposition to normativity may, in the same breath, legitimate these norms. At the same time, the liminality of the performance spaces empowers Muslims to assert their bodies, voices, and identities on their own terms. Ultimately, this essay has aimed to construct a novel approach to examining space, performance, and ritual as scenes where Muslims may creatively and ritualistically perform their narratives and identities in order to affirm their nonnormative existence.

NOTES

1. A *qawwali* is a form of Sufi devotional poetic performance that is done in remembrance and praise of God, Prophet Muhammad, or Ali. This form of performance originates in the Indian subcontinent.

2. *Dhikr* can be described as a rhythmic chant or recitation in remembrance and praise of God, Prophet Muhammad, or Ali.

3. Sylvia Chan-Malik, *Being Muslim: A Cultural History of Women of Color in American Islam* (New York: New York University Press, 2018), 10.

4. Sultan Jahan Begum, "We Sinful Women ('Hum Guneghaar Aurtain')—Transgressing Temporality and Poetic Form," *Literature and Transgression*, April 17, 2014.

5. Hussein Rashid, "Qawwālī in America: Making Space," *Muslim World* 107, no. 2 (2017): 271–86.

6. Amiri Baraka, "Expressive Language," in *Home: Social Essays* (1963; reprint, New York: Akashic Books, 2009).

7. Timothy D. Knepper and Leah E. Kalmanson, *Ineffability: An Exercise in Comparative Philosophy of Religion*, vol. 1. (Cham, Switzerland: Springer, 2017), 241.

8. James Baldwin, *The Cross of Redemption: Uncollected Writings* (New York: Vintage, 2010), 100.

9. Audre Lorde, "Poetry Is Not a Luxury" (1985), in Lorde, *Sister Outsider: Essays and Speeches* (Berkeley: Crossing Press, 2007).

10. Nitasha Tamar Sharma, *Hip Hop Desis: South Asian Americans, Blackness, and a Global Race Consciousness* (Durham, NC: Duke University Press, 2010).

11. Su'ad Abdul Khabeer, *Muslim Cool: Race, Religion, and Hip Hop in the United States* (New York: New York University Press, 2016).

12. Murray Forman and Mark Anthony Neal, eds., *That's the Joint! The Hip-Hop Studies Reader* (New York: Routledge, 2004), 274.

13. Hisham D. Aidi, *Rebel Music: Race, Empire, and the New Muslim Youth Culture* (New York: Pantheon Books, 2014), xxvi.

14. bell hooks, *Yearning: Race, Gender, and Cultural Politics* (New York: Routledge, 2014), 166–67.

15. Saba Mahmood, "Rehearsed Spontaneity and the Conventionality of Ritual: Disciplines of 'Ṣalāt,'" *American Ethnologist* 28, no. 4 (2001): 827–53.

16. Khabeer, *Muslim Cool*, 8.

17. Clifford Geertz, *The Interpretation of Cultures: Selected Essays* (New York: Basic Books, 1973).

18. Sara Ahmed, *The Cultural Politics of Emotion* (Edinburgh: Edinburgh University Press, 2014).

19. The convention of using an asterisk when writing "trans*" is taken from Jack Halberstam's *Trans**, not only to upend colonial strictures of naming and classifying bodies, but also to situate a transformative, perpetually continuous becoming. See Jack Halberstam, *Trans*: A Quick and Quirky Account of Gender Variability* (Berkeley: University of California Press, 2018).

20. Veena Das, *Life and Words: Violence and the Descent into the Ordinary* (Berkeley: University of California Press, 2007).

21. Kathleen Stewart, *Ordinary Affects* (Durham, NC: Duke University Press, 2007).

22. "The Muslim Protagonist: Centering the Margin," *PEN America*, March 6, 2017.

23. I use her name by permission. Mahmoud believes using her name is an important facet of the subjectivity she seeks to employ.

24. Stéphane de Freitas, dir., *On Est Ensemble/We Are One*, Netflix, 2020.

25. Freitas, *Ensemble*.

26. "Masjid Al-Rabia," Masjid Al-Rabia website.

27. "Masjid Al-Rabia," Masjid Al-Rabia website.

28. "The MASGD," MASGD website.

29. I utilize the word "sectarian" here for the sake of legibility. I do contend that the word "sect" can be problematic, as the word stems from Protestant origins and often holds negative connotations. A more neutral term to describe the diversity of Islamic practice may be "branch."

30. Anna Piela, *Muslim Women Online: Faith and Identity in Virtual Space* (New York: Routledge, 2012); Kayla Renée Wheeler, "Remixing Images of Islam: The Creation of New Muslim Women Subjectivities on YouTube," *Online—Heidelberg Journal of Religions on the Internet* 6 (2014); Krista Melanie Riley, "'You Don't Need a Fatwa': Muslim Feminist Blogging as Religious Interpretation," PhD diss., Concordia University, 2016; Donna Auston, "Prayer, Protest, and Police Brutality: Black Muslim Spiritual Resistance in the Ferguson Era," *Transforming Anthropology* 25, no. 1 (2017): 11–22.

31. I honor Waggeh's chosen pronouns by noting them here and by using both alternatively in my discussion.

32. Regie Cabico, ed., *Stoked Words: An Anthology of Queer Poetry from the Capturing Fire Slam and Summit* (Washington, DC: Capturing Fire Press, 2018), 154.

33. Cabico, ed., *Stoked Words*, 154–55.

34. Cabico, ed, *Stoked Words*, 155.

35. Eve Kosofsky Sedgwick, *Tendencies* (London: Taylor and Francis, 2014).

36. Alberto Fernández Carbajal, *Queer Muslim Diasporas in Contemporary Literature and Film* (Manchester, UK: Manchester University Press, 2019).

37. "Reconstructed," *Reconstructed Magazine*, website.

38. Catherine M. Bell, *Ritual Theory, Ritual Practice* (New York: Oxford University Press, 2009).

Guilt, Anxiety, and S(h)ame-Sex Attraction

The Affective Economies of Heteronormativity and Conversion "Therapy" at Liberty University

Lucas F. W. Wilson

In their study of LGBTQ+ students at religious colleges and universities, Shelley L. Craig and colleagues explain: "For some, the choice to attend religious school was an attempt to seek cover and avoid or hide their LGBTQ identities.[1] To many outside the religiously conservative fold, however, the question of what would drive LGBTQ+ students to "seek cover" in educational settings that actively discriminate against them is puzzling. It would seem as though most religious schools, specifically those of the Christian fundamentalist[2] variety, would be some of the *last* places students of nonnormative sexual and gender identities would choose to study. But regardless of the discrepancy between these students' identities and their schools' opinions of them, there is a significant LGBTQ+ population at religious colleges and universities,[3] and many of these students have chosen not only to attend but also to remain in these institutional settings.

Despite the number of LGBTQ+ students in these spaces, there is "limited research on LGBTQ students in religious schools."[4] As Jonathan S. Coley explains, not only are Christian colleges and universities "often ignored sites" of academic inquiry, but the "issues facing LGBT students on Christian campuses have historically been hidden from public [and scholarly] awareness."[5] I seek to further this field of inquiry by fleshing out the impetuses behind LGBTQ+ students' decision to have attended one specific, and prominent, fundamentalist school, located in Lynchburg, Virginia: Liberty University. Bracketing off those who attended the school because of scholarships or those who attended because their parents would only finance their education if they were to go to Liberty, I specifically aim to untangle queer male[6] students' motivations for having remained at the world's largest fundamentalist university—a school that has actively subjugated (and, to this day, continues to subjugate) its queer students. I assume a Foucauldian approach in this study, endeavoring to parse out "how things work[ed] at the level of on-going subjugation, at the level of those continuous and uninterrupted processes which subject[ed queer students'] bodies, govern[ed their] gestures, dictate[d their] behaviours."[7] Further, I seek to examine many of these queer students' decision to attend Liberty's gay conversion therapy program, which until recently was led by a member of the so-called "ex-gay" movement,[8] Dane Emerick.[9] As it is currently unknown if the school still has an active conversion therapy program on campus, my study discusses Liberty from the early 2000s until 2020—the period when Emerick ran his on-campus operation.

Of course, the extent to which queer students *chose* to study at Liberty, along with their *choice* to have been part of the school's conversion therapy program, is complex. These students' capacity to have chosen to attend and remain at Liberty was shaped by what Talal Asad refers to as the "theatrical context" of human agency. In general terms, Asad compares agentic subjects to a professional actor who willfully chooses to perform roles that have been given to them: "The actor's agency consists not in the actions of the role she performs but in her ability to *disempower* one self for the sake of another. Her action is not solely her own. It is at the same time that of the dramatist who has written the script and of the director who mediates between script and performance . . . In an important sense the actor is a part subject; her actions are not fully her own."[10] Asad's actor resembles, in many ways, queer students at Liberty. Although they were the ones who ultimately attended and remained at Liberty, these students were part of a larger fundamentalist system that scripted, directed, and coerced them to do so in the first place.

Moreover, they performed according to the scripts of heteronormativity that the university championed. These students' performance of such heteronormative scripts—scripts that actively disempowered them—points to how their actions were indeed "not fully [their] own." Insofar as these queer students acted according to scripts of heteronormativity—which covered over and/or elided their queer subjectivities—it can be said that they were "part subject[s]" while in attendance. Understanding them as docile, pliant, "part subjects," this study demonstrates how Liberty governed and controlled queer students who were part of the Christian fundamentalist tradition into staying at the university and in turn seeking their own queer erasure—that is, the eradication of their queer orientations and identities.

These students' motivations to have chosen Liberty and to have been a part of its conversion therapy program become clearer when we take into consideration how fundamentalists conceptualize homosexuality. Fundamentalists firmly believe that queer individuals are not actually queer but are, as Mel White puts it, "heterosexual[s] struggling against an odious, sinful, straight-from-the-devil sexual preoccupation."[11] According to the fundamentalist imagination, homosexuality is not an intrinsic part of queer subjects' God-given personhoods, not an inherent or constitutive aspect of their subjectivities. In line with the theories of sexuality that undergird conversion therapy practices, fundamentalists argue that "same-sex attraction" (the phrase commonly used to describe queer desire in fundamentalist and conversion therapy circles) is largely a function of having an absent or emotionally distant father, in tandem with having an overbearing mother.[12] It is said that such family dynamics preclude individuals "struggling" with same-sex attraction from aligning themselves with so-called "proper masculinity" (or "godly masculinity," as defined by Lynne Gerber, below) at a young age. Queer men's predilection for other men is therefore believed to be, at its root, a function of misaligned gender identification. Because of their supposed misaligned gender identification, queer men crave what they apparently lack—masculinity—which they eventually seek out sexually after puberty in "unhealthy" ways. Over time, as the theory goes, they habitually search for masculinity and masculine connection through sexual fantasy and activity, which further solidifies their same-sex attraction.[13]

This understanding of same-sex attraction as habituated *action* and *thought* unconnected to queers' *beings* affords fundamentalists and conversion therapists the misconception that queer individuals, "through religious and/or psychological interventions,"[14] can change their gender identities and thus their sexual orientations. Shedding light on the heteronormative scripts in fundamentalist communities, Christine Robinson and Sue Spivey discuss how the ex-gay movement has understood sexual orientation and gender identity: "Ex-gay etiologies of homosexuality presume a natural link between sex (male), normative gender identity (masculine), and its progeny, heterosexual desire. Ex-gay discourses identify sex differences as the most basic, defining feature of humanity and conflate biological sex with gender identity."[15] According to such thinking, failure to follow particular gendered scripts may lead individuals down the path to same-sex attraction; however, as conversion therapists argue, if queer individuals are to perform according to scripts of heteronormativity, they still have the chance to become attracted to the opposite sex. Conversion therapists push queer men into attempting to realign their gender identification through a prescribed program of habituated performance of "masculinity." That is to say, they teach queer men that if they are to participate in the so-called "activities of men,"[16] and if they are to approximate the supposed "discourse of men" (that is, to talk about "manly things"),[17] they will then begin to feel more masculine and will thus begin to reorient their sexuality. The undergirding belief behind this thinking is that speaking like "real men" and doing the things that "real men" do allows queer men not only to *act* like "real men" but also to *become* "real men." It is argued that performing "masculinity" in an embodied sense over time leads to a habituated heterosexual persona that eventually allows each individual to find attraction to women (or, at least, *one* woman).[18] Such views on queerness, heteronormativity, and the possibility to change underlay Liberty's conversion therapy program—a program that was symptomatic of the heteronormative and homophobic culture of the university as a whole.

To flesh out this study of Liberty, I draw upon oral histories of five queer alumni—Adam A., Ryan D., Sebastian C., Jude H., and John J.—[19]who attended the school between the early 2000s and 2019, the period when Emerick ran his university-sanctioned conversion therapy program. This study centers on these five queer men who attended Liberty and who lived according to the school's dogmatic anti-LGBTQ+ teachings, and who were nonetheless cognizant of how the school's theology, with which they largely aligned, was incompatible with their sexual desires and/or gender identities. Although they came to accept the fundamentalist dogma that attempted to negate their queer subjectivities, they knew that they were indeed attracted to men. For instance, Adam A. (he/him) recounts, "I knew that I fantasized about men, but I didn't know that I was actually gay at the time"; he perceived himself "as somebody who was struggling with lust for men." Similarly, Ryan D. (they/them) did not consider themself gay; rather they saw themself as "same-sex attracted." In other words, these students denied the reality of their sexual desires, regardless of their lived experience of these desires, which led to a profound sense of cognitive dissonance. Their theory of human sexuality and their embodied experience directly contradicted one another, resulting in an ontological split between their queer selves and who they longed to be. White offers insight into these queer students' cognitive dissonance, stating: "We [queer Christians] are trapped between two uncompromising forces: our parents' or our pastor's determination to follow a 'traditional values' standard based on a literal interpretation of select biblical passages and our natural, God-given needs and passions."[20] However, this cognitive dissonance between these "two uncompromising forces" did not deter many queer students from believing anti-LGBTQ+ theologies at Liberty. Rather, their cognitive dissonance, ironically, functioned as an effective—and *affective*—tool that solidified their anti-LGBTQ+ beliefs, binding them all the more strongly to Liberty's heteronormative ideals despite their conflicting sexualities and/or gender identities. By *affective*, I mean to communicate emotions and/or intensities of energy that are registered prelinguistically and are communicated viscerally and corporeally—what many Christian fundamentalists understand as the "conviction" of the Holy Spirit. Because of the culture of "traditional values"—that is, of homophobia—in which they were raised and in which they lived at Liberty, these queer students felt spiritual conviction that acting on their sexual desires was sinful. In large part as a function of the university's affective world-building project, they experienced a heightened sense of so-called conviction because of the school's intensified campus culture of shame, guilt, and anxiety—an affective campus culture that I elucidate throughout this essay. These queer students attempted to suppress their desires in hopes of becoming attracted to women, with the assistance of Emerick (and, it ought to be noted, other conversion therapists on [and off] campus).[21]

I argue that Liberty's subjugation, governance, and dictation of queer students, by way of a series of theological and moralizing discourses and practices, pushed queer students to self-subjugate, self-govern, and self-dictate, which determined and controlled how they conducted themselves while at Liberty—all in order to reorient these students' sexual orientations and/or gender identities. Though I focus on Liberty in this project, the institution is representative of a larger network of Christian fundamentalist colleges and universities in the United States, along with the wider Christian fundamentalist world. Liberty serves as a microcosm for Christian fundamentalism as a system, one of many examples of how fundamentalist institutions have pushed their queer members further into the closet and further from living authentically as queer individuals.

LIBERTY'S HETERONORMATIVE CAMPUS CULTURE

Liberty—cofounded in 1971 by the late Jerry Falwell Sr.—was and is a significant religious, political, and educational institution. A prominent Southern Baptist university, Liberty has maintained a distinctly fundamentalist ethos throughout its history, in order to train up, as the university motto proclaims, "champions for Christ." Over the past several decades, Liberty students have been guided by the student code of conduct handbook, known as *The Liberty Way*. Failure to abide by *The Liberty Way*'s rules and regulations has resulted in financial penalties, mandatory community service, and even expulsion. These rules and regulations have assisted in shaping what has commonly been referred to as the "Liberty bubble." The Liberty bubble can be understood as a sphere of insulated existence apart from the off-campus, secular world, which has allowed for a collective religious identity therein. Of course, many institutions, particularly US colleges, refer to "bubbles" that surround their individual campuses. Differing from many secular campus "bubbles," however, the Liberty bubble is of specific interest because of the affective tools the university employed to further its religious, world-building project. Indeed, the circulation of shame, guilt, and anxiety within the Liberty bubble served as the university's modus operandi, which assisted in sustaining a cohesive atmosphere that is in line with the school's conservative, Southern Baptist brand.

Maintaining the Liberty bubble has been, like all world-building projects, "a collective enterprise."[22] As students have corporately followed *The Liberty Way* and in turn have assisted in maintaining the Liberty bubble, the university has been able to construct a "cultural world [that was] not only collectively produced, but it remain[ed] real by virtue of collective recognition. To be in culture means to share in a particular world of objectivities with others."[23] The collectively constructed "world of objectivities" of Liberty's campus life constitutes the school's *plausibility structure,* that is, the school's particular view of reality that stands in contradistinction to other, opposing views of reality.[24] The Liberty bubble has served to shield students from the perceived sinfulness of the outside world, and thus helped create a sacred order on campus that established strict boundaries for "upright" living. To remain within these boundaries was to remain within the good graces of the Liberty community (and, in the estimation of many at the school, of God), while to transgress these boundaries was to threaten the university's moral order.

To protect against such supposed ungodly living, the university fortified the Liberty bubble by forcing its students to align with their moral code. This created what Jude H. described as an "isolationist environment," engendering what Ryan D. identified as an "insulated way of thinking and way of seeing the world that is specific to that space." Such isolation and insulation from the outside world assisted in fortifying the plausibility structure, which helped protect "against the nightmare threats of chaos [or, otherwise put, of sin]. To fall out of such a 'right' relationship [with God was] to be abandoned on the edge of the abyss of meaninglessness."[25] This sense of "meaninglessness" was what is understood by fundamentalists as life without Christ, a state of being without divine relationship and thus without a clear purpose or teleology. Thus, *The Liberty Way*—which prompted students to police themselves and each other—functioned as the glue that held the school's moral community intact and meaning*ful.*[26] Because the secular world lay immediately beyond the perimeter of campus, the Liberty bubble required constant maintenance and fortification, for the university knew that students were prone to off-campus "temptation." *The Liberty Way* indeed pushed the collective student body to act according to the same moral scripts, thereby reinforcing the campus's sacred order.

Along with this proper, godly conduct came what Sara Ahmed refers to as *the promise of happiness*. Such is the promise that, if one is to orient oneself toward a particular, socially agreed-upon object of happiness (which, in the context of Liberty, was godly living), one will achieve a state of happiness that is perceived to be the "good life" (or at Liberty, following John 10:10, "life to the full"). Ahmed explains that "the public [or the social] investment in happiness is an investment in a very particular and narrow model of the good."[27] At Liberty, happiness was framed as contentment with one's active and ongoing relationship with God. The implicit argument behind *The Liberty Way*, therefore, was that those who followed the code of conduct would find happiness, since they were oriented "rightly."

As Liberty's perception of happiness was indeed narrow, this narrowness gave shape to the rigid, demanding contours of Liberty's moral community. The university's moral order was defined by and organized around a series of binary oppositions: right and wrong, good and bad, of God and of the enemy, and so on. There is little room within the black-and-white fundamentalist cosmology for moral or ethical ambiguity. According to such thinking, moral and ethical boundaries are clear-cut imperatives that require strict obedience. Moreover, to question or doubt Christian teachings was often understood as identical to questioning or doubting *God*. As fundamentalist doctrines at Liberty were inextricably linked to literalist understandings of scripture, and as scripture was understood to be the very words of God,[28] questions and doubts were coded as spiritually dangerous. In such an intellectually restrictive culture, students were discouraged from exploring ideas outside fundamentalism. Instead of pursuing questions and doubts—specifically and especially in regard to sexual orientation—students were trained to submit to dogmatic teachings and religious authority. This was particularly the case because of their unabating anxiety that they could lose their salvation if they were to find answers to their questions or doubts that differed from answers found in their fundamentalist tradition. Despite the common avowal of "once saved, always saved," the ever-present possibility of not actually being saved kept the fires of hell just beneath their feet in their theological imagination. Anxiety about hell thus eclipsed all other competing theological or epistemological concerns, which was integral to maintaining the Liberty bubble.

But for students whose subjectivities or identities differed from other students', the Liberty bubble proved to be a site of struggle and a source of anxiety, especially for queer students. Though referring to the ex-gay movement in particular, Spivey and Robinson's reflections can be aptly applied to Liberty: as being a Christian and being gay are considered mutually exclusive, "anyone who embraces a[n] LGBT identity is considered 'non-Christian,' regardless of that person's own religious identity, and such non-Christians are accused of embracing entirely different values and worldviews."[29] By way of example, Jude H. remembers being taught at Liberty "that queer culture is evil. It is a mockery of *Imago Dei*. It is an affront to the image of the unseen" (a reference to Colossians 1:15), and he was convinced that "to give in to 'the gay lifestyle' would be eternal damnation. It would be soul-sucking torment. It would be hell." Because of such thinking, queer students abided by the narrow sexual ethic that the university required. The university made explicitly clear that any form of nonnormative sexual activity was immoral and therefore not permitted. *The Liberty Way* states: "Sexual relations outside of a biblically-ordained marriage between a natural-born man and a natural-born woman are not permissible at Liberty University . . . Activities inconsistent with these standards and guidelines are violations of the Student Honor Code."[30] As is evidenced by its narrow definition of marriage, the school held heterosexual marriage up as not only the ideal sexual ethic but the *only* possible sexual ethic—precisely the reason why Sebastian C. married a woman while at Liberty (he is now divorced). This narrow definition of marriage was used as "a cover, a way of covering over what resists or is resistant to a view of the world"[31] that would otherwise afford queer individuals the possibility of living authentic, queer lives.

The university's heavy emphasis on heterosexual marriage amplified the circulation of anxiety on campus (for both queer and straight students alike). The school recurrently reminded them about straight marriage, which evoked a moral panic of sorts, where students sought out opportunities to follow this nuptial script. In his undercover investigative study of Liberty, Kevin Roose—an agnostic and a critic of fundamentalism—explains how even he experienced such marriage-related panic when he was at Liberty, which reveals the potency and contagion of such anxiety: "I've never felt particularly rushed about getting married (probably because I've never taken an abstinence pledge), but when you're surrounded by nuptial-crazed Christians, it forces the issue. Every few days, I hear about another Liberty guy who popped the question, and I spend a few minutes feeling panicked. I'm almost twenty! Shouldn't I at least have someone in mind?"[32] By placing this emphasis on marriage, the university created a culture of anxiety on campus, and it was this culture of anxiety that, in the words of Ryan D., was "even more complicated" for queer students.

Surrounded by the school's constant emphasis on heterosexual marriage and heteronormative culture in general, queer students were recurrently reminded of a nuptial script that they did not actually desire. Ryan D. describes the campus: "You look around, and you don't see yourself reflected anywhere as far as the kind of love and the kind of relationship that you would want—that just doesn't exist." The complete dearth of queer representation and expression, *via negativa*, placed an emphasis on straight relationships and underscored how queer relationships were entirely outside the realm of possibility, if one were to remain within the fundamentalist fold.

Yet, despite and because of their lack of attraction to women, queer students felt the need to try to convince both themselves and others of their feigned attraction in order to "pass," which further heightened their on-campus anxiety. First, they had to convince themselves of their heterosexuality by adopting what Jeffrey A. Bennett refers to as an "illusory ontological identification," an erroneous self-estimation that they were attracted to women.[33] Second, these queer students tried to convince others that they were heterosexual, so as to further solidify their self-deceit. As James Baldwin, who draws on Charles Cooley's theory of the looking-glass self, reminds us, "we all exist, after all, and crucially, in the eye of the beholder. We all react to and, to whatever extent, become what that eye sees."[34] At Liberty, inasmuch as students policed the conduct of their fellow students in the name of "Christian accountability,"[35] their perceptions of themselves were constantly filtered through how other students and Liberty as an institution saw them. Indeed, when heterosexuality was "internalized as God's will and natural, individuals police[d] their own and each other's conduct accordingly."[36]

Queer students therefore were pushed to conform their gender and sexual presentations to match the mutually agreed-upon standards of what Lynne Gerber refers to as "godly masculinity." Gerber describes godly masculinity as "an idealized maleness drawn from fundamentalist discourse that appropriates some aspects of hegemonic masculinity while criticizing others."[37] Adam A. details one example of how Liberty communicated its prescribed brand of masculinity: by means of a frequently invited guest speaker/pastor, Clayton King. King often preached at Liberty and commonly spoke during Liberty's twice-annual "Spiritual Emphasis Week," a week devoted to focusing students' attention on God and all things spiritual. Adam A. remembers King saying "that those types of guys who care about their hair and their appearance, etc., are not real men, as if they are worthy of being targeted for one reason or another." The targeting to which Adam A. refers points to an affective push of nonnormative students toward so-called godly masculinity. This can also be seen in Ryan D.'s explanation: "There was pressure for me to date women—that was hinted to me as something I should do by the men I had come out to, these people that I would consider mentors. There was pressure to date women in order to change your sexuality—that narrative was very common." But as they were only open about their sexuality to this small group of "mentors," Ryan D. also had the rest of their social contacts to convince of their "heterosexuality." The pressure to play straight for those not privy to their sexuality, in tandem with the pressure to appease their mentors, pushed Ryan D. to exert a large measure of emotional labor as they repressed their sexual desires for men and feigned attraction to women. In response to the school's ring-by-spring culture, Jude H. remembers "finding [him]self anxious several Aprils in a row that [he] still hadn't found the one that was going to make it all make sense." Here, "the one" to which Jude H. refers was a woman for whom he was searching, a woman to whom he would be attracted and who would become his wife; the expectation was that he would find a wife who would afford him heterosexual attraction and therefore a life of nuclear normalcy. But as his wife-to-be remained a chimerical fantasy, the pressure to find her increased over his time at Liberty, compounding his already-present anxiety that he was not living up to God's will for his life. And in order to both become attracted to women and find a wife, he had to approximate the prescribed brand of heteronormativity. Like the LGBTQ+ students surveyed in Craig and colleagues' study, queer students at Liberty were resigned to perform on a daily basis: "given that school policies and practices punished students for having, displaying, or acting on an LGBTQ identity, hiding their identities was a pervasive concern."[38]

This constant, forced performance resulted in an anxious paranoia of sorts, where these students scrutinized and rescrutinized all their actions to ensure that they were passing as straight. In reference to his apprehension of being identified as gay, John J. (he/him) explains this experience of anxious paranoia: "I walked around constantly as though I was being judged and condemned. No one was ever like, 'You're going to hell.' But at the same time, everyone was saying that, even though no one was saying it. I know that doesn't make sense, but that's how it felt constantly. So, it was like low-level stress all the time for me because I never knew what should I or shouldn't I say, how should I or shouldn't I sit, how do I . . . act? So, it was a lot of trying to conform to absolutely everything that everybody wanted you to be." For John J., like other queer students, the transmission of affect, communicated by way of other students' gazes, created a palpable environment that made clear that he was noticed, exceptional (in the literal sense of the word), and thus unwelcome as he was. John J. remembers thinking: "I'm just under a tremendous amount of pressure to not ruin my own life by everyone finding out I'm gay." Ryan D. echoes this sentiment: "I felt that queerness would be the literal death of me. I felt that if anyone ever knew [that I was gay] that my life would be over." They go on to say, "I had . . . the threat of exposure, the threat of being cast out from that system—that was always hanging over me." The potential consequences of their sexualities and gender identities being revealed by way of their aberrant queer embodiment evoked a constant, lingering anxiety that pushed them to perpetually analyze their self-presentations, so as to conform to institutionally accepted forms of godly masculinity. Thus, in order to resist being a spectacle, queer students had to weigh, measure, and control their bodily comportment, not to mention their diction and way of speaking, so as to pass.

Compounding this catalytic source of anxiety were the mental gymnastics that came part and parcel with attempting to understand their sexualities and gender identities through a restrictive fundamentalist doctrine. Painting an illustrative portrait of the psychological and emotional exertion that queer fundamentalists undergo, White presents what it was like having to strive for heterosexuality without any success: "I thought I was a sinner who just hadn't disciplined my mind or body long or hard enough. I thought if I prayed and fasted, if I witnessed to my faith and 'led enough people to Christ,' . . . maybe then I would please God enough to be sure that my soul wasn't lost in hell for all eternity."[39] White's presentation of his experience points to queer fundamentalists' self-perception that is defined by their supposed lack. As queer students at Liberty perceived themselves as not having enough discipline or not having done enough spiritual work to become opposite-sex attracted, they also understood their desire for men as a function of their dearth of masculinity. Such a perceived lack often resulted in queer male students attempting to compensate largely by way of supposedly "manly" activities, to make up for this supposed masculine insufficiency. The emotional labor involved in such compensation created an affective cycle that perpetuated these queer students' anxieties.

Ahmed offers insight into how shame specifically works "as a deterrent," which is useful when looking at how shame, like anxiety, served as one of the central affective tools that drove queer students to pursue heteronormativity at Liberty. She states that "in order to avoid shame, subjects must enter the 'contract' of the social bond, by seeking to approximate a social ideal. Shame can also be experienced as *the affective cost of not following the scripts of normative existence*."[40] Of course, many students who attended Liberty were straight and, as such, already followed heteronormative scripts willingly. But, for queer students, in order to fit in and operate in a socially and institutionally acceptable way on campus, they were forced to enter into a heteronormative social contract and live in queer subterfuge as they fought against their sexual and gender identities. After explaining that there was a lot of shame surrounding how they understood their queerness, Ryan D. notes how at Liberty, "there is a lot of social reward from looking a certain way and fitting into a very specific path . . . There were a lot of goodies for being 'straight.'" Being recognized as "straight" was one of these "goodies." For queer students (or even for those who were straight but did not align with the prescribed masculinity that Liberty espoused), any deviation from heteronormative scripts further registered as a source of shame, for their identities did not align with the fundamentalist ideal.[41]

The university's stance on sexuality was of death-dealing consequences for queer students because of the ontological split that was brought about by such a contracted perception of godly sexuality. Sebastian C. explains his experience on campus this way: "I had a strong war inside me between what I was taught to believe and what I was starting to believe—a strong war inside me between who I was attracted to and who I was told I had to be attracted to. And every time when I would try to be more honest, I don't know—I couldn't fully breathe—there was no room to be fully honest." This feeling of not being able to breathe, which he also described as "feeling suffocated," points to the affective pressure on queer students explored here. Queer students were divided between who they were and who they believed they "ought" to be; they recognized and were of course cognizant of their queer desires but were precluded from acting on them; and coupled with their forced renunciation of their sexual and gender identities, they were directed to pursue romantic relationships with women to whom they were not attracted (a subject that will not be discussed in detail here).[42] Yet, despite this cognitive, emotional, and spiritual push and pull, many queer male students not only remained at Liberty but intentionally sought out the services of Emerick's conversion therapy program or other conversion therapy services offered on- and off-campus. This affective campus culture that I have detailed thus far was indeed compounded by Emerick and the specious therapy he offered.

LIBERTY'S CONVERSION THERAPY PROGRAM

Though conversion therapy has been repudiated by all reputable professional and scientific associations, and in spite of the known harms of such practices,[43] Liberty housed a conversion therapy program. The program was designed to train queer male students to resist their "sinful" sexual desires and embrace adopted—and *affected*—heteronormative identities. Emerick led these students through weekly one-on-one sessions that involved detailed questions about their family dynamics and sexual histories and activities, in addition to prayer, Bible study, and discussion of assigned readings. Through his conversion therapy program, Emerick conceptually separated students' same-sex attraction (the supposed sin) from the students themselves (the so-called sinners saved by grace), a move that was intended to absolve them of their guilt but which nonetheless created a culture of guilt. Although he offered students space to confess their "sins," he also guilted them into feeling negatively about specific actions and thoughts that did not align with the school's fundamentalist ethic—all in order to deter them from acting on their queer identities. But when queer students inevitably could not change their sexualities or gender identities, the economy of guilt Emerick created became a profound source of shame, insofar as these students came to perceive their inability to change as a reflection of *themselves* as defective, as deficient, and ultimately as failures. Here, I elaborate on Emerick's use of guilt and how it led, albeit indirectly, to shame.

One-on-one meetings with Emerick can be understood as concentrated expressions of cultural and religious homophobia. In addition to highlighting the main scriptures that, according to a fundamentalist hermeneutic, condemn homosexuality,[44] Emerick began his initial sessions with students by taking stock of how they were raised (specifically in regard to their relationship with their parents) and by asking detailed questions about their sexual histories and proclivities. After the first few sessions, Emerick began meetings by taking a weekly inventory of how students had "slipped up," that is, how they had recently acted upon their sexual desires. Some "slip-ups" consisted of looking lustfully at other men, while others involved looking at gay pornography, masturbating, or making intimate contact with other male students—issues that were considered more egregious. Emerick recurrently assessed students' supposed progress in changing their gender identities and sexual orientations, while identifying how they could avoid temptations in the future. To help frame his meetings with students, he drew upon assigned readings of conversion therapy manuals, such as Alan Medinger's *Growth into Manhood: Resuming the Journey*. Such texts promoted the idea that homosexuality is a result of, to borrow Medinger's words, "underdeveloped manhood" that required healing in order to "grow into full, comfortable, complete manhood."[45] This rhetoric of queer men being underdeveloped and lacking in their manhood further pushed queer students to perform according to scripts of godly masculinity.

Since Emerick taught students that their queer desires were not a part of who they were, it cannot be said, in a strict sense, that he directly shamed them for any slip-ups. Shame communicates to individuals that their very person, their selfhood, is faulty, dirty, or tarnished. But based on his separation of queer students' sexual *activities* from their *identities*, Emerick guilted queer students for the discrete "sinful" sexual activities; he taught them that, though their activities were "sinful," such activities did not define them as individuals (whom he considered new creations in Christ),[46] arguing that their sexual activities were separate from their personhood. With such an understanding of "sinful" sexual activity, Emerick differentiated himself from many others within fundamentalist communities who—despite touting the idea that all "sin" is equal—often identify queer individuals as intrinsically perverted or damaged, or at least more so than their straight counterparts. He was able to present himself as seemingly less judgmental, as one who was supposedly "on their side" as he pushed them to feign heteronormativity.

Emerick's self-presentation as a loving guide—a fatherly or grandfatherly[47] figure who accepted queer students "despite" their same-sex attraction—established a power dynamic that affectively bound students to him. Adam A. remembers his time with Emerick as "very buddy-buddy . . . like hand on the shoulder or hand on my knee, or he would call me 'boy,' which is a very 'daddy' thing to do, which I did not realize then—I thought it was just a Southern thing." According to Ryan D., Emerick "presented himself as very grandfatherly, very nurturing"; this is in line with Jude H.'s description of how he saw Emerick as a "genuine, caring individual." Emerick's paternal (and tactile) approach helped establish trust between him and many of the queer students with whom he worked, cultivating a large measure of belonging, ostensible acceptance, and Christian accountability. In addition to establishing himself as a paternal figure, Emerick also served as a mentor—or, to borrow a phrase from Freud, as an "ego-ideal," the embodiment of what queer students sought to emulate. This was in large part because Emerick himself claimed to be an "ex-gay," one who professed to have rejected his queer desires in favor of his new identity in Christ. Adam A. notes how Emerick said "that he used to live a 'homosexual lifestyle,'" a point Jude H. also discusses. Because of Emerick's specious success in becoming an "ex-gay," Jude H. remembers thinking, when meeting with Emerick: "There's hope for me—that's going to be me one day!" With Emerick having carved out this paternal mentor role for himself, many queer students thus did not want to disappoint him.

For the queer students, recounting to Emerick any slip-ups, which can be understood as a form of Christian confession, was framed as an avenue to alleviate the students' guilt, but it actually served to compound their guilt. Foucault explains that Christian confession, which he describes as exhaustive (in light of the amount of detail it requires), produces a truth "that will, in some way, constitute the bond between the shepherd [*berger*] and his flock, and each member of his flock."[48] Queer students' bond of "truth" with Emerick, a man who was known as "Pastor Dane," was perceived, at least in part, as an opportunity to absolve them of their guilt for their "sins." Ryan D. describes their bond this way: "I had access to everything on my phone at that point and was still looking at porn and felt very guilty about that. The cycle was looking at porn and then after cumming feeling very dirty and very much like you needed to confess to someone—that kind of thing. That was the cycle, and I think I would maybe write down or journal how many times and the thoughts I was having—very much like collecting research, like data, and then I would come back to him. He set himself up as like a—in Catholicism—as like the priest, as someone that could release you from your sins, if you would confess—kind of like an in-between-you-and-God." Whereas their confession may have temporarily attenuated their guilt, the fact that Ryan D. continued to look at pornography and masturbate recurrently reanimated that guilt, which in turn led them back again and again to Emerick in order to alleviate their guilt. This dynamic affectively bonded Ryan D. and other queer students all the more to Emerick and created a sense of dependency on him, so that the students believed him to be the one who would lead them to opposite-sex attraction in the long term and the one who would absolve them of their guilt in the short term.

Yet, despite how Emerick seemed to offer a sense of absolution, the homophobic theology he espoused was in actuality the *source* of these queer students' guilt. Although this homophobic theology was (and is) pervasive throughout the Christian fundamentalist world, Emerick's conversion therapy program was the concentrated expression thereof, wherein Emerick emphasized a hamartiology of guilt for any and all queer actions. Thus, it can be said that Emerick was both the salve to alleviate queer students' guilt and a central catalyst for why they felt as guilty as they did. Offering insight into how Emerick guilted queer students into acting contrary to their queer selves, Roose offers a particularly illustrative conversation between him and Emerick. Emerick "says that his first job, first and foremost, is to provide emotional support for gay Liberty students. 'The problem is, the church has been too busy condemning kids for having these feelings, and now they won't come for help. My pastorate is not like that at all. It's an affirmation. There's a difference between saying "it's sin," and saying, "I love you, dude. I want to work through this with you."'"[49] Emerick assumed the all-too-familiar posture of "love the sinner, hate the sin." As Spivey and Robinson explain: "If homosexuality is a condition, 'treating' people with same-sex attractions is reconstructed euphemistically as compassionate and humane [and loving], not dehumanizing."[50] However, Emerick's "love" for his queer students was emphatically misleading. His "love" bifurcated queer students into two compartmentalized parts: the "sinful" part (students' actions that were said to be separate from their personhoods) and the nonsinful part (that is, the supposed latent heterosexual within each of them). The former was condemnable, the latter lovable.

Such "love" did not embrace queer students as such; rather, it embraced them for who they *could be*. Emerick's "love"—his largely hollow sentiment masquerading as care for queer students as queer students—was insidiously lacking.[51] When these students (inevitably) failed to meet the standards of sexual "purity" that he "lovingly" established, they came to experience profound guilt. The guilt they felt was, of course, in part a function of their belief that homosexual activity is immoral, but Emerick's "love" amplified such guilt, compounding their negative response to their sexual activity, especially given his role as mentor and ego-ideal. Contrary to Roose's evaluation that Emerick "shows his students compassion" and that his "love with strings attached seems better than no love at all,"[52] Emerick's conversion therapy program was significantly lacking compassion, and his "love" indeed had *many* strings attached. Instead of directly communicating that queers were unwelcome in the fundamentalist community (a common phenomenon), Emerick covertly communicated—in the false robes of his "love"—that queer students were *very much* unwelcome as they were. Such a qualified acceptance, *which is in truth no acceptance at all*, was deficient of compassion as it disregarded the totality of the individual in the name of promised change. Emerick's "love" affectively promised so much (the possibility of heteronormativity that many queer students, at least initially, desired while on campus), but delivered so little.

Emerick's meetings with students rejected the possibility of queer subjectivity, thereby gaslighting the students into believing that their lived realities as queer men were false consciousnesses. Emerick touted the belief that heterosexuality is an ontological part of every individual's subjectivity. Roose quotes Emerick's thoughts on homosexual desire: "I don't use the word *homosexuality*. I say *same-sex attraction*. If I say I'm homosexual, I'm something that I can't help. Now, I may fall into the sin of homosexuality, but same-sex attraction just means I'm attracted to another man."[53] Emerick refused to acknowledge homosexuality as an authentic category of human sexuality because such an acknowledgment would have served to confirm that queer subjectivity was, after all, possible—that homosexuality exists and is indeed a constitutive part of many individuals' identities. In refusing to use the word "homosexuality," Emerick effectively rejected the reality of queer students' queer identities, "thus denying the personhood, indeed the existence,"[54] of each of these students. This ontological denial further communicated to them that their attractions were not a function of their identities. As a result, Emerick's words (along with his omission of certain other words) led queer students not to interrogate the reality or the authenticity of their feelings and attractions, but to believe that they could change their orientations, particularly by what they *did.*

Building on the code of conduct specified in *The Liberty Way,* Emerick taught queer students how to structure their conduct around what Foucault describes as *disciplinary methods,* which assisted in governing how these students conducted themselves on campus. Such disciplinary methods—techniques that assure "the ordering of human multiplicities"[55] (in this case, the number of queer students on campus)—require "meticulous control of the operations of the body."[56] Indeed, queer male students were subjected to a strict regimen, as set forth by Emerick. From how to sit "like a man" to how to play sports "like men," the bodily disciplines Emerick encouraged queer students to adopt were legion.

Internalizing these disciplinary methods, these students came to control their conduct and thought-life by way of what Foucault further describes as *techniques of the self.* Such techniques of the self "permit individuals to effect, by their own means, a certain number of operations on their own bodies, on their own souls, on their own thoughts, on their own conduct, and this in a manner so as to transform themselves, modify themselves, and to attain a certain type of perfection, of happiness, of purity, of supernatural power, and so on."[57] The point of contact between the abovementioned disciplinary methods and techniques of the self constitutes Foucault's notion of *government.* Foucault is wont to make clear that government, broadly defined, is not always purely violent or coercive;[58] however, the techniques of the self that queer students employed to transform, modify, and sanctify themselves in order to align with the university's conceptions of happiness and sexual purity were largely a function of what they learned about homosexuality throughout their lives, at Liberty, and in a concentrated form through Emerick's conversion therapy program. In regard to Emerick specifically, it can be said that the disciplinary methods he coerced students into adopting pushed them to act according to the norms established by the university and, over time, to view these excessive requirements as normal, if in fact they did not already perceive them as such.[59]

When these rules became normalized as unexceptional, students came to police themselves. Each queer student, as Sandra L. Bartky explains in a different context, "[became] to himself his own jailer [or monitor]. This 'state of conscious and permanent visibility' [was] a sign that the . . . disciplinary control of the body has gotten a hold of the mind as well."[60] As queer students had to align themselves with the particular standard of decorum that Emerick and Liberty demanded, they began to internalize the scripts of "proper Christian conduct."[61] In doing so, they internalized the panoptic gaze of the school and became implicated in their own self-governance. The university's disciplinary methods, articulated in *The Liberty Way*, which Emerick further discussed and concretized in his meetings with students, over time and with a large measure of habituation, produced self-policing part-subjects who employed techniques of the self in order to hold themselves to a strict standard of what they believed to be "morality."

Emerick's hollow promise for change mirrored what Lauren Berlant refers to as *cruel optimism*. Berlant suggests that cruel optimism "names a relation of attachment to compromised conditions of possibility whose realization is discovered either to be *im*possible, sheer fantasy, or *too* possible, and toxic. What's cruel about these attachments, and not merely inconvenient or tragic, is that the subjects who have *x* in their lives might not well endure the loss of their object or scene of desire, even though its presence threatens their well-being."[62] For queer students, their object of desire that evoked a sense of cruel optimism was heterosexuality itself. Emerick told these students that by performing scripts of godly masculinity they could not only live like straight men, but also become attracted to a woman or women. It can thus be said that this cruel optimism maintained an attachment to queer students' problematic object they so desired—heterosexual attraction—"*in advance* of its loss."[63] In other words, as they were promised heterosexual attraction, something that was impossible to attain for these students from the onset, they continued to believe in its potentiality despite any change in their sexual orientation. The cruelty of this optimism was compounded by the fact that the so-called "conversion process" had (and continues to have) "no endpoint,"[64] leaving these students with a goal that had (and has) no possibility of being actualized. As a result, Emerick's promise of heterosexual attraction and all that came along with it (supposed godliness, a nuclear family, and so on) led to the death-dealing cycle of frustration that was perpetuated by such cruel optimism.

Although Emerick claimed that he attempted to make queer students feel loved and supported, his efforts returned to him void, so to speak. That queer students never saw change in terms of their orientation evoked a heightened sense of anxiety and, eventually, after no change occurred, shame—a point that Craig and her colleagues also discuss in the context of their study.[65] Jude H. offers insight into Emerick's approach to queer students: "To this day, I can honestly say that I never really felt shamed by him—directly"; the use of the qualifier "directly" is significant when considering the affective economy of Emerick's conversion therapy program. Although Emerick was a catalyst for anxiety (and guilt), as explored above, he did not *directly* shame queer students (in light of his separation of their actions from their personhoods). However, the anxiety of not seeing any orientational change eventually led these students to be ashamed of themselves, and such shame intensified their anxiety—a phenomenon that pushed them to submit to the campus culture of heteronormativity all the more in order to fit in. It thus makes sense why Sebastian C. describes how he felt during and after conversion therapy: "In the moment, I felt like I was feeling better. In the aftermath, that's when I started to experience increased symptoms of depression, hopelessness, [and] powerlessness." As queer students mistakenly believed that their performance of masculinity would lead to heterosexuality, their inevitable failure to cultivate and achieve heterosexual desire resulted in recurrent frustration that eventually led to self-abnegation and self-hatred. These students' shame that issued forth from their lack of change was indeed a function of Emerick's cruel promise of heterosexual attraction.

Emerick's gay conversion therapy program intensified the affective environment of Liberty for queer students. As queer students attempted to live "the (straight) 'godly' life," they predicated their attempts on both a false consciousness and a false ideal. This desired straight, godly life turned out to be "a bad life that wears out the subjects who nonetheless, and at the same time, find their conditions of possibility within it."[66] Queer students chased after heteronormativity, which precluded authentic subjectivity, but they did so because they understood heteronormativity as the only possible way of living and being if they were to follow the teachings of Christian fundamentalism. The cruelty of their affective attachment to heteronormativity lay in part in the accompanying anxiety that if they did not live according to so-called "biblical teachings," then they would forfeit their ability to have any relationship with God at all. Rejecting one's commitment to God becomes, according to the fundamentalist imagination, a one-way ticket to hell. Belief in such an anxiety-inducing theology for these queer students could be understood as punishment in and of itself. Of course, students were not and would not be institutionally punished for renouncing their faith, but it was the *possibility* of eternal punishment, in concert with the *possibility* of losing their fundamentalist community, that punished them while affectively binding them to such a restrictive theology. Indeed, to live and to identify as queer, in their estimation, was to reject their faith wholesale, as explored above. As a result, they persisted in their affective attachment to and pursuit of heteronormativity, despite never experiencing change in terms of their sexual or gender identities.

CONCLUSION

Exploring Liberty's culture of heteronormativity and its gay conversion therapy program through the lens of affect theory offers scholars a way to analyze how Christian fundamentalism—along with religious communities more broadly—deploys emotion to cause its moral communities to cohere. Indeed, serving as a generative case study, Liberty is one of many examples of Christian fundamentalist institutions across the globe that govern queer (not to mention straight) believers by way of manipulating affect. Of course, much of what convinces queer believers in these spaces to pursue heteronormativity and to reject their queer desires is communicated through antiqueer sermons, doctrinal teachings, and modern translations of scripture. However, not only do these linguistic modes of communication carry affective stock, but much of what is said is also affectively compounded by what is *not* said, that is, by the affects these institutions create and circulate, as explored throughout this essay. This affective communication is one of the many mechanisms of governance and subjugation that Liberty and institutions like it continue to employ in order to regulate and control queer believers' sexual orientations and gender expressions today.

NOTES

1. Shelley L. Craig et al., "Fighting for Survival: The Experiences of Lesbian, Gay, Bisexual, Transgender, and Questioning Students in Religious Colleges and Universities," *Journal of Gay and Lesbian Social Services* 29, no. 1 (2017): 10.

2. George M. Marsden defines "fundamentalists" as "a subtype of evangelicals," and a group for whom "militancy is crucial to their outlook. Fundamentalists are not just religious conservatives, they are conservatives who are willing to take a stand and to fight." See George M. Marsden, *Understanding Fundamentalism and Evangelicalism* (Grand Rapids, MI: William B. Eerdmans Publishing Co., 1991), 1. Though Marsden explains that evangelicalism is difficult to define, he posits that "essential evangelical beliefs include (1) the Reformation doctrine of the final authority of the Bible, (2) the real historical character of God's saving work recorded in Scripture, (3) salvation to eternal life based on the redemptive work of Christ, (4) the importance of a spiritually transformed life. By this account evangelicalism includes striking diversities: holiness churches, pentecostals, traditional Methodists, all sorts of Baptists, Presbyterians, black churches in all these traditions, fundamentalists, Anabaptists such as Mennonites, Churches of Christ, Christians, and some Episcopalians, to name only some of the most prominent types" (4–5). For the purposes of this essay, I employ the

term "fundamentalism" to name the brand of Christianity at Liberty University.

3. A recent study by the Religious Exemption Accountability Project and College Pulse found that "12% of students identify as LGBTQ+, and nearly one-third (30%) of students at these Christian colleges and universities describe experiencing some amount of non-heterosexual attraction or experience." See "The LGBTQ+ Student Divide: The State of Sexual and Gender Minority Students at Taxpayer-Funded Christian Colleges," report, Religious Exemption Accountability Project (REAP), 2021.

4. Craig et al., "Fighting for Survival," 2.

5. Jonathan S. Coley, *Gay on God's Campus: Mobilizing for LGBT Equality at Christian Colleges and Universities* (Chapel Hill, NC: University of North Carolina Press, 2018), 11, 12.

6. In this study, I am exploring the experiences of biological males who are queer, and not biological females, because the university's gay conversion therapy program, led by Pastor Dane Emerick, is only for male students. Moreover, as Christine M. Robinson and Sue E. Spivey explain, not only does conversion therapy "focus primarily on male homosexuality," but also the ways in which conversion therapy attempts to "repair" lesbians "is qualitatively different." See Christine M. Robinson and Sue E. Spivey, "The Politics of Masculinity and the Ex-Gay Movement," *Gender and Society* 21, no. 5 (2007): 655. I therefore seek not to overextend my argument by homogenizing queer female students and queer male students.

7. Michel Foucault, *Power/Knowledge: Selected Interviews and Other Writings 1972–1977*, ed. Colin Gordon (New York: Pantheon, 1980), 72–73.

8. As Sue E. Spivey and Christine M. Robinson explain, "the ex-gay movement is predominantly an evangelical Christian Right social movement which aims to purge society of homosexuality." See Sue E. Spivey and Christine M. Robinson, "Genocidal Intentions: Social Death and the Ex-Gay Movement," *Genocide Studies and Prevention* 5, no. 1 (2010): 70.

9. Ted Allen, "Longtime Campus Counselor and Mentor Leaves Legacy of Love at Liberty," January 13, 2021.

10. Talal Asad, *Formations of the Secular: Christianity, Islam, Modernity* (Stanford: Stanford University Press, 2003), 75–76.

11. Mel White, *Stranger at the Gate: To Be Gay and Christian in America* (New York: Plume, 1995), 67.

12. Robinson and Spivey, "The Politics of Masculinity and the Ex-Gay Movement," 656–57.

13. Robinson and Spivey, "The Politics of Masculinity and the Ex-Gay Movement," 657.

14. Spivey and Robinson, "Genocidal Intentions," 70.

15. Robinson, and Spivey, "The Politics of Masculinity and the Ex-Gay Movement," 658.

16. For instance, in *Growth into Manhood*, Alan Medinger states that "*we grow into the fullness of our manhood by doing the things that men do*," and that "we are changed by what we do! Our actions change our thinking and our perspectives. Act as though a woman is something special, and she will become that to you." See Alan Medinger, *Growth into Manhood: Resuming the Journey* (Colorado Springs, CO: WaterBrook Press, 2000), 8 (original emphasis) and 202; also 34.

17. See Medinger, *Growth into Manhood*, 161.

18. According to gay conversion therapy teachings, a man struggling with "same-sex attraction" has the potential to become sexually attracted to women. However, it is also argued

that after "therapy" sometimes men will not be attracted to women in the traditional sense, but will only become attracted to *one* woman or *particular* women.

19. The names of the five oral history narrators have been pseudonymized for this study.

20. White, *Stranger at the Gate*, 52.

21. Sebastian C., Ryan D., Jude H., and John J. all explained how they met with other on- and/or off-campus counselors, therapists, or pastors in order to become straight. However, for the purposes of this study, I focus specifically on Emerick's conversion therapy program.

22. Peter L. Berger, *The Sacred Canopy: Elements of Sociological Theory of Religion* (New York: Anchor Books, 1990), 7.

23. Berger, *The Sacred Canopy*, 10.

24. Peter L. Berger and Thomas Luckmann, *The Social Construction of Reality* (New York: Doubleday, 1967), 154–55.

25. Berger, *The Sacred Canopy*, 26–27.

26. This is the same kind of governance one finds in, say, Puritan faith-testing.

27. Sara Ahmed, *The Promise of Happiness* (Durham, NC: Duke University Press, 2010), 70.

28. Spivey and Robinson, "Genocidal Intentions," 73.

29. Spivey and Robinson, "Genocidal Intentions," 72.

30. "The Liberty Way: Student Honor Code," Liberty University, August 8, 2019.

31. Ahmed, *The Promise of Happiness*, 83–84.

32. Kevin Roose, *The Unlikely Disciple: A Sinner's Semester at America's Holiest University* (New York: Grand Central Publishing, 2009), 74.

33. Jeffrey A. Bennett, "Love Me Gender: Normative Homosexuality and 'Ex-gay' Performativity in Reparative Therapy Narratives," *Text and Performance Quarterly* 23, no. 4 (2003): 332.

34. James Baldwin, "Here Be Dragons," in *The Price of the Ticket: Collected Nonfiction, 1948–1985* (New York: St. Martin's Press, 1985), 670.

35. See Prov. 27:17.

36. Robinson and Spivey, "The Politics of Masculinity and the Ex-Gay Movement," 669.

37. Lynne Gerber, "Grit, Guts, and Vanilla Beans: Godly Masculinity in the Ex-Gay Movement," *Gender and Society* 29, no. 1 (2015): 27.

38. Craig et al., "Fighting for Survival," 9.

39. White, *Stranger at the Gate*, 40.

40. Sara Ahmed, *The Cultural Politics of Emotion* (London: Routledge, 2004), 106–7 (original emphasis).

41. Ahmed, *The Cultural Politics of Emotion*, 107.

42. Craig and colleagues ("Fighting for Survival," 11–12) discuss this phenomenon of queer students pursuing relationships with the opposite sex.

43. See Djordje Alempijevic et al., "Statement on Conversion Therapy," *Journal of Forensic and Legal Medicine* 72 (2020): 1–6, at 3.

44. See Gen. 9:20–27; Gen. 19:1–11; Lev. 18:22, 20:13; 1 Cor. 6:9–10; 1 Tim. 1:10; Rom. 1:26–27.

45. Medinger, *Growth into Manhood*, 2, xii.

46. See 2 Cor. 5:17.

47. This self-presentation is in line with Joseph Nicolosi's influential pseudoscientific work. Nicolosi argues: "The therapist takes on a mentor role, while providing the masculine perspective. *The therapist is the 'father,' the masculine frame of reference from which the client learns how to be a man.*" Joseph Nicolosi, "A Developmental Model for Effective Treatment of Male Homosexuality," *American Journal of Pastoral Counseling* 3, nos. 3–4 (2001): 96 (emphasis added).

48. Michel Foucault, "Sexuality and Power (1978)," in *Religion and Culture*, ed. Jeremy R. Carrette (New York: Routledge, 1999), 125.

49. Roose, *The Unlikely Disciple*, 185.

50. Spivey and Robinson, "Genocidal Intentions," 74.

51. There is perhaps a parallel to be drawn here between this sort of "love" and the "love" that is expressed in evangelical prison ministries. In such prison ministries, although they do not try to convince people to feign another identity, the counselors do fail to account for the structural racism in the criminal justice system (in which they are complicit) that puts people in prison in the first place.

52. Roose, *The Unlikely Disciple*, 189.

53. Roose, *The Unlikely Disciple*, 184 (original emphasis).

54. Spivey and Robinson, "Genocidal Intentions," 74.

55. Michel Foucault, "Panopticism," in *The Foucault Reader*, ed. Paul Rabinow (New York: Pantheon, 1984), 207.

56. Michel Foucault, "Docile Bodies," in *The Foucault Reader*, ed. Rabinow, 181.

57. Michel Foucault, "About the Beginning of the Hermeneutics of the Self (1980)," in *Religion and Culture*, ed. Jeremy R. Carrette (New York: Routledge, 1999), 162.

58. Foucault, "About the Beginning of the Hermeneutics of the Self (1980)," 162–63.

59. Indeed, many incoming students take little issue with these requirements, as they are similar to those with which the students grew up.

60. Sandra L. Bartky, "Foucault, Femininity, and the Modernization of Patriarchal Power," in *Feminist Social Thought: A Reader*, ed. Diana Tietjens Meyers (New York: Routledge, 1990), 95.

61. Craig and colleagues explain that "consistent internal monitoring" is common on religious campuses across the United States ("Fighting for Survival," 10).

62. Lauren Berlant, "Cruel Optimism," in *The Affect Theory Reader*, ed. Melissa Gregg and Gregory J. Seigworth (Durham, NC: Duke University Press, 2010), 94 (original emphasis).

63. Berlant, "Cruel Optimism," 94 (original emphasis).

64. Tanya Erzen, *Straight to Jesus: Sexual and Christian Conversions in the Ex-Gay Movement* (Berkeley: University of California Press, 2006), 3.

65. Craig et al., "Fighting for Survival," 17.

66. Berlant, "Cruel Optimism," 97.

"Truth is Never Ridiculous"

Social Territory and the Cartography of Ridicule

Joshua Urich

In late February 1843, someone adopting the name "Irenaeus" sent a long, satirical letter to the Charleston, South Carolina, *Mercury* in response to the city's recent interest in mesmerism. Mesmerist practitioners were "apostles of quackery," he warned, so "let the jackasses look out." The author's *nom de plume* was apt: the second-century writer Irenaeus is best remembered for his anti-Gnostic polemic, *Against Heresies.* Our southern "Irenaeus" obviously considered himself something of a heresiologist, but, unlike his namesake, "Irenaeus" was uninterested in philosophical arguments. For this author, proofs of mesmerism's foolishness were unnecessary because "there *is* a feeling or a principle, that growth of all our past experience, which enables us sometimes to say . . . that the thing cannot be, and without examining evidence or discussing proofs, that the thing is on its face impossible."[1] "Irenaeus" gave that feeling a name—he knew mesmerism was illegitimate because it felt "ridiculous," and "truth is never ridiculous."

Mesmerism was but one of the three "M's and the Isms" drawing the ire of "Irenaeus." He also had unkind words for the apocalyptic prophet William Miller and a curio marketed as a veritable mermaid corpse. I find "Irenaeus's" choice of penname curious because, aside from Millerism, neither mesmerism nor "mermaidism" is heretical in the usual sense of the word. They irked "Irenaeus" because they "bid Common Sense defiance," made a mockery of *real* scientists with "a mission and a destiny," and gave the lazy a tool to exploit the foolish. While the connection between common-sense realism and evangelicalism,[2] and the Protestant impulses behind vocational callings[3] clearly influenced "Irenaeus's" opinions," his complaints against mesmerism or the mermaid had no explicit connection to Christian theology. Nevertheless, for this southerner, to expose—and more important, to ridicule—the "M's" felt like the second-century Irenaeus's defense of Christian orthodoxy. For this author, ridiculing the "Three M's" felt religious.

Rather than arguing for or against the authentic religiosity of a taxidermic mermaid or a mesmerist mountebank—or, for that matter, the authentic religiosity of their denunciation—this essay instead uses religious studies theories and methodologies to better understand "Irenaeus's" impulse to ridicule, what social work that ridicule did, and why that work felt religious enough to warrant adopting the name of a famous heresiologist. "Irenaeus's" chosen genre, heresiology, offers a helpful entry point for these questions. According to Todd Berzon, early Christian "heresiologies identified the similarities and differences among Christians by creating a categorical framework, even if just discursive, within which to house them," and in so doing they "produced a textual world and worldview driven by the comparison of theologies and dispositions."[4] Berzon's interpretation of heresy aligns with J. Z. Smith's view of religion as a fundamentally cartographic enterprise in which chaotic or dynamic social "territory" is translated into a comprehensible and navigable "map." For Smith, religion is "among other things, an intellectual" process of mapmaking, but he only vaguely signals what those "other things" might be—an omission encouraging almost exclusively intellectualist, discursive analyses of religion.[5] For the second-century Irenaeus, who was primarily engaged in the logical refutation of heretical *belief*, an intellectualist, discursive approach makes sense. Such an approach is less appropriate for the latter-day "Irenaeus," for whom the categorization of social differences happened on a physical and emotional level more than on an intellectual one. I therefore suggest a slight modification to Berzon's understanding of heresiological activity: the categories heresiologists create may be carnal, not discursive.

Like many of his contemporaries, "Irenaeus" used ridicule to try to naturalize social boundaries that felt jeopardized during the "market revolution," a time of intense and rapid social change in the United States. The completion of the Erie Canal in 1825 opened vast markets for an increasingly consumer-capitalist system, far larger and more anonymous than anything Americans had experienced before. The local, agricultural market system was being replaced by an anonymous, nationwide marketplace, and the relationship between worker, work, and product was becoming increasingly alienated and anonymized. Through newspaper advertisements and traveling salesmen, someone could hawk a never-before-seen product in a place where no one knew them, effectively insulating them from any repercussions if the product was shoddy or even a scam. The older system of intracommunity commerce and reputation-based credit was being replaced with banks and a "buyer beware" mentality, forcing Americans to be on the lookout for con artists and impostors.[6]

In small prayer groups and large associations, evangelicals advocated for radical social changes, such as temperance and abolition, drawing new lines between sinners and saints. Jacksonian democracy convinced white men of middling and lower classes that their opinions were every bit as valuable as those of the white elite, erasing traditional class divisions. Finally, in the late 1830s, the United States Exploring Expedition began surveying the islands of the Pacific Ocean and cataloguing their peoples, flora, and fauna. In the 1830s and 1840s, in short, Americans were literally and figuratively mapping out their place in the world.

To make these new maps, antebellum Americans relied on gut feeling as much as intellect—to paraphrase "Irenaeus," if something *felt* "ridiculous," then it could not be "true." But nothing is inherently ridiculous, so how did one know that something felt ridiculous? This essay aims to answer that question by excavating the socially constructed feelings associated with ridicule.[7] To do so, I pay special attention to the affects attached to antebellum instances of ridicule. Affects, as defined by psychologist Silvan Tomkins, are precognitive bodily experiences that motivate action.[8] While affects are experienced in an individual body, they are nevertheless deeply social: they transfer easily from person to person, and they can also intentionally be invoked to effect social change.[9] Identifying affects as the basic components of the experience of ridicule makes it possible to trace how things were *made* to feel ridiculous through their manipulation.

This essay comprises two case studies in which ridicule mobilized affects to draw or redraw social boundaries. The first examines David Meredith Reese's 1838 *Humbugs of New-York*, a kind of capitalist heresiology in which Reese catalogued the various frauds, or "humbugs," he thought plagued New York City.[10] Through this analysis, I demonstrate how affective undercurrents give ridicule power to effect social change at the level of the individual physical body. The second case study centers on the "three M's" that so irritated "Irenaeus," with special attention paid to the mermaid. Arguments over the mermaid's veracity grew so tenacious, and the ridicule was heaped so high by skeptic and supporter alike, that two gentlemen nearly dueled over the issue. Analysis of the mermaid conflict reveals that social maps are palimpsests. For skeptics, the mermaid *felt* like a violation of racial boundaries in the South. To restore those boundaries, she needed to become ridiculous.

FIT SUBJECTS FOR RIDICULE

In 1838, just as the United States Exploring Expedition was setting sail, David Meredith Reese (1800–1861) published *Humbugs of New-York*, a taxonomy of the "most successful, and the most mischievous among the reigning" humbugs in the center of American commerce, New York City.[11] Reese felt compelled to compile this list because, in his words, "there is high *and even sacred* authority for the employment of ridicule against acknowledged *evils*, and popular infatuation."[12] Like "Irenaeus," then, Reese considered his heresiological enterprise religious. That is because Reese understood a "humbug" to be, fundamentally, "*an imposture*," or "any system of science, philosophy, or religion, which 'seems to be what it is not.'"[13] For Reese, dissimulation is the humbug's defining feature: it is "evil" because it intentionally masquerades as something else. "Humbuggery on a large scale" had left America in a state of "commercial distress," and these impostures needed to be exposed if the country were to thrive once again.[14]

Each chapter of Reese's book tackled a different humbug, ranging from animal magnetism to homeopathy, from "Ultra-Temperance" to "Ultra-Protestantism." Here, I explore how Reese used ridicule to expose what he considered "the present reigning humbug in the United States": mesmerism.[15] I argue that, for Reese, exposure through ridicule generated what Eve Sedgwick called "paranoid knowledge," knowledge that came not from the discovery of something new, but instead through the confirmation of what one suspected all along.[16] I suggest that Reese generated paranoid knowledge by successfully mobilizing affects, leading to a kind of paranoid *carnal* knowledge—the *feeling*, more than the logically demonstrable proof, that mesmerism and its adherents were ridiculous.

Reese made clear at the beginning of his text the result of the paranoid carnal knowledge he hoped to generate: laughter. It is too common for Americans to laugh at the victims of "popular delusions," Reese wrote, but it was the perpetrators who most deserved Americans' "risible faculties."[17] Laughter, according to Silvan Tomkins, is a byproduct of the joy affect. While we tend to equate joy with happiness, Tomkins suggests that the two are not necessarily related. Rather, Tomkins paired joy with relief because joy is the result of a reduction of affective overstimulation. Scary movie jump scares are pleasurable because they lead to a brief spike in affective input, which subsides into joy-relief, which may result in a smile or laughter. For something to be ridiculous—for it to elicit laughter, however derisive or mocking that laughter may be—it first needs to generate a glut of affective stimulation.

In his study of mesmerism, Reese built to laughter by cultivating the affect of disgust. Disgust, according to Tomkins, is tied to consumption and digestion. The taste of sour milk on one's tongue triggers disgust: one coughs, sputters, even retches in order to get the offending substance out of the body before it can cause harm.[18] And, what is more, disgust is easily provoked. One need not drink lumpy, rotten milk to feel ill enough to vomit. Remembering a similar experience—or even visualizing the vomit mentioned here—may inspire a disgust reaction. Disgust is also easily transferable. A single hair discovered on a dinner plate might ruin a whole meal for a person, even if the hair only touched a small portion of the food on the plate.

The relative ease with which disgust can be triggered and transferred makes it a powerful political affect. According to affect theorist Sara Ahmed, shared disgust provokes a collective disgust response: the community expels, often violently, the disgust object. Disgust's political impact is even greater because it transfers so easily among objects. For example, India's Dalits are considered "untouchable" because they themselves have been rendered disgusting through close contact with substances considered disgusting.[19] Through the shared experience of disgust, in other words, groups come to define themselves as a pure community in opposition to a polluted other.[20] For Reese, therefore, disgust was an important component in crafting a social map with clear boundaries.

Reese made mesmerism disgusting by connecting it to disease. In the late eighteenth century, he wrote, mesmerism "spread rapidly over France, Germany, Switzerland, Russia, and Sweden . . . with the rage of an epidemic."[21] An American named Elisha Perkins began practicing mesmerism, even adding the use of special metal wands called "tractors." Like a poisonous miasma, "Perkinsism found its way into some of the most important of our public charities," including the New York Hospital, through Perkins's claim that his wands could cure all manner of diseases.[22] Reese took care to point out that Perkins "seems ultimately to have *swallowed* his own humbug" when he used his wand to treat victims of New York's yellow fever epidemic of 1799. Perkins himself caught the illness and died.[23] For his contemporary readers, combining the "swallowed" metaphor with Perkins's own death from yellow fever would have been profoundly disgusting: the stricken turn yellow; bleed from their nose, mouth, and eyes; and finally vomit black blood—the symptom that gave the disease its other name, "the Black Vomit."[24]

By associating mesmerism with a disgusting disease, Reese rendered mesmerism itself "a contagious fever" threatening the health of the nation.[25] Both by metaphor ("the rage of an epidemic," "swallowed") and by proxy (a mesmerist himself dying of the Black Vomit), mesmerism—and mesmerists—became an object of disgust. Establishing mesmerism as a disgust object made it feel more like something that had violated an established border. That border, perceived in the body more than apprehended in the mind, meant that the "third rate doctors, merchants and mechanics [who], having failed in their *appropriate* employments" and turned to fraud were *felt* to be impostors.[26] Like the "pestilential fever[s]" they claimed to cure, these con men infected "the most important of our public charities; and the New-York Hospital."[27] Reese's prolonged disease analogy made mesmerism *feel* like something that needed to be purged from the social body.

Ostensibly, Reese's remedy for the mesmerism imposture was pointing out logical fallacies in mesmerists' claims. His arguments, however, often centered on minute points open to interpretation. For example, a blind woman claimed that, in a mesmeric trance, she could only hear someone if he spoke to her directly. If he failed to address her by name, the woman would only see his lips move. Reese pounced on an apparent discrepancy in the story. How could a blind woman—whose eyes were nevertheless blindfolded—see lips move?[28] For him, it was nonsense. For a mesmerism supporter, however, the answer would be obvious: the woman was clairvoyant. Reese's litany of examples and refutations may have had the veneer of logical analysis, but it is unlikely that his book would have changed a mesmerist supporter's mind, just as it is unlikely that any other heresiology would change their target "heretic's" mind. But again, heresiologies are not meant to change minds, they are meant to make maps.

It is not the content of Reese's arguments that renders mesmerism ridiculous, therefore, but the mode of their delivery. Structurally, Reese's examples take the shape of a joke, in which small details build to a grand reveal. Reese's punchline in the case of the blind clairvoyant, for example, was that the woman was never blind.[29] Each example drips with sarcasm, and Reese liberally employed rhetorical questions, italics, and exclamation points to convey his tone: "How strange, that this *blind* lady, *asleep*, and with her eyelids closely shut, and bandaged with cotton waddings, can, nevertheless, *see* through her green spectacles, whether the *lips move*!" In some cases, Reese explicitly described laughter at the mesmerist impostors' expense. In one story, for example, Reese relayed witnesses' laughter at a spectacularly failed attempt at clairvoyance.[30] Like cued audience laughter in a televised sitcom, Reese's inclusion of this detail invited his audience to share in the laugh at the mesmerists' expense. In Reese's heresiology, therefore, laughter was not the result of relief-joy, but its cause. Reese's descriptions of laughter were akin to speech acts, whose illocutionary force served to manifest the very thing they described.

Another instance underscores Reese's aim in stoking laughter. Reese described a mesmerism demonstration he attended and, anticipating his audience's disdain, begged that, "if the reader is disposed to laugh at those of us who witnessed this scene, and marvel that men should waste time in being so outrageously humbugged," then the reader should "suspend his ridicule" because Reese was only there to "open the eyes of a worthy friend." The reader, Reese concluded, "will find a new reason for his risibility when he is informed" that the friend failed to see the light.[31] Reese's mock concern that his audience might misclassify him and his redirection of their mirth draw our attention to ridicule's efficacy: laughing at someone—being "in on the joke"—makes one feel like part of a community by drawing categorical boundaries between "us" and "them."

In affective terms, Reese's aim was to shame the victims of his ridicule. Silvan Tomkins wrote that, of all the negative affects, "shame strikes deepest into the heart of man" because it is inherently isolating.[32] The ashamed person feels that all eyes, even those of friends and family, *see* them without *recognizing* them. They have become a stranger, exposed and vulnerable with no one to comfort them, and so they retreat into themself, lowering their gaze and hiding their face so that those unfamiliar eyes no longer burn on their skin.[33] Sara Ahmed noted that the experience of collective shame unites people into communities.[34] I suggest that *shaming* does the same thing by rendering the shamed object contemptible. Tomkins, in fact, suggests that shame and contempt are inextricably linked: if one is treated with contempt, one feels shame; if one feels shame, one sees oneself as contemptible.[35] And, more significantly, Tomkins also argues that contempt—a close relative of disgust—is a necessary component of any hierarchical relationship. Contempt makes one feel oneself *above* the object of disdain.[36]

Ridicule, in Reese's words, acted as an "antidote against public credulity and popular delusion." It was effective because it united people *in opposition to* mesmerism, alchemizing the disgusting disease that must be expelled into an object of contempt, barely worth one's notice.[37] "Henceforth," Reese decreed at the end of his exposé, anyone who perpetuates or is taken in by this "contemptible humbug" should be considered "uniformly and infallibly either a *knave* or a *fool*."[38] Mocking mesmerism and shaming its advocates created a new social map, with new lines separating social territory. The world made sense once more.

In the other chapters in *Humbugs of New-York*, Reese used ridicule to restore what the world should feel like by carving lines into New York's shifting territory. Those who were too Protestant, too teetotaling, or too abolitionist shifted the boundaries of the Protestant, temperance, and abolition movements he knew and felt comfortable with. Fake doctors, snake oil salesmen, and outrageous advertisements crossed the line between real and fake, legitimate medicine and quackery, erasing important lines on Reese's social map as they did so. As Reese ridiculed his way back to normalcy, he was feeling a new map into existence.

THAT MERMAID

Four years after David Meredith Reese published *Humbugs*—and just as the United States Exploring Expedition ships were sailing into New York harbor after four years at sea—a mermaid was visiting New York City.[39] It belonged to Boston museum owner Moses Kimball, who claimed to have acquired it from a sailor who had purchased it in Calcutta in 1817. While it may have been true that someone bought the mermaid in India, it most likely originated from Japan, where merchants sold desiccated fish tails sewn to mummified monkey torsos as tchotchkes. Kimball knew this ugly creature could be valuable, but it also seems he knew his own limitations, because instead of trying to make use of it himself, he traveled to New York City to meet with a rising star in the world of showmanship: P. T. Barnum.

Barnum had made a name for himself with his first foray into show business in 1835, when he purchased an enslaved elderly woman named Joice Heth and exhibited her as the world's oldest woman. Through this exhibition, Barnum learned the value of sowing doubt and exploiting boundaries. When ticket sales slumped, for example, he sent anonymous letters to local papers claiming that the world's oldest woman was not a woman at all but instead an automaton. Since an exhibition of an automaton chess player called The Turk immediately preceded the Heth exhibit, Barnum's claim tapped into the public's piqued curiosity about the limits of technological advancement.[40] Barnum was successful not only because he raised doubts about Heth—was she human or machine?—but also because he invited the public to come and decide for themselves how to classify her. As they practiced their own mapmaking in this new world of traveling curiosities and exaggerated advertisements, Barnum's audience got the chance to practice classifying consumer items as real or fraudulent, an important skill in the market revolution.

Barnum agreed to lease the mermaid from Kimball, exhibit it, and give Kimball a share of the profits. Barnum drew several lessons from the Joice Heth hoax, as well as The Turk who preceded her. He claimed the mermaid was from "FeeJee," situating her as an outsider—in terms of both geographic origin and the hegemonic social formations of the white, masculine, and Protestant United States—that was in need of classification. Barnum emphasized the mermaid's categorical ambiguity in his advertisements: "naturalists and scientific men who have examined [the FeeJee Mermaid] assert that it is absolutely the work of Nature. Others, however, insist that its existence is a natural impossibility. When doctors disagree, the PUBLIC must decide."[41]

Barnum's tactics worked, and the mermaid had a successful run in New York City during the summer and fall of 1842. Some viewers were inclined to accept Barnum's claims, while others were more skeptical. The latter had no hesitation in airing their displeasure at the aquatic imposture. On one occasion, for example, while the exhibitor's back was turned, a group of medical students lifted the glass case enclosing the mermaid and placed a cigar in her mouth. More visitors approached, and the exhibitor launched into an explanation of the mermaid's discovery as bombastic as it was fictitious. He did not notice the prank until someone in the crowd asked if the mermaid died clutching the cigar. Sweat dripped down the mortified exhibitor's face while the crowd laughed at him.[42] Some New Yorkers had apparently learned from David Meredith Reese: the best way to handle an imposture was ridicule.

In 1981, Neil Harris published the earliest, the most sustained, and arguably the most thorough examination of the FeeJee Mermaid in relation to the humbuggery rampant in antebellum America.[43] Barnum's genius as a showman, Harris argued, was manifold. First, he cultivated just enough doubt to entice his audience to come and see for themselves whether they were being deceived.[44] Second, like the most successful humbugs of the era, Barnum's claims were "couched in the bland neutrality of a technological vocabulary."[45] Finally, Barnum's invitation to debate the scientific or technological validity of his claims appealed to Jacksonian egalitarianism and the confidence common people felt in weighing evidence and expressing opinions.[46] Harris argued that these factors combined, almost synergistically, to inspire in Americans a love for learning how deceptions worked.[47] For Harris, Barnum's appeal to the public revealed the popularity of that period's "aesthetic of the operational": Americans enjoyed detecting deception because, doing so "relieved [them] from the burden of coping with more abstract problems. Beauty, significance, spiritual values, could be bypassed in favor of seeing what was odd, or what worked, or was genuine."[48] Harris's analysis of the mermaid and Barnum's other humbugs suggests, in other words, that Barnum succeeded in New York because he offered an opportunity to make maps that better suited the market revolution.

One of Harris's claims is worth special interrogation: that Barnum's "realization that men took instinctive pleasure in uncovering . . . fundamental but hidden relationships" was the ultimate source of his success.[49] Two words stand out here: "instinctive pleasure." The latter implies there is some animal pleasure humans feel in revealing hidden things, whether intentional deceptions or simply hitherto unknown connections or causalities. This aligns with Tomkins's thinking, as he attributed human intelligence to the affect system, which inspires us to pursue interests with both passion and creativity.[50] The word "pleasure" reaffirms the power of revelation to trigger affects; at the same time, however, it needs some clarification.[51] As I argued in the previous section, there are many kinds of pleasure, and different pleasures have different social origins and consequences. The "instinctive pleasure" that comes from revealing hidden relationships is hardly "instinctive," therefore; it is social, and it changes in timbre and intensity depending on the social context, the kinds of relationships involved, and how those relationships overlap. These social questions, I argue, are key to understanding why the reaction to the mermaid was so different in Charleston.

After the mermaid's profitable run in New York, Barnum sent the mermaid on a national tour. She arrived in Charleston, South Carolina, in January 1843. Local naturalists, led by the Reverend Dr. John Bachman—most famous for his rejection of polygenism and his work with John James Audubon—urged Charlestonians to skip the mermaid exhibit. It was clearly an imposture, Bachman wrote in a letter published in the *Mercury*.[52] Other members of the community were less sure, especially Richard Yeadon, a lawyer and editor for a rival newspaper called the *Courier*. Yeadon insisted the mermaid was the genuine article. Even though the mermaid left Charleston after only a few weeks, Bachman and his allies engaged in a three-month-long print battle with Yeadon and his allies over the mermaid's authenticity and origins. As the conflict wore on, the *Mercury* took increasing pleasure in exposing the mermaid as another of P. T. Barnum's frauds—the paper explicitly mentioned Joice Heth[53]—and in mocking Yeadon, the *Courier*, and anyone fooled by the mermaid. Things became so tense, in fact, that a third party had to intervene to stop Bachman and Yeadon from dueling.

Two historians have examined the social components of the mermaid controversy in depth, though both fail to explain its intensity. Kenneth S. Greenberg, a historian of the US South, highlighted the role of honor in the conflict.[54] What he found "most startling about the debate over the Feejee mermaid is the lack of interest in the mermaid itself . . . The central concern of these men was to have their words, names, and pseudonyms treated with respect. Honor was at stake."[55] Honor was certainly an important feature of the mermaid controversy, but it was not the only one; Greenberg's analysis fails to account for the presence of the other two "M's" exacerbating the conflict or the way the conflagration came to involve others besides Bachman and Yeadon. Put another way, Bachman and Yeadon were symptoms of a broader issue.

Historian of medicine Peter McCandless addressed those concerns by situating the mermaid within the context of a broader social conflict in South Carolina.[56] Specifically, McCandless argued that the factions in the mermaid controversy aligned with the factions in an earlier and longer lasting controversy over mesmerism and phrenology. Conservative members of Charleston's medico-scientific elite ridiculed the two emerging "sciences" almost as soon as they were popularized in 1836. Like Reese, these men saw in mesmerism a threat to the social order because, besides challenging their own authority as scientific experts, it promoted radically materialist religious ideas and radically egalitarian racial ides—and so they mocked it mercilessly.[57] For their part, Yeadon and his allies were trying to get their own opinions heard and respected, and thereby break the control Bachman and the other members of the elite held over scientific expertise and the authority it granted.[58] The mermaid's arrival reignited that controversy. Though it is more holistic, McClandless's argument nevertheless leaves unanswered questions, such as how authority was conferred or revoked, and why this particular battle for authority was so heated.

Though Greenberg's and McClandless's analyses are both convincing to an extent, they nevertheless fail to explain adequately how and why the conflict grew so heated and lasted so long. I suggest that is because these scholars were only looking at one map at a time: Greenberg read the mermaid conflict using the "map" of southern honor culture, while McCandless superimposed the mermaid on the controversy over mesmerism. At the end of his essay on religious cartography, J. Z. Smith suggested that different maps "remain coeval possibilities which may be appropriated whenever and wherever they correspond to man's experience of the world."[59] Such imagery suggests that, like a physical atlas, scholars can leaf through maps one at a time until the proper one can be identified and usefully applied to a situation. I think this is precisely why Greenberg and McCandless fell short: they were only ever looking at a single map. Furthermore, the mermaid conflict was not a rational conflict, as both participants and observers admitted. Both the Bachman and Yeadon camps referred to their emotional states as much as their reasoning. If the conflict itself was not solely rational, then reason cannot adequately explain it.

Like Reese's *Humbugs*, the mermaid controversy created social maps to deal with changing territory. But, as a lived example of heresiology, as opposed to a monograph, the mermaid conflict adds another layer to our understanding of how ridicule makes social maps. Maps are palimpsests: even if two situations have nothing in common rationally, they might *feel* similar. As one map overlays another, borders can overlap and appear darker and thicker. Social divisions would feel more natural and more significant because the boundary-making affects involved resonate even if they do not connect logically.[60]

Because I have already briefly outlined the Charleston controversy—and it has already been described at length in the works I have cited—I will not rehash the words or deeds of its participants. Instead, I attempt to draw out affective affiliations elicited by the mermaid ad appearing in the Charleston *Mercury*. I break the advertisement into sections according to theme. After introducing a section of the advertisement, I include peripheral primary sources that might have resonated with contemporaneous readers on a particular theme; these are closely related in time and space to that winter in Charleston, though occasionally I refer to primary source material from a different year or location to offer broader context. I have also added commentary to help clarify the affective components of these resonance points.

Readers of the *Mercury* tended to be more skeptical of mermaids and mesmerists, and in their attempts to paint their rivals as ridiculous, these men leveraged other social divisions—particularly racial ones. It is possible, even likely, that some of the affective themes might cause discomfort in modern readers, for whom a southern white elite's social maps are anathema. I urge the reader to pause at these moments of discomfort—the boundary violation that triggers unease in the modern reader nestled comfortably into the contemporaneous reader's worldview. Believing the mermaid to be two separate animals sewn together instead of the genuine article, the skeptical camp made her ridiculous by appealing to social divisions surrounding the South's Peculiar Institution. As the foundational aspect of southern social life, slavery and the color line it drew offered skeptics a master atlas against which to compare the mermaid and render her ridiculous.

The first FeeJee Mermaid advertisement appeared in the *Mercury* on January 17, 1843, and ran every day for a week. It began:

> **Grand Exhibition!!!**
>
> *Wonders of Nature!!!*
>
> Will be exhibited at Masonic Hall . . . that most wonderful object of creation the real "MERMAID," taken near the FeeJee Islands . . .[61]

In 1840, a group of Fijians lured the then-famous United States Exploring Expedition into a trap—or so thought the Americans. Upon landing, "the natives received them with seeming kindness, but told them they had nothing there for them, and that they must go around to the other side of the island, as the Chief was there with a number of presents for them, such as hogs, yams, &c. Not suspecting any treachery, they pulled around as directed . . . They had been on shore but a short time, when the natives manifested their hostility to them."[62] Two Americans were killed.

The day after the supposed treachery, the American sailors "marched immediately towards the town where the massacre took place, which was well secured from an attack . . . but it did not resist our tars, who burnt that and another of their towns . . . fifty-seven of the cowardly barbarians were made to expiate with their lives their murder[s]."[63]

In 1842, around the same time that the FeeJee Mermaid debuted in New York, national papers reported on the court-martial of expedition commander Charles Wilkes. The articles' tone was one of sordid yet gleeful fascination.[64] "Such an expose we have not seen for many a day," wrote one paper. "The history of the Exploring Expedition is here embodied and it opens deliciously."[65]

In late June 1842, one South Carolina newspaper reminded readers of the expedition and the "treacherous nature of the natives" of Fiji.[66]

In contemporaneous stories, mermaids rested with their torsos out of the water and lower body hidden beneath the waves. They were always seen "stroking their faces and breasts with their hands, or something resembling hands" and in so doing they looked like "Indian women bathing"—until they dove into the water and revealed their tails.[67] According to legend, mermaids used their beauty to lure sailors into dangerous waters. When the hapless men saw the tail, it was too late. Like the portrayal of the native Fijians, accounts of mermaids combined racial otherness with deception and danger.

Grand Exhibition!!!

Wonders of Nature!!!

Will be exhibited at Masonic Hall . . . that most wonderful object of creation the real "MERMAID," taken near the FeeJee Islands, and whose recent exhibition in New York, Boston, Baltimore, Washington, &c. &c . . .

Reflecting on the significance of the Mason-Dixon line in 1854, John Latrobe wrote, "there is, perhaps, no line, real or imaginary, on the surface of the earth—not excepting even the equator and the equinoctial—whose name has been oftener in men's mouths during the last fifty years"[68]

George Howard, 7th Earl of Carlisle, known in America as Lord Morpeth, wrote to a Boston abolitionist in support of the cause. The Mercury picked up the story, claiming Lord Morpeth had turned on its head "the spirit of chivalry . . . the impulse that liberated lovely maidens from giants and griffins" by claiming that freeing the slaves would be a chivalrous act. Lord Morpeth, in "a ludicrous absurdity on a parallel with negro intellect, classes chivalry among those impulses that would, in the long run, tend to make the Southern States a second St. Domingo in horrors, idleness, ignorance, and folly."[69]

Unsurprisingly, a nation born of a slave revolt terrified southerners. St. Domingo—or Haiti, as it is now known—was an affectively potent reference. Arguing against recognition of Haitian independence, one southerner revealed his own feelings of disgust when he warned Congress that interactions with the island would "introduce a moral contagion, compared with which physical pestilence, in the utmost imaginable degree of its horrors, would be light and insignificant."[70]

Slavery's stability depended on a rigid social map, divided by a clear color line that simultaneously delineated divisions of labor. Crossing that line could shake the rest of society. The *Mercury* kept abreast of the danger: "The Abolitionists have now been busily engaged for some ten or fifteen years in distracting the Church, and convulsing the State."[71]

The *New York Evening Post* criticized South Carolina senator John C. Calhoun, who was particularly beloved by the *Mercury*. "This attack upon our Senator and upon the South altogether was unexpected by us: it was illiberal, treacherous, ungenerous, and unbecoming a noble rivalry," the *Mercury*'s editor opined, but rather than jeopardize the Democrat's presidential aspirations on "this side of the Mason and Dixon's line" or "divide the Democracy by a section feud, we will let it pass."[72]

Almost as soon as the mermaid arrived in Charleston, "No Humbug," the Reverend Doctor John Bachman's *nom de plume*, connected her to the sectional feud. "The seams are not sufficiently covered to conceal the point of union between Fish and Monkey," he wrote. "Our Yankee neighbours usually show more ingenuity, and they ought to have recollected that although we poor simpletons of Charleston" are far from northern waters, "we are not to be imposed on by the tail of a Codfish."[73]

Perhaps some southerners felt the union between North and South was every bit as ludicrous—and, considering daily attacks on Calhoun and the constant meddling of abolitionists, as offensive—as the union between fish and monkey.

Headline, January 27: "Another Assault on the South."[74]

The next day: "The Anti-Slavery Assaults on Mr. Calhoun and the South—Again."[75]

Grand Exhibition!!!

Wonders of Nature!!!

Will be exhibited at Masonic Hall . . . that most wonderful object of creation the real "MERMAID," taken near the FeeJee Islands, and whose recent exhibition in New York, Boston, Baltimore, Washington, &c. &c, has utterly dispelled the doubts of thousands and thousands of naturalists and other scientific persons regarding the real existence of such an animal!

The *Mercury*'s editor seemed to realize the mermaid might spark serious conflict. When the first letter was published on January 20, the editor added this warning: "We have been advised to use soft words, and hard arguments; but it is quite common to reverse the order; and use hard words and soft arguments. Men rail when they cannot reason."[76]

Despite the admonitions to keep the arguments rational, things got emotional. On January 26, Bachman signaled his contempt by proclaiming the mermaid's exhibitor as "clearly beneath my notice."

Though the exhibitor may be dismissed as contemptible, the real threat came from Bachman's fellow Charlestonians: Richard Yeadon and the other mermaid supporters in the *Courier* who might threaten the status quo.

It was time for Bachman to draw his own line separating the wise from the fools: "Our community has been too often imposed on by the loafer and imposter. Let not the cause of science be degraded by the exhibition of a despicable fraud."[77] It is unclear what Bachman meant by "our community." The white South? The white, elite community in Charleston to which he belonged? The medico-scientific community in which he was a leading figure?

Perhaps to Bachman it felt like all at once, and so the mermaid felt like a much bigger threat than the cheap hoax he believed she was.

In the beginning of February, Bachman began referring to the mermaid's exhibitor as "the Imposture," and he called the mermaid a "vile caricature of nature." She was not simply a fake—she was a *vile* one, an object of disgust. "The system of nature is beautiful, harmonious and perfect," Bachman wrote. "Naturalists feel it is their duty to defend [nature] against those who, with barbarous hands, would mutilate the symmetry of her works."[78] The mermaid had, in other words, profaned the sacred, and anyone who defended her was a heretic.

Émile Durkheim wrote that any violation of the sacred must be punished.[79] Bachman felt that impulse keenly, and it was only through the intervention of a "mutual friend" on "neutral ground" that Bachman and Yeadon avoided a duel. After a long, productive conversation, Bachman said, the two men left on good terms. Bachman concluded his letter with two Parthian shots. First, he noted that Yeadon "now talks less confidently of Mermaids, and I hope he will soon treat the matter as a joke." Second, he signaled his intention to write another letter to the paper describing a rival of the FeeJee Mermaid called the "*fudge* Mermaid."

Bachman was referring to the "Fud-ge Mermaid" exhibited by Peale's Museum in New York City. Unknown to Bachman, Barnum had recently acquired Rubens Peale's museum and debuted a rival mermaid to drum up even more interest in the FeeJee Mermaid. In choosing the name "Fud-ge," Barnum was doing more than playing on the word "FeeJee"—he was reverting to his usual tactic of boundary-blurring. The word "fudge" was antebellum slang meaning, among other things, "to conceal the defects of (a map or other drawing) by adjustment of the parts."[80] For Barnum, "fudging" the mermaid's seam made her a success; for Bachman, it made her a threat to the "natural" order—which, for him, was the slave system. Treating "the matter as a joke" robbed her of her power.

After un-fudging the boundaries of his social map, Bachman was contented enough to let the matter rest as a joke. Yeadon was far from satisified. The following day, he took to the *Courier* to express his displeasure; Bachman had not apologized, he merely behaved politely.

As Bachman decided the mermaid was too ridiculous to worry over, his ally Lewis R. Gibbes was becoming more incensed that Yeadon, a lawyer, would presume to correct a learned naturalist like Bachman. Gibbes reminded Yeadon that "facts are in their nature unalterable," but they are not equally apparent to everyone because people are not equal. Some people simply had more astute senses owing to the "course of education they have undergone . . . the relative degree of exercise in which [their senses] have been maintained, and the consequent dexterity with which [their senses] are applied." Bachman's well-trained eye saw the seam because he was a naturalist. Yeadon was a lawyer, and therefore unqualified to weigh in on the presence of the seam.[81]

Like the mermaid, then, Yeadon was an impostor straying into territory where he did not belong.

Grand Exhibition!!!

Wonders of Nature!!!

Will be exhibited at Masonic Hall . . . that most wonderful object of creation the real "MERMAID," taken near the FeeJee Islands, and whose recent exhibition in New York, Boston, Baltimore, Washington, &c. &c, has utterly dispelled the doubts of thousands and thousands of naturalists and other scientific persons regarding the real existence of such an animal! Also will be exhibited the ORNITHORYNCUS, from New Holland, OURANG OUTANG, &c.!

Barnum intentionally exploited the taxonomical paradox the mermaid posed. The mermaid appeared some seventeen years before Charles Darwin's *On the Origin of Species*, and during this period many naturalists adhered to the classical belief that existence was an unbroken, linear chain from God to the lowest of animals. The great chain of animated nature, as Barnum called it in his New York advertisements, was not a perfect system, since it was sometimes difficult to connect disparate species. What connected birds and mammals, for example? Barnum suggested the "ornithorhynchus," commonly known as the platypus, as a possible link. The flying fish—which was, coincidentally, the name of one of Wilke's ships on the United States Exploring Expedition—connected the birds and fish. Both creatures were on display next to the

"FeeJee Mermaid," adding just enough credibility to Barnum's implied missing link hypothesis.

The ourang outang (orangutan), as it was known at the time, was just as great a taxonomic challenge as the mermaid, and for many of the same reasons. The year before the mermaid arrived in Charleston, one South Carolina newspaper published an article about the "*ourang outang*, which literally means a wild man [and] has been classed as a species of the . . . ape genus, though it is generally admitted by zoologists to have much more resemblances to human beings." There were even stories of "a family . . . which sprang from a female ourang outang that was married by a Melay. She soon followed the customs of other women in her mode of living and working" and, after several generations, "many of the old men on the coast more resemble ourang outang than they do men."[82] Such stories suggest that, like the mermaid, the ourang outang was a potential imposture: a man pretending to be an ape or an ape pretending to be a man. From the nineteenth-century perspective, rumors about marriages between the ourang outang and people in distant foreign lands meant that the ourang outang was not simply an imposture—it was an object of disgust.

Both the mermaid and the ourang outang were racialized, canvases upon which white Americans could experiment with or negotiate the social classification of peoples.

Charlestonians were constantly forced to confront and justify the classification of racial others. On January 18, for example, the following ads ran in the Charleston *Mercury*, immediately adjacent to an image of the FeeJee Mermaid: "Negroes Wanted—Negroes of both sexes, from the age of 12 to 25 years, will be purchased" and "At Private Sale.—A smart active BOY between 16 and 17 years of age, brought up in the House, and also accustomed to the care of horses." The buying and selling of Black bodies, advertised with such matter-of-fact simplicity in the daily paper, reinforced the classification of enslaved Black people as property. "A mortgage of the property and personal security required," demanded another seller in that same issue.

Free Black and mixed-race peoples, however, challenged the classification system by crossing boundaries between free and slave, white and Black.

As the mermaid controversy continued to simmer in March 1843, the *Mercury* published a letter to the *Boston Medical Journal* from the previous year.

In "Vital Statistics of Negroes and Mulattoes," the pseudonymous "Philanthropist" explained that the "mind cannot have a sublunary existence independent of the body; and the intellectual character generally, and often wholly, depends upon the condition of the animal system." If either the mind or the body is in the wrong condition, the misplaced person will suffer disease or death. The author asserted that his data would help "decide upon a question, which is now being agitated with intense interest through the whole length and breadth of our union"—that is, slavery. "Mulattos," he wrote, were, by far, the "shortest lived of any class of the human race," especially whites or Blacks. Mixing races, according to this "Philanthropist," literally led to death. White southerners understood that the issue was not biological, it was social. Violating social boundaries was just as deadly as violating biological ones: "the mortality of the free people of color . . . is more than 100 per cent. greater than that of the slaves."[83]

With Yeadon and his allies defending the authenticity of the boundary-blurring mermaid, platypus, and ourang outang, and with the sectional and abolition controversies intensifying, it is no coincidence that the *Mercury* editor published this example of rigid cartography from the previous October.[84] Bachman and his allies were angry because the map they lived by was being challenged. Their world was falling apart.

A few years later, another South Carolina scientist worried that the map was being downright erased. "Positive historical facts prove too, that Egypt has been conquered in early times by various inferior tribes, and the blood of her people adulterated," race scientist Josiah Clark Nott lectured. Greeks and Romans conquered Egypt, but even their "pure blood . . . could not wash out the black stain, both moral and physical, which she has received . . . This adulteration of blood is the reason why Egypt and the Barbary States never can again rise, until the present races are exterminated, and the Caucasian substituted." Anywhere that Blacks have mixed with whites, "the latter have sunk into barbarism."[85]

When the mermaid left Charleston, she was replaced by the next attraction:

LECTURES ON MESMERISM.

or Animal Magnetism.

Mr. Learned having practiced MESMERISM in private circles, with much success, will in compliance with the solicitations of many friends, deliver a

> course of five or six Lectures, on this new and interesting science, accompanied and illustrated by Experiments—a young Lady, found to be highly susceptible of the Mesmeric influence, having kindly consented to sit for this purpose . . . Subjects for the first Lecture include "Increased Mental action, manifested by Phreno-Magnetism."[86]

In the early 1840s, mesmerists began experimenting with the direct manipulation of the phrenological organs, the sections of the mind phrenologists thought controlled different aspects of a person's character. Through magnetic manipulation of these organs, the mesmerist could restore balance to unbalanced minds.[87] Put another way, the mesmerist could align the organic territory of the mind with the correct map as laid out by phrenologists. The insane could be restored to sanity.

As it happens, phrenomesmerists could not have come at a better time. South Carolinians were going mad.

By early 1843, the Lunatic Asylum in Columbia, South Carolina, had filled up and needed to be expanded. For several weeks, the *Mercury* ran an advertisement seeking bids for the construction of a new wing.[88]

According to the polygenist Josiah Nott, species (by which he meant races) of humans that strayed outside of their divinely appointed regions became "insane or idiot." The number of insane Black people in the North vastly outnumbered those of the South because God had created Blacks for hotter climates.[89] Likewise, because of the inappropriate mixing of species, mulattos were also "probably more prone to insanity."[90] In this environment, boundary-crossing was dangerous. It drove people insane.

By late February, the ridicule process was entering the mockery and derisive laughter stage in the *Mercury*. A new map was being asserted to contain the dangers, and anyone who crossed the lines it drew was worthy of ridicule.

Enter "Irenaeus."

"Father Miller ought to come himself," he quipped, "to take advantage of the paroxysm of isms, and complete the three M's." The "Asylum at Columbia is quite full," he continued, "but the peripatetic philosophers of the black art [mesmerism] will pick up the quarter dollars notwithstanding, and depart from among us, not caring what afterwards becomes of their deluded proselytes whose brains were not at home to keep their money from being magnetized from their pockets."[91]

Like crossing racial boundaries, accepting William Miller's (1782–1849) assertion that Christ would return circa 1843 not only disrupted the social order, but also made people insane—a common accusation levied against Miller's followers.

A comet slowly streaked across the sky in March 1843, convincing some of Miller's followers that his predictions were coming true. On March 10, the Mercury ran a report from New York describing "a number of instances" in which "poor children have been sent home in hysterical convulsions" after being taught of Miller's prophecies. "This is really shocking, and measures should be taken to put a stop to such insane conduct."[92]

On March 16, the *Mercury* echoed the *New York Plebeian*'s sentiments: "We deplore all this sincerely. While we laugh at, we pity these delusions . . . Every age has its prophecies and its impostures. Millerism is but a revamped humbug."[93]

The mermaid conflagration was dying by the end of March, smothered by the stream of puns, jokes, and jabs directed at the Three M's. Accompanying Bachman's penultimate letter on the subject of the mermaid, there was a fanciful story of a Millerite who was in such a hurry to get to heaven that he jumped out of a tree, and another of a mesmerist who put himself in a trance so powerful it sent his soul and body out of the city without paying his bills.94 The next day, another author mocked amateur mesmerists for using slaves as mesmerism subjects, implying that slaves were simultaneously prone to laziness and to extreme obedience, and again linking mesmerism to racialized conceptions of racial others.[95]

After the mess with the mermaid, Barnum was more careful with his next exhibition in Charleston, which followed on the mesmerists' heels:

> No Humbug,
> Mr. Editor:—I visited yesterday the exhibition of the Dwarf—Genl. Tom Thumb, Jr . . . There can possibly be no imposition as regards his weight . . . This little stranger is well worth a visit from our Citizenship who, I can assure them, will not be humbugged this time.[96]

Though the anonymous author—very likely either Barnum or someone in his employ—called Tom Thumb a "little stranger," he was nowhere near as strange as the mermaid and everything she represented. The exhibit was uneventful.

CONCLUSION

This essay explored how antebellum Americans used ridicule to feel social differences into existence. For Reese and "Irenaeus," humbugs threatened the world as they knew it, and fixing them in a suitable place felt significant enough that they reached for religious idioms to explain their endeavors. Setting aside questions of authentic religiosity, I excavated the feelings that made their chosen humbugs so dangerous—and how ridicule resolved the threat. Beneath the arguments and ratiocinations that made up *Humbugs of New York* ran a current of affect—disgust, joy, and contempt—and it spread from Reese to his readers as he invited them to join in the mocking laughter. Similarly, the Charleston controversy cannot be boiled down to a matter of honor or an argument over authority, though these were certainly crucial components. Rather, the fake mermaid *felt* familiar to some Charlestonians. In her, skeptics saw signs of a mounting sectional conflict—attacks on slavery and the South as a whole. They saw signs of a social order, neatly divided by color lines, crumbling under the weight of impostures from north of the Mason-Dixon line. Though tensions briefly came to a boil, ultimately it was ridicule, not violence, that redrew the fudged lines of Charleston's social map.

NOTES

1. "Mesmerism," *Charleston Mercury*, February 24, 1843.

2. Mark Noll, "Common Sense Traditions and American Evangelical Thought," *American Quarterly* 37, no. 2 (Summer 1985): 216–38.

3. Max Weber, *The Protestant Ethic and the Spirit of Capitalism*, trans. Stephen Kalberg, (New York: Oxford University Press, 2011).

4. Todd Berzon, *Classifying Christians: Ethnography, Heresiology, and the Limits of Knowledge in Late Antiquity* (Berkeley: University of California Press), 9.

5. J. Z. Smith, *Map Is Not Territory: Studies in the History of Religions* (Chicago: University of Chicago Press, 1993), 293–94.

6. Charles Sellers, *The Market Revolution in Jacksonian America, 1815–1846* (New York: Oxford University Press, 1991), 46–54.

7. For a brief introduction to emotionology, or the social construction of emotion, see Carol Z. Stearns and Peter N. Stearns, *Anger: The Struggle for Emotional Control in America's History* (Chicago: University of Chicago Press, 1986), 14.

8. Eve Kosofsky Sedgwick and Adam Frank, eds., *Shame and Its Sisters: A Silvan Tomkins Reader* (Durham, NC: Duke University Press, 1995). For affect theory and the study of religion, see Donovan O. Schaefer, *Religious Affects: Animality, Evolution, and Power* (Durham, NC: Duke University Press, 2015); and Kevin Lewis O'Neill, "Beyond Broken: Affective Spaces and the Study of American Religion," *JAAR* 81, no. 4 (December 2013): 1093–1116.

9. Sara Ahmed, *The Cultural Politics of Emotion* (Edinburgh: Edinburgh University Press, 2014).

10. David Meredith Reese, *Humbugs of New-York: Being a Remonstrance against Popular Delusion; whether in Science, Philosophy, or Religion* (New York: John S. Taylor, Brick-Church Chapel, 1838).

11. Reese, *Humbugs*, vii.

12. Reese, *Humbugs*, 16 (my emphasis).

13. Reese, *Humbugs*, vi–vii (original emphasis).

14. Reese, *Humbugs*, 23.

15. Reese, *Humbugs*, 27.

16. Eve Sedgwick, *Touching Feeling: Affect, Pedagogy, Performativity* (Durham, NC: Duke University Press, 2003), chap. 4.

17. Reese, *Humbugs*, 2.

18. Sedgwick and Frank, *Shame and Its Sisters*, 22.

19. Ahmed, *The Cultural Politics of Emotion*, 89–92.

20. Mary Douglas, *Purity and Danger: An Analysis of Concepts of Pollution and Taboo* (London: Routledge and Kegan Paul, 1978).

21. Reese, *Humbugs*, 27.

22. Reese, *Humbugs*, 30.

23. Reese, *Humbugs*, 33 (my emphasis).

24. See "Black Vomit," *Gazette of the United-States*, September 14, 1793, 539.

25. Reese, *Humbugs*, 34.

26. Reese, *Humbugs*, 35 (my emphasis).

27. Reese, *Humbugs*, 30.

28. Reese, *Humbugs*, 40.

29. Reese, *Humbugs*, 44.

30. Reese, *Humbugs*, 48.

31. Reese, *Humbugs*, 50.

32. Sedgwick and Frank, *Shame and Its Sisters*, 133.

33. Sedgwick and Frank, *Shame and Its Sisters*, 134–35.

34. Ahmed, *Cultural Politics of Emotion*, 102.

35. Sedgwick and Frank, *Shame and Its Sisters*, 139–44.

36. Sedgwick and Frank, *Shame and Its Sisters*, 139.

37. Reese, *Humbugs*, 45.

38. Reese, *Humbugs*, 53, 61 (original emphasis).

39. "That Mermaid," *Charleston Mercury*, January 20, 1843; hereafter cited as the *Mercury*.

40. On the saga of Joice Heth, the "world's oldest woman," see Phineas Taylor Barnum, *The Life of P.T. Barnum* (New York: Redfield, 1855), 155–59 and 172–75; and James Cook, *The Arts of Deception: Playing with Fraud in the Age of Barnum* (Cambridge, MA: Harvard University Press, 2001), chap. 1.

41. Advertisement, *New-York Daily Tribune*, September 11, 1843.

42. Barnum, *The Life of P.T. Barnum, Written by Himself* (New York: Redfield, 1855), 239–40.

43. Neil Harris, *Humbug: The Art of P. T. Barnum* (Chicago: University of Chicago Press, 1981).

44. Harris, *Humbug*, 75.

45. Harris, *Humbug*, 72.

46. Harris, *Humbug*, 75.

47. Harris, *Humbug*, 77.

48. Harris, *Humbug*, 79.

49. Harris, *Humbug*, 82.

50. Sedgwick and Frank, *Shame and Its Sisters*, 39.

51. Kimerer L. LaMothe, "What Bodies Know about Religion and the Study of It," *JAAR* 76, no. 3 (September 2008): 573–601.

52. "The Mermaid," *Mercury*, January 20.

53. "Joice Heth," *Mercury*, February 7.

54. Kenneth S. Greenberg, "The Nose, the Lie, and the Duel in the Antebellum South," *American Historical Review* 95, no. 1 (February, 1990): 57–74.

55. Greenberg, "The Nose, the Lie, and the Duel," 61.

56. Peter McCandless, "Mesmerism and Phrenology in Antebellum Charleston: 'Enough of the Marvellous,'" *Journal of Southern History* 58, no. 2 (May 1992): 199–230.

57. McCandless, "Mesmerism and Phrenology," 211.

58. McCandless, "Mesmerism and Phrenology," 224.

59. Smith, *Map Is Not Territory*, 309.

60. Susan Lepselter, *The Resonance of Unseen Things: Poetics, Power, Captivity, and UFOs in the American Uncanny* (Ann Arbor: University of Michigan Press, 2016), 4.

61. "Grand Exhibition!!!" *Mercury*, January 17, 1843.

62. "Latest from the Exploring Squadron—Massacre of Two of the Officers of the Peacock at the Feejee Islands," *Richmond* [VA] *Enquirer*, February 23, 1841.

63. "Latest from the Exploring Squadron," *Richmond Enquirer*, February 23, 1841.

64. "Naval General Court Martial on Board of the U.S. Ship North Carolina," *New York Herald*, August 23, 1842.

65. "Trial of Lieut. Charles Wilkes, U.S.N.," *New-York Daily Tribune*, August 26, 1842.

66. "The Return of the Exploring Expedition," *Camden* [SC] *Journal*, June 22, 1842.

67. "The Mermaid," *New York Herald*, July 17, 1842.

68. John H. B. Latrobe, *The History of Mason and Dixon's Line* (Philadelphia: Lippincott, Grambo, and Co., 1855), 5.

69. "Lord Morpeth on Slavery," *Mercury*, January 12, 1843.

70. Quoted in Mary Treudly, "The United States and Santo Domingo 1789–1866," *Journal of Racial Development* 7, no. 2 (October 1916): 226.

71. "The Domestic Institutions of the South," *Mercury*, January 14, 1843.

72. "The South Proscribed," *Mercury*, January 19, 1843.

73. "The Mermaid," *Mercury*, January 20, 1843.

74. "Another Assault on the South," *Mercury*, January 27, 1843.

75. "The Anti-Slavery Assaults on Mr. Calhoun and the South—Again," *Mercury*, January 28, 1843.

76. *Mercury*, January 20, 1843.

77. "To the Editor of the *Mercury*," *Mercury*, January 26, 1843.

78. "To the Editor of the *Charleston Courier*," *Mercury*, February 1, 1843.

79. Émile Durkheim, *The Elementary Forces of Religious Life* (New York: Free Press, 1965), 52–55.

80. "fudge, v.," OED Online, June 2022.

81. *Charleston Courier*, February 13 and 14, 1843.

82. "The Orang Outang of Malacca," *Farmers' Gazette and Cheraw* [SC] *Advertiser*, April 19, 1842.

83. "Vital Statistics of Negroes and Mulattoes," *Mercury*, March 3, 1843.

84. Vital Statistics of Negroes and Mulattoes," *Boston Medical Journal*, October 12, 1842.

85. Josiah Clark Nott, *Two Lectures, on the Natural History of the Caucasian and Negro Races* (Mobile: Dade and Thompson, 1844), 16.

86. "Lectures on Mesmerism," *Mercury*, February 11, 1843.

87. Emily Ogden, *Credulity: A Cultural History of US Mesmerism* (Chicago: University of Chicago Press, 2018), 164–69.

88. "Lunatic Asylum," *Mercury*, January 31, 1843.

89. Nott, *Two Lectures*, 29–30.

90. Nott, *Two Lectures*, 30. John Bachman vehemently disagreed with the methodology polygenists used to make their arguments and asserted the unity of humanity on the basis of divine creation. John Bachman, *The Doctrine of the Unity of the Human Race Examined on the Principles of Science* (Charleston, 1850).

91. "Mesmerism," *Mercury*, February 24, 1843.

92. "Millerism in Brooklyn," *Mercury*, March 10, 1843.

93. "Millerism—The Comet—Signs and Wonders," *Mercury*, March 16, 1843.

94. "The Sequel to the Mermaid Controversy," "Practical Millerism," and "Mesmerism—Important Circumstance," *Mercury*, March 29, 1843.

95. "Mesmerism Confirmed," *Mercury*, April 1, 1843.

96. "No Humbug," *Mercury*, April 19.

The Black Queer Theological Tradition of Abolition

Zilpha Elaw's Nineteenth-Century Ministry of Spectacle

Jaimie D. Crumley

The Ethiopian eunuch was adopted as a son and heir of God.
Zilpha Elaw, 1846

Women of African descent in the United States have historically practiced evangelical Christianity[1] in Black queer and abolitionist ways. One such was the nineteenth-century transnational itinerant preaching woman, Zilpha Elaw. Her theological vision, as she presented it in her 1846 spiritual autobiography and travel narrative, *Memoirs of the Life, Religious Experience, Ministerial Travels, and Labours of Mrs. Elaw* (hereafter *Memoirs*), provides one example of how nineteenth-century Black religious women approached transnational abolitionist politics. Scholarly work on nineteenth-century Black women's literature rarely considers Elaw's *Memoirs*. An examination of this text written by a freeborn Black Methodist widowed woman provides rare insight into the harrowing experiences of nineteenth-century people who participated in a dominant American faith tradition while belonging to multiple marginalized groups.

In her *Memoirs*, Elaw indicates that when those who were most marginalized in the nineteenth century sought a place within American institutions, they found only closed doors. Although she worked to conform to the dominant religious traditions of her time, Elaw was frequently reminded that she would never be accepted because of her race and gender. *Memoirs* reflects her frustration that of all the doors she wished to enter, the doors of the Methodist Church seemed to be the heaviest of all. Because the denomination would not endorse her, she created her own ministry that boasted open doors for all people no matter their social standing. By choosing not to seek approval within Methodism, she redefined what it meant to belong. She believed this was work God called her to undertake.

In *Memoirs*, Elaw shared her story of conversion and transatlantic itinerant Christian ministry. Her writing is both a spiritual autobiography and a travel memoir in which she shares wisdom from the journey of her soul as a spiritual person and as a transnational voyager. She addressed her self-published writings to the "Saints and faithful Brethren in Christ . . . in London and other localities of England" with whom she spent five years. In *Memoirs*, Elaw discussed the early years of her Christian itinerant ministry in the United States and her years as an itinerant preacher in England.[2] The narrative concluded in 1845 as she prepared to cross the Atlantic again to return to the United States.

Elaw adopted a Black queer posture toward dominant white masculine perspectives on Christian theology. Her epistemology was Black queer because it defied sexual, gender, and racialized norms simultaneously. The Black queerness of her faith and intellect emerged in her framing of the positionality of Black Americans in *Memoirs*. Elaw wrote, "The Almighty accounts not the black races of man . . . as inferior to the white . . . the Ethiopian eunuch was adopted as a son and heir of God."[3] Elaw described persons of African descent as those who shared the social positionality of the Ethiopian eunuch in Acts 8:26–40.

In the book of Acts, the Ethiopian eunuch appears only briefly. He is described as a cultural outsider and a sexually nonnormative figure. While there are many definitions of the term "eunuch," the most common understanding is that eunuchs were castrated men. The belief was that, unless they were castrated, they could not be trusted to serve high-ranking women of noble birth. Elaw's description of all Black persons in the Americas as cultural others who were sexually violated indicates that she believed that all people of African descent, regardless of their gender or social class, were caught in what contemporary Black feminists have called "interlocking" oppressive systems.[4] However, the eunuch's acceptance into God's family points to the radical possibilities for marginalized people to become spiritual insiders. Elaw believed that through conversion and baptism, the Ethiopian eunuch was adopted as God's son and heir. Although she herself lived through times when race and gender inhibited her everyday life, Elaw did not believe these social constructs were something to be overcome. Her ministry was insistent that social constructs, including race, gender, and class, must be abolished. Everyone belonged in God's family.

This essay characterizes Elaw's theology as Black queer and abolitionist. The term "Black queer" describes sexual or nonsexual intimacies between

Black people of the same sex or gender identity. However, it also describes the shared outsider political and cultural positionality occupied by Black persons in the nineteenth-century United States. In Elaw's case, the term "Black queer" describes her private experience of isolation from her family of origin, her husband, and other Methodists. While Elaw fails (or refuses) to speak openly about her sexuality in *Memoirs*, the subtext of her writing indicates the depth of her concern about the violation of Black people's bodies, both sexually and nonsexually. A Black queer approach to Christianity shares direct ideological links to an abolitionist approach to Christianity.[5] Therefore, this essay frames Elaw's Black queer approach to Christian theology as a contribution to the abolitionist tradition. Elaw was an abolitionist theologian. She maintained a Christian theological belief that a greater world was to come. Meanwhile, she maintained a belief in abolition, that is, the destruction of racism and white supremacy and a new day of justice. Through her writing and preaching, she declared herself to have as much a place in God's family as any other convert. When people discouraged her work as an itinerant minister, she accused them of being "of the world" and said that they had no faith at all.[6]

This essay contributes to current conversations at the intersection of African American studies, queer of color critique, and religious studies. Leading voices at this intersection include E. Patrick Johnson, José Esteban Muñoz, Ashon Crawley, Kelly Brown Douglas, and Ahmad Greene-Hayes. This essay is also guided by Alice Walker's theorization of womanism. Together, Black queer theory and womanist theory, alongside a close reading of *Memoirs*, demonstrate that Black queer approaches to Christianity are not about death and impossibility.[7] Black queer Christian theology is about traditional communalism, that is, the practice of being attuned to collective values and shared history.[8] Black queer theology is an abolitionist political theory that is committed to otherwise possibilities and hope in the not yet.

This essay proceeds in five sections. First, it explores what it meant for a Black woman to preach to people of all races and genders, and across geographic bounds. Second, it considers the particularity of Elaw's Black, female body. Her distinct social positionality rendered her both the perpetual outsider and an effective Christian minister. Third, this essay examines how free Black persons found a sense of kinship or belonging in the nineteenth century. Fourth, it studies Elaw's call to Christian ministry, which demonstrates the Black queer nature of conversion. Elaw released herself from the demands of nineteenth-century marital expectations and wed herself to her faith instead. Finally, this essay examines how Elaw and other Black preaching women remade gender. Nineteenth-century Black women's lives were rife with contradictions. Her Black womanhood and her commitment to creating kinship bonds rendered Elaw, to borrow the words of Black feminist Audre Lorde, a "sister outsider."[9]

THE GEOGRAPHY OF BLACK FREEDOM

For Zilpha Elaw and many other free and quasi-free Black people, the "space of freedom" was "at the same time a space of captivity."[10] Elaw and other Black preaching women spoke from the outskirts of traditional power. They reinterpreted Christian theology to help them organize against oppression. They deployed a Black queer hermeneutic that allowed them to critique the Atlantic world's capitalist structure that placed Black laborers below all other laborers because of their Blackness.[11] Their Black queer performances allowed them to create new social worlds. Despite the state's best efforts to render them civilly dead, they did not allow their lives to be defined by loss, failure, or impossibility.

Elaw's itinerant preaching ministry, which she began in 1817, led her to travel throughout the northeastern United States and even into the southern states, which she called the slave states. When traveling through the South, she was at risk of capture and sale.[12] Even in the North, free Black people faced segregation, few professional opportunities, kidnapping, and sale into the slave market.[13] As a Black woman, Elaw was at risk no matter where she went. When she preached, she traveled without her husband, a fuller named Joseph Elaw, and their young daughter. After her husband's untimely death on January 27, 1823, she continued to travel and preach, both to follow her calling and to provide financially for her family. During her travels, she left her daughter with friends or sent her to be employed as a domestic servant.

After she was widowed, Elaw balanced the practical demands of her life as a now unmarried working-class woman with what she believed to be a divine call to become an itinerant preacher. Her limited professional options after her husband's death reveal the precarity of nineteenth-century Black women's lives. She entered the masculine world of itinerant preaching more forcefully than she had before she was widowed. At the crossroads between a life of domestic servitude or a life fueled by what she perceived to be a higher calling, Elaw made a choice that for most nineteenth-century American women, especially Black women, was unthinkable.

In 1840, Elaw expanded her itinerancy by traveling across the Atlantic Ocean to preach throughout England. She was not the only Black woman who pursued foreign missions during the nineteenth century, but she was unique among her female preaching contemporaries because she pursued her missionary ventures without the support of a denomination or supervisory board. Black Methodist itinerant preaching woman Jarena Lee also traveled widely and took an extensive voyage through Canada. However, Lee's call, unlike Elaw's, was endorsed in 1819 by Reverend Richard Allen, the bishop of the African Methodist Episcopal Church.[14] How Zilpha Elaw safely navigated her journeys in the United States and abroad to England without any outside support is almost unfathomable. Her pursuit of her dangerous and isolating call to itinerant preaching indicates the depth of her commitment to abolishing all white supremacist power structures. She would not wait for institutional acceptance. Instead, she followed the path she believed God had placed before her.

Her transatlantic journey began on June 10, 1840, at nine o'clock in the morning, when she met her daughter and grandsons who were "entwined in the strongest affections of [her] heart" to bid them farewell.[15] The affection she felt for her daughter and grandsons was profound. However, she maintained her commitment to her preaching ministry. Through her preaching, she hoped all who heard her would know that people of all races, including people of African descent, were part of God's family. For Zilpha Elaw, Christianity was not about restricting people's rights and privileges based on their placement in a social hierarchy that was emerging through the nineteenth-century formation of the social constructs of race, culture, and gender. She worked against the exclusionary understandings of Christianity in the United States that had been introduced by English Protestants who arrived in the early seventeenth century to begin their "errand into the wilderness."[16] Elaw believed that Christianity was for all people.

Elaw wanted her English listeners to have the same "powerful and converting" reaction to the Gospel as she had experienced among her American listeners. In England, she found the "mental soil" to be unyielding, but she continued to preach as often as she could because she believed that God was for everyone. In Elaw's mind, Christians were people who were faithful to God even when that faithfulness required them to defy the world.

A MINISTRY OF SPECTACLE

Elaw possessed extraordinary, perhaps even otherworldly, faith that compelled her to flout every social expectation placed upon nineteenth-century Black women. Instead of conforming to American Protestant Christian admonitions to be "mild, dependent, and softening" and to maintain the character that was most "natural" for women, she lived according to a proto-Black feminist, biblical set of guidelines that she herself devised.[17] Elaw's most substantive spiritual guidelines for women concerned the issue of marriage. She wrote, "That woman is dependent on and subject to man, is the dictate of nature; that the man is not created for the woman, but the woman for the man, is that of Scripture." She encouraged women to wed men who shared their beliefs because a woman could not be the "help-meet" of someone who led her astray.[18] She justified her preaching despite her husband's objections because of her perception that he failed to conform to her belief system. Elaw offered an early manifestation of biblical Black feminist principles in that she depended on biblical teachings to guide her life. However, she interpreted the Bible through the lens of her lived experiences as a free Black woman born in Philadelphia in the late eighteenth century.

While notions of race, as we understand them today, were still being created during Elaw's time, English intellectuals and travelers used gendered and theological language with great frequency in their writing to create and maintain a strict social order. Encounters with non-English people, especially non-English women, complicated their social order.[19] Freeborn women of African descent like Zilpha Elaw were caught in the balance. She flouted the social order at great risk to herself and her daughter at a time when free Black people were at greater risk than ever before. Since Elaw's childhood, the Fugitive Slave Law of 1793 had been in place, which allowed the arrest of "fugitives from justice" based on no more than the oral testimony of an agent or attorney working for a slaveholder.[20]

By the 1830s, people of African descent in the United States faced new crises. Free Black people from the North were at constant risk of capture and sale into slavery. When their family members disappeared, free Black people were left grieving and fearful.[21] The race-based violence of the late eighteenth and early nineteenth centuries forced Black people in the United States to create rival geographies to practice freedom within enclosures of unfreedom.[22] Churches, private homes, literary societies, and even public spaces became their rival geography where they reveled in the freedom possibilities that were yet to be made manifest.

Despite the risk of openly enjoying her freedom, Elaw traveled as the Spirit of God compelled her. She moved freely during some of the most repressive years for Americans of African descent. These were also years during which abolitionists were divided about whether the abolitionist platform ought to include women's rights.[23] Ironically, she felt called by God to travel to the intellectual home of the oppressive social order she endured in the United States. Her experiences are a reminder that theologically justified white supremacy was a transatlantic crisis; her body and epistemology functioned as the ultimate critique of the English imperial social order.

Elaw successfully preached to many people during her time in England. In *Memoirs* she wrote, "My reader may perceive that I have not been an idle spectator in my Heavenly Master's cause. During my sojourn in England, I have preached considerably more than a thousand sermons."[24] This figure indicates that on an average of twice a day for six years, Elaw found an audience that would be receptive to hearing a message from her. Even if Elaw's estimation of how many times she preached during her England years is hyperbolic, her contributions to nineteenth-century religious history, transnational feminist history, the Black literary tradition, and diasporic Black history are undeniable. Elaw could undertake her transnational preaching ministry because she existed in a liminal Black queer space which was socially constructed to enclose her. Yet, she leveraged it to develop a Black queer counterpublic sphere within which she taught other minoritized people that freedom was possible. Her life was a delicate choreography of survival and Black feminist leadership.

In the eyes of the white people in the United States and England who encountered her during her travels, Elaw's mobile body produced what literary theorist Kimberly Blockett describes as "a spectacle."[25] However, Elaw deployed her spectacle-inducing positionality to attract her "white brethern and sisters" who, she writes, "flocked to [her] ministry."[26] English people would not have been entirely surprised by her presence, as other people of African descent also traveled from the United States during the eighteenth and nineteenth centuries.[27] However, Elaw was unique among her contemporaries because she did not travel as an enslaved person to be exhibited or as a formerly enslaved person to protest the injustice of slavery. Rather, she traveled exclusively for evangelical purposes.

While Blackness and womanhood are both social constructions that exist to foreclose the social possibilities of Black women, they opened a new set of social and political possibilities for Elaw. She eagerly pursued each of the possibilities she believed God laid before her. She believed that God had called her to preach because she was a blessing to "many who were living in sin and darkness before they saw [her] coloured face." She found that the novelty of her body drew people who had "scarcely heard a sermon in their lives" but wanted to see the "coloured female preacher."[28] Her listeners' racist ideologies about Black women meant that they often expected to witness an amusing performance when they heard her preach. Yet, Elaw was not an object who intended to entertain her listeners. She understood her subjectivity as a nineteenth-century freeborn Black woman from the imagined bedrock of liberty. She deployed her subjectivity to compel transformations of the soul.

A HOME IN GOD'S FAMILY

Zilpha Elaw was born free in Pennsylvania in 1790 to religious parents. She does not divulge her natal family's surname in her autobiography, which emerges as a Black queer practice intended to reject the limitations of the here and now in favor of a more hopeful future.[29] Her story is about her personal conversion, and about a journey she believed Black people must take to achieve fuller freedoms in society. While the idea that the preconversion life is irrelevant is a common theme of evangelical conversion narratives, Elaw's identity as a Black woman on the fringes of her religious tradition makes her silence on these topics especially telling. Her choice not to include the full name of any member of her family of origin left her with an uncertain past and gave her the agency to shape her own future. She wrote her "humble memoirs" so they might "continue to be read long after [she] shall have ceased from [her] earthly labours and existence."[30] Her story was not about her uncertain past; it was about the certain future promised to God's followers.

Elaw was separated from her brother at a young age by her maternal grandparents who took him hundreds of miles away to work on their farm. When she was twelve years old her mother died while giving birth to her twenty-second child. Only Elaw and two of her siblings survived beyond their infancy. From her childhood, Elaw was well acquainted with premature loss and death. She writes nothing of the toll that the loss of eighteen children and eventually her mother took on her and her family, but it is clear that her experiences shaped the woman she became. After her mother's death, Elaw's father placed her younger sister in an aunt's care. Meanwhile, she was sent to work as a domestic servant for Pierson and Rebecca Mitchel, where she remained until age eighteen. Her father died soon after he sent her away.

Without familial support, Elaw experienced religion differently. The Mitchel family were Quakers, and Elaw wrote that she never saw them participate in religious exercises, and that if they did perform any religious exercises, they happened in "the secret silence of the mind."[31] Elaw had experienced religion differently before living with the Mitchel family. She explains little about the "family devotion," prayers, and "praises of God," to which her family "regularly attended . . . morning and evening" during her early childhood, but she returned to these rituals during her challenging teenage years.[32] Elaw needed a more emotive and public spiritual practice than Quakerism allowed. Based on her experiences of familial loss, it is no wonder that the evangelical idea of adoption into God's family appealed to her.

As a teenager, Zilpha Elaw drifted from her Christian faith, but she felt that God appeared to her to return her to her path. At age fourteen, she had a dream about the Christian notion of a Judgment Day. When she awoke, she felt guilty and terrified. Despite Rebecca Mitchel's attempts to comfort her, she continued to feel a sense of "incompetency to meet [her] Judge."[33] Her concerns about the eschaton are rooted in Pauline and Johannine theology in the Christian scriptures.[34] Like many of her contemporaries, Elaw feared eschatological judgment and wanted to avoid permanent separation from God. Around the same time, the Methodists began to preach in her area, and she attended "their meetings once a fortnight,[35] on the Sabbath afternoons." Although the gatherings appealed to her, she did not feel fully converted. She felt her conversion was completed one day when she was milking a cow and the "manifestation of [God's] presence was so clearly apparent, that even the beast of the stall turned her head and bowed herself upon the ground." In response to the incident, Elaw sang a hymn about Jesus's love. She writes that "as [she] was milking the cow and singing, [she] turned her head, and saw a tall figure approaching . . . [she] was overwhelmed by astonishment at the sight." She explains, "this . . . was the manner of [her] soul's conversion to God."[36]

In 1808, Elaw joined the Methodist Episcopal Society with the full support of others who were present.[37] Elaw understood Christianity to be about God's acceptance of and love for all living creatures. Although her moments of discovery, or conversion, happened privately, she took the lessons she learned from her experience and shared them with others. Her ministry was a spectacle not because of her choice to preach as a Black woman, but because she insisted that there was a place for all people within God's family.

THE BLACK QUEER CALL

Elaw first perceived her call to preach at a camp meeting near Burlington, New Jersey, in 1817. Her memory of the camp meetings provides a clear distillation of the environment of the religious revival services that were common in the nineteenth-century United States. She likely wrote about the meetings in such detail in part because she wrote to her supporters in England. While we can assume that they were familiar with American evangelicalism, Elaw's writing offered them a rare opportunity to learn about the religious fervor of the early nineteenth-century United States from the perspective of a converted American Christian who was also a woman of African descent. Camp meetings were riveting spiritual gatherings that changed many lives in the eighteenth and nineteenth centuries. Of the 1817 gathering Elaw wrote, "the hardest hearts are melted into tenderness; the driest eyes overflow with tears, and the loftiest spirits bow down."[38]

Elaw explained that to form a camp meeting, the date and time of the meeting was published extensively, and each family that planned to attend would bring their own tent with seats and the provisions they needed. Thousands descended upon the meeting site for the meetings that frequently lasted a week or longer. The group formed circular enclosures, where they pitched tents. The space in the center was reserved for the minister. Worship commenced before sunrise. Men with trumpets used the sound of their music to manage the various activities, including meals and socializing, that participants did during the day. On the last morning of the meeting, all the attendees gathered for a love feast. After the feast, everyone said farewell and marched away from the campground in the minister's presence.[39] Elaw's description also illustrates the liminal space between order (trumpets and processions) and disorder (passionate and emotive experiences of worship) that characterized life in the antebellum United States.

Elaw believed that during the 1817 camp meeting, God revealed to her that she was like another Phoebe, a female deacon in the early Church who is referenced in Romans 16. Elaw believed God was calling her to a ministry that entailed visiting families to speak to them about salvation. She also believed she was called to visit the sick. She followed her perceived call by visiting people of all social classes to discuss salvation with them.[40] Her choice to follow her call to preach within the Christian tradition was a Black queer practice that frustrated the customs of her time, which discouraged women's public speaking. Given the social mores of the time, it is perhaps no surprise that the person who was most angered by Elaw's preaching was her husband, Joseph Elaw, whom she had wed in 1810. Joseph Elaw worked in the shipping industry, and his steady employment allowed his wife the time to pursue her interests. Her husband's profession meant that, unlike many other Black women in the nineteenth century, she herself did not need to pursue paid employment. However, Joseph Elaw could not have expected that his wife would take up preaching. Even before she followed her call to preach, Joseph Elaw encouraged his wife with some frequency to "renounce [her] religion."

Although her husband's commands to desert her faith infuriated her, she clung to nineteenth-century notions of a respectable woman by keeping her "mouth as with a bridle" to prevent herself from speaking harshly to him, despite her certainty that his opinions were incorrect.[41] In *Memoirs*, she indicates that when she first began to preach, she did not tell her husband. She recounts a time in the early 1820s when a friend mocked her husband after discovering that she was a preacher. Joseph Elaw was surprised to learn that his friend's words were true. To her surprise and great delight, he told her that he would come hear her preach. She preached in his presence with joy. However, after hearing her, he declared, "We are undone." He urged her to stop her speaking publicly altogether.[42] Despite his best efforts to discourage her, however, she was not dissuaded by her husband's disdain for her work.

Elaw knew the Christian theological teachings that mandated women's subordination to men. However, she found the epistemological loophole, which she unabashedly shared with her readers. After discussing the challenges of being married to a man who did not share her faith, she explained to her readers that she believed that a Christian who was married to someone with a different faith could not share the "mutual sympathy and affectionate accordance" that Christian couples enjoyed. She understood that a wife was "destined to be the help-meet of her husband." However, she believed that if the husband did not share her faith, she could not be "his instrument or abettor in worldly lusts and sinful pursuits." Likewise, if the husband were a Christian while his wife was not, Elaw explained that she was "not his help-meet, but his drawback and curse."[43] For Elaw, marriages were partnerships in which two people agreed to pursue a common goal. In her case, she expected her spouse to join her theological vision. Because her husband refused to share what she understood to be a biblical vision for the world, she justified her audacious choice to continue to preach despite his objections.

Only one thing made Elaw hesitant to disobey her husband. Throughout *Memoirs*, a key theme is Elaw's desire to have the family she was denied as a child. Therefore, she longed for the kind of close bond that a marriage might provide. Despite her consistently thwarted desire for familial love, Elaw believed that she was uniquely equipped to serve as a Christian minister, even if she did so without the support of her life partner or the formal support of an institutional church. Despite the dangers of disobeying her husband who, through his labor to provide for their small family, defended her livelihood, she clung to a Black queer and eschatological hope in the not yet. As a proto–Black feminist intellectual, she held tightly to what Black feminist cultural theorist Tina Campt has called the future real conditional, or that which will have had to happen for Black women to become free.[44] Although her life was marked by loss, despair, and impossibility, she held an unwavering belief in a future that she believed must happen. This was a Black queer theological possibility, rooted in the impossibility that Elaw refused to accept.

Soon after he lamented that his wife's preaching would be their undoing, Joseph Elaw fell ill, and Zilpha Elaw's life changed forever. Now that her husband was ill and could not financially support them, it was her responsibility to support her family emotionally, physically, and financially. As he died, Joseph Elaw recognized that his behavior toward his wife had been too harsh.

He admitted that her behavior during their marriage was above reproach and wished her well in life. On January 27, 1823, he died, leaving her with debt and deep sorrow. Despite their disagreements about religion and preaching, theirs was a mutually beneficial union that they both honored.[45] As it had in her childhood, the death of a close relation remade Zilpha Elaw's life.

Elaw's pre-1823 decision to enter public life was one she had made entirely by choice, but now she was without other options. Accordingly, for the sake of her daughter's survival and her own, she entered public life. All that was left to decide was what kind of public life she would cultivate. She chose to expand her ministry. Now, her preaching would take her throughout the East Coast of the United States and across the ocean to England. She traveled alone, often leaving behind her young daughter. As she went, extraordinary risks followed her, but she believed that the Spirit of God guided her actions. Her itinerant preaching ministry allowed her to reimagine the meaning of family, sisterhood, and maternity, and invited others to do likewise.

REMAKING GENDER

The remaining concern is how Elaw, a nineteenth-century Black woman who was orphaned, widowed, and without support from an institutional church, fashioned her successful and spectacle-inducing transnational Christian itinerant ministry. There are many ways of responding to that question, but I propose that her survival and success hinged on her Black queer theological approach to life and faith. Since the colonial period, women in the Americas have defied gender norms to speak theologically and politically.[46] By doing so and maintaining that despite their gender, they had a God-ordained right to be heard, they remade gender.

The experience of being remade in the social and theological sense was something that Black women in the Americas had had before, as those ripped from their indigenous homeland and converted from human to chattel on the voyage across the Atlantic. Through her public preaching ministry, Elaw worked toward repairing the harm slavery had inflicted. She joined a tradition of proto–Black feminist preaching women who remade social mores that did not serve them. The tradition included Sojourner Truth, Jarena Lee, and Rebecca Cox Jackson, Black women who preached in the northeastern United States in the late 1820s and throughout the 1830s. The Black queer theological tradition also includes Black women who did not leave behind extant writings, whose extant writings are attributed only to a first name, or who wrote anonymously.

Rebecca Cox Jackson made the clearest contributions to the nineteenth-century Black queer Christian theological tradition. Like Elaw, Jackson was born free in the late eighteenth century outside Philadelphia. Jackson was also married when she began to preach. Unlike her well-known Black woman preaching contemporaries, Jackson split from her husband when he antagonized her for her public preaching career and theological ideas. Rather than conforming to the heteronormative expectations of her time, she refused heteronormativity because it failed her. She ended her marriage, became a Shaker, and took a strict vow of celibacy. After splitting from her husband, she maintained a close and intimate relationship with her lifelong disciple, Rebecca Perot.[47] Archival records reflect that although the bond between the Rebeccas was close, it was not necessarily sexual in nature because of their shared spiritual commitment to celibacy.

The intimate relationship between the Rebeccas indicates that Black Christian women in the nineteenth century formed private worlds of proto–Black feminist erotic and nonerotic love. Their theologies were born of violence and shared intimate bonds; their theologies offered them a reprieve from sexual, racial, and gendered terror. Nineteenth-century Black women itinerant preachers were the first in a legacy of Black women within the Christian ethical tradition to balance a profound dilemma. They balanced their desire to speak universally about how God intervened in the human condition and their need to speak with specificity about the distinct experiences of Black women whose theology began from a need to disentangle centuries of historically conditioned value judgments based on race, gender, and class.[48]

After her husband died in 1823, Elaw did not immediately begin her life as an itinerant minister. Instead, she and her daughter worked as domestic servants to liquidate their debts. When her health became too impaired for her to continue as a domestic servant, Elaw opened a school, which became successful because of support she received from the Society of Friends (Quakers). In *Memoirs*, Elaw remembered a time when members of the Society of Friends invited strangers to come to her school in Burlington, New Jersey. She recounted that the white onlookers were gratified to see the Black children, who, because of their race, were turned away from most schools, being taught by a woman of color. Although she enjoyed her work as an educator, she soon remembered her "commission . . . from the Lord" to be an itinerant preacher.

A few years later, Elaw submitted to her compulsions to preach. When she resumed her preaching ministry, she placed her daughter under a relative's care and traveled to Philadelphia to begin preaching.[49] While her preaching was about walking with all people on their journey to God, her race, gender, class, and marital status shaped each step. Now, without the judgment of her husband, and with her daughter receiving care from a loving relative, she felt free to travel as God compelled her. Her early itinerant ministry was completely self-supported. She visited and preached to people of all races in Baltimore; Washington, DC; Alexandria, Virginia; Annapolis, Maryland, and elsewhere throughout the upper South. She also traveled freely in the mid-Atlantic and northeastern states, and met with considerable ministerial success.

When she wrote about the time after her husband's death and reflected on the nature of white supremacy, she wrote that the "pride of a white skin is a bauble of great value with many in some parts of the United States." She accused people with white skin of being willing to "sacrifice their intelligence to their prejudices." However, she dismissed white supremacy as both anti-intellectual and ungodly. She wrote, "The Almighty accounts not the black races of man either in the order of nature or spiritual capacity as inferior to the white; for He bestows his Holy Spirit on, and dwells in them as readily as in persons of whiter complexion: The Ethiopian eunuch was adopted as a son and heir of God; and when Ethiopia shall stretch forth her hands . . . their submission and worship will be graciously accepted."[50]

Elaw's assertion that she and other Black Americans were like a dark-skinned, sexually nonnormative man in the ancient world indicates that she thought Black people were far from recognized in seats of power in the United States. Elaw was not alone among Black American theological thinkers and religious groups who frequently referred to Black Americans as the Ethiopians of the Christian Scriptures. However, she diverges from her contemporaries because she contended that Black Americans shared the social positionality of the converted Ethiopian eunuch. Her comparison indicates that Elaw tied Blackness in the United States to experiences of sexual and gender violence.

Through her comparison, Elaw argued that all Black people, regardless of gender, shared the social positionality of a socially ostracized dark-skinned male stranger. Her words indicated that she believed that experience of slavery both ungendered and hyper-gendered enslaved people of African descent.[51] However, her words also compared all Black Americans to a man who was socially othered because he was sexually nonnormative. She might have believed that Black Americans were violated, not just by the Middle Passage, slavery, and slavery's afterlife, but also by sexual terror enacted upon them by those who exercised power over them. While her reference to the Ethiopian eunuch is brief, it indicates that Black Christian women in the United States participated in what historian Darlene Clark Hines has called a "culture of dissemblance." Nineteenth-century free Black women carefully navigated a culture of sexual violation that disempowered Black people of all genders in the nineteenth century.[52]

The figure of the Ethiopian eunuch in Acts 8 is a complicated one. In the fourteen-verse passage, he is described only by the region from which he came, his position in the royal court, and his sexual nonnormativity. We do not learn the details of his story or what he did after his encounter with an early Church evangelist named Philip. In the first century, the word "Ethiopian" referred to anyone with dark skin, and especially those from south of Egypt. They were considered to be those who lived at the end of the earth.[53] To call a person an Ethiopian did not indicate their nationality. Rather, it situated them as a social and cultural other. Therefore, the biblical term "Ethiopian" is not synonymous with understandings of Blackness in the nineteenth century. Elaw did not necessarily compare Black Americans to the Ethiopian because of their shared complexion. Rather, she offered an astute theory that, as in the case of the Ethiopian man in the Acts 8 story, slavery made all Black people strangers in a strange land.[54] Like the Ethiopian figure in Acts, they existed at the ideological ends of the earth.

In addition to being described as an Ethiopian, the Acts 8 eunuch was othered by his status as a servant to "the Candace." This was the title bestowed on the queen of Meroe, a Nubian realm on the upper Nile.[55] The Candace was the queen of those who lived at the end of the earth. Many Hebrew Bible scholars agree that eunuchs were high-ranking male officials in a royal court, but they disagree about their sexual status. However, most Greek audiences would read the Acts 8 eunuch as a castrated man who served in a queen's court.[56] The Ethiopian eunuch had substantial power as the manager of the queen's treasury. In Acts 8, he was returning home from Jerusalem where he had gone to worship. A cultural outsider wherever he went, he found that his belief in the God of Israel created a sense of home and belonging for him.

Zilpha Elaw longed to receive the acceptance from her racial and religious communities that the Ethiopian eunuch received from Philip in Acts 8. As he traveled home from Jerusalem, the Ethiopian eunuch read from Isaiah (53:7–8). The Isaiah passage encouraged the Israelites as they suffered. It asserted that those who suffered well would be uplifted. In the Isaiah passage, the suffering servant was opposed and afflicted, and through it all he remained silent. Instead of receiving justice, he was led away and killed because of the transgressions of others. Philip believed his encounter with the pious Ethiopian eunuch to be an evangelistic opportunity. Philip approached the eunuch's chariot to inquire whether he understood what he was reading. The eunuch asked how he could understand the words if no one interpreted them for him. He invited Philip to help him interpret what he read. Philip responded by teaching him the Christian theological perspectives on the passage from Isaiah. After learning Philip's Christian theological perspective, the eunuch asked to be baptized in a body of water. Baptism is a spiritual practice that indicates that the believer has died to their old self and is prepared to become a new person in Jesus. Philip agreed to perform the Ethiopian eunuch's baptism in a body of water they passed during their travels. After his baptism, the eunuch emerged from the water to find that Philip was gone. Although Philip was no longer with him, the Ethiopian eunuch felt accepted into God's family. Perhaps Elaw could relate to this part of the eunuch's story. She too felt deeply connected to the Christian faith despite the ephemerality of God's presence in her life. From her youth, she saw visions of God's glory. Although the visions were fleeting, they inspired her to a life of service to God.

The Ethiopian eunuch's story and Elaw's reference to it introduces an array of contradictions about who could belong in the early Christian community. The Ethiopian eunuch was an outsider who was marked by his nationality, skin color, and status as a sexually nonnormative person. However, he also had close proximity to extraordinary wealth. Although he was culturally different from the people he encountered on the road between Jerusalem and Gaza, he was also in a different socioeconomic class. As he traveled, he rode in a chariot. Meanwhile, Philip presumably traveled on foot. The Ethiopian eunuch's proximity to wealth begs the question of whether Philip would have interpreted the Christian scriptures and welcomed into the Christian community an Ethiopian stranger who was not easily identifiable as an elite.

Like the Ethiopian eunuch, Elaw had relative privilege when compared to other nineteenth-century African diasporic people in the United States. She was born to free parents in Philadelphia, educated by Quakers, and stayed at home to raise her child until her husband's untimely death compelled her to speak boldly about her beliefs and publish her writings. Opportunities to share ideas in public and self-publish them for an audience were not available to most people of any race in the 1830s and 1840s. Despite the complications of comparing Black people to a person who enjoyed relative privilege in his time, Elaw's Black queer theological response to claims of white superiority in the United States exposed the idea of white superiority as a farce. Her evocation of the eunuch figure allowed her to demonstrate the irrationality of anti-Blackness. In a society that was settled by white Europeans, people of African descent were culturally othered. However, Elaw's use of the story also indicates that she believed that people of all ethnicities and cultures must be introduced to Christianity. Through his radical welcome of the Ethiopian stranger, Philip introduced the Christian tradition to people who lived at the proverbial ends of the earth. These newest potential converts brought their rich cultural traditions. Their contributions served to expand and complicate the Christian theological story. Elaw indicated that if they were open to doing so, white American Christians had a unique opportunity to open their faith to those who were strangers in a strange land. She also gestured toward the unique contributions that people who possessed an outsider status would bring to the Christian "family." She believed that if more people knew of God's love for the most degraded people in society, those who held to racial myths could also believe that God loved them.

Elaw's exegesis of the Ethiopian eunuch passage in Acts 8 did not end with an expectation that white Americans would be convinced that they must overturn white supremacy. Instead, she encouraged other Black people to turn to God for help. Borrowing Psalm 63:8, she wrote, "Let Ethiopia hasten to stretch out its hands to God." Her use of this verse placed her within the African diasporic tradition of rhetoricians and preachers in the nineteenth century who also used God's love for Ethiopia to cultivate a sense of racial pride.[57] Elaw stated that she wrote *Memoirs* for her friends in England, but she also hoped that other African diasporic people would be inspired by her words and experiences. She encouraged people who shared her race not to wait passively for equality. She urged them to follow her example by asking God to help them. She assured them that when they turned to God, "their submission and worship will be graciously accepted."[58]

CONCLUSION

Through her Black queer and abolitionist ministry of spectacle, Zilpha Elaw drew many people into the Christian faith. Her theology inspired and converted others, but it also helped her navigate the losses she had experienced during her life. In the narrowest sense of the term, Elaw was not an abolitionist. In her spiritual autobiography she never explicitly called for slavery's abolition, nor did she write at length about her attitudes about the institution of slavery. However, this essay has argued that a Black queer approach to Christianity is a critical, albeit overlooked, aspect of the abolitionist tradition. Elaw's Black queer refusal to conform to any of the social inhibitions of her time and her determination to courageously pursue an itinerant preaching ministry, despite encountering closed doors at every turn, reveal that abolition is both a theory and praxis. Her way of navigating in the world demanded that all people who called themselves Christians create alternative forms of sociality in which all people were radically free.

In the social world that Elaw created through *Memoirs* and in her boundary-defying preaching ministry, the categories of male and female, enslaved and free, rich and poor, Black and white, do not exist. Her writing breaks down the socially constructed differences between humans, dismissing them all as "nursery prejudices" that must be outgrown.[59] Her theology, which is categorized as Black queer, allowed her to cast off such prejudices. Zilpha Elaw used her ministry, her life experiences, and her written description of the movements of her soul to work toward a world that was more whole, more free, and more spectacular.

NOTES

1. In this essay, I use the word "evangelical" in the form it took in the first century CE. It derives from the Greek word *euangelion*, which roughly translates to "gospel" or "good news." Elaw proclaimed what she believed was the "good news" of Jesus's love for all people, regardless of their social status.

2. See Elaw's "Dedication" in "Memoirs of the Life, Religious Experience, Ministerial Travels, and Labours of Mrs. Elaw," in *Sisters of the Spirit: Three Black Women's Autobiographies of the Nineteenth Century*, ed. William L. Andrews (Bloomington: Indiana University Press, 1986), 51–52.

3. Zilpha Elaw, "Memoirs of the Life, Religious Experience, Ministerial Travels, and Labours of Mrs. Elaw," in *Sisters of the Spirit*, ed. William L. Andrews, 85 (hereafter cited as Elaw, *Memoirs*).

4. Beverly Guy-Sheftall, "The Combahee River Collective," in *Words of Fire: An Anthology of African-American Feminist Thought* (New York: New Press, 1995), 231–40.

5. See Marquis Bey and Jesse A. Goldberg, "Queer as in Abolition Now!" *GLQ: A Journal of Lesbian and Gay Studies* 28, no. 2 (April 1, 2022): 159–63.

6. Elaw, *Memoirs*, 141.

7. I engage with José Esteban Muñoz, *Disidentifications: Queers of Color and the Performance of Politics* (Minneapolis: University of Minnesota Press, 2009); Muñoz, *Cruising Utopia: The Then and There of Queer Futurity* (New York: New York University Press, 2009); E. Patrick Johnson, *Honeypot: Black Southern Women Who Love Women* (Durham, NC: Duke University Press, 2019); Ashon T. Crawley, *The Lonely Letters* (Durham, NC: Duke University Press, 2020); Kelly Brown Douglas, *Sexuality and the Black Church: A Womanist Perspective* (Maryknoll, NY: Orbis Books, 1999); Ahmad Greene-Hayes, "'Queering' African American Religious History," *Religion Compass* 13, no. 7 (2019); and Alice Walker, *In Search of Our Mothers' Gardens: Womanist Prose* (New York: Harcourt, 1983).

8. I borrow this idea from Stacey M Floyd-Thomas, *Mining the Motherlode: Methods in Womanist Ethics* (Cleveland: Pilgrim Press, 2006), 9.

9. Audre Lorde, *Sister Outsider: Essays and Speeches* (Berkeley: Crossing Press, 2007).

10. See Saidiya V. Hartman, *Scenes of Subjection: Terror, Slavery, and Self-Making in Nineteenth Century America* (New York: Oxford University Press, 1997), 9.

11. Here I refer to the theory of racial capitalism by building on Cathy Cohen's work in "Punks, Bulldaggers, and Welfare Queens: The Real Radical Potential of Queer Politics?"

in *Black Queer Studies: A Critical Anthology*, ed. Mae Henderson and Patrick E. Johnson (Durham, NC: Duke University Press, 2005), 21–51; and Cohen, "The Radical Potential Of Queer? Twenty Years Later," *GLQ: A Journal of Lesbian and Gay Studies* 25, no. 1 (January 1, 2019): 140–44. See Grace Kyungwon Hong, *Death beyond Disavowal: The Impossible Politics of Difference* (Minneapolis: University of Minnesota Press, 2015), 157n29.

12. Such actions were legal because of the Fugitive Slave Acts of 1793. Abolitionist newspapers and antislavery reports from the 1830s, 1840s, and 1850s frequently shared the harrowing reports of what they called "man-stealing" in New England and throughout the South, even of free Black Americans.

13. "The Annual Report of the American and Foreign Anti-Slavery Society, Presented at New York" (William Harned, for the American and Foreign Anti-Slavery Society, May 7, 1850), American Congregational Library.

14. Andrews, ed., *Sisters of the Spirit*, 2, 6.

15. Elaw, *Memoirs*, 138.

16. The phrase "errand into the wilderness" was often used in New England. It originates from a sermon delivered before the General Assembly of the Massachusetts Colony on the Day of Election in 1670 by Samuel Danforth. *American Sermons: The Pilgrims to Martin Luther King Jr.* (New York: Library of America, distrib. Penguin Putnam, 1999), 151–71.

17. See "Document 21: General Association of Massachusetts Congregational Churches, 'Pastoral Letter,' 28 June 1837," Alexander Street Documents.

18. Elaw, *Memoirs*, 61–62.

19. Kathleen M. Brown, *Good Wives, Nasty Wenches, and Anxious Patriarchs: Gender, Race, and Power in Colonial Virginia* (Chapel Hill: University of North Carolina Press, 1996); and Jennifer Lyle Morgan, *Laboring Women: Reproduction and Gender in New World Slavery* (Philadelphia: University of Pennsylvania Press, 2004).

20. "The Constitution of the United States with All the Acts of Congress in Relation to Slavery" (D. M. Dewey: Arcade Hall, Rochester, NY, 1854), Boston Athenaeum, 16–17.

21. "Annual Report of the American and Foreign Anti-Slavery Society," 86.

22. On rival geographies, see Stephanie M. H. Camp, *Closer to Freedom: Enslaved Women and Everyday Resistance in the Plantation South* (Chapel Hill: University of North Carolina Press, 2004).

23. "Report of the Boston Female Anti-Slavery Society with a Sketch of the Obstacles Thrown in the Way of Emancipation by Certain Clerical Abolitionists and Advocates for the Subjugation of Woman" (Boston, No. 25, Cornhill, 1837), American Congregational Library.

24. Elaw, *Memoirs*, 158.

25. Kimberly Blockett, "Disrupting Print: Emigration, the Press, and Narrative Subjectivity in the British Preaching and Writing of Zilpha Elaw, 1840–1860s," *MELUS: Multi-Ethnic Literature of the United States* 40, no. 3 (September 2015): 96.

26. Elaw, *Memoirs*, 83.

27. Perhaps the most influential of these visitors were poet Phillis Wheatley and Olaudah Equiano. Wheatley visited with her owners' son in 1773 to improve her health and meet with people of high social standing to show them her poetry. Her poetry is published in one volume called *Poems on Various Subjects, Religious and Moral by Phillis Wheatley, Negro Servant to Mr. John Wheatley, of Boston, in New England*, which was published in London. Olaudah

Equiano is often described as the author of the first slave narrative. His autobiographical *The Interesting Narrative of the Life of Olaudah Equiano, or Gustavus Vassa, the African* was also published in London in 1789.

28. Elaw, *Memoirs*, 141.

29. See Muñoz's theorization of the possibilities of queerness in Muñoz, *Cruising Utopia.*

30. Elaw, *Memoirs*, 160.

31. Elaw, *Memoirs*, 54.

32. Elaw, *Memoirs*, 53–54.

33. Elaw, *Memoirs*, 55.

34. For example, in Romans 14:10–12; 2 Corinthians 5:10; and Revelation 11:18.

35. She was allowed (likely by the Mitchel family) to attend meetings once every fourteen days.

36. Elaw, *Memoirs*, 55–57.

37. Elaw, *Memoirs*, 58.

38. Elaw, *Memoirs*, 64.

39. Elaw, *Memoirs*, 64–66.

40. Elaw, *Memoirs*, 70–71.

41. Elaw, *Memoirs*, 63.

42. Elaw, *Memoirs*, 84.

43. Elaw, *Memoirs*, 62.

44. Tina Marie Campt, *Listening to Images* (Durham, NC: Duke University Press, 2017), 17.

45. Elaw, *Memoirs*, 85.

46. See Catherine A. Brekus, *Strangers and Pilgrims: Female Preaching in America, 1740–1845* (Chapel Hill: University of North Carolina Press, 1998).

47. Rebecca Jackson and Jean McMahon Humez, *Gifts of Power: The Writings of Rebecca Jackson, Black Visionary, Shaker Eldress* (Amherst: University of Massachusetts Press, 1987), 8–9.

48. Katie G. Cannon, "Hitting a Straight Lick with a Crooked Stick: The Womanist Dilemma in the Development of a Black Liberation Ethic," *Annual of the Society of Christian Ethics* 7 (1987): 165–77.

49. Elaw, *Memoirs*, 85–89.

50. Elaw, *Memoirs*, 85.

51. Hortense Spillers, "Mama's Baby, Papa's Maybe: An American Grammar Book," *Diacritics* 17 (Summer 1987): 65–81.

52. The culture of dissemblance is a practice Black women adopted to help them survive violent experiences by masking their true feelings. See Darlene Clark Hine, "Rape and the Inner Lives of Black Women in the Middle West," *Signs* 14, no. 4 (1989): 912–20. On sexuality and Black life in the Americas, see Daina Ramey Berry and Leslie M. Harris, eds., *Sexuality and Slavery: Reclaiming Intimate Histories in the Americas* (Athens: University of Georgia Press, 2018).

53. Jouette M. Bassler et al., "Acts 8:27 Note," in *The HarperCollins Study Bible: Fully Revised Standard Version, with the Apocryphal/Deuterocanonical Books Student Edition* (New York: HarperCollins, 2006).

54. "The most universal definition of the slave is a stranger . . . the slave defines the position of the outsider." In the sixteenth and seventeenth centuries, slavery created the color line, but processes of othering existed throughout human history. See Saidiya V. Hartman, *Lose Your Mother: A Journey along the Atlantic Slave Route* (New York: Farrar, Straus, and Giroux, 2007), 5.

55. See notes to Bassler et al., "Acts 8:27 Note."

56. Sean D. Burke, *Queering the Ethiopian Eunuch: Strategies of Ambiguity in Acts* (New York: Fortress Press, 2013), 19–38.

57. Lena Ampadu, "Maria W. Stewart and the Rhetoric of Black Preaching: Perspectives on Womanism and Black Nationalism," in *Black Women's Intellectual Traditions: Speaking Their Minds*, ed. Kristin Waters and Carol B. Conaway (Burlington: University of Vermont Press, 2007), 38–54.

58. Elaw, *Memoirs*, 85.

59. Elaw, *Memoirs*, 86.

Vessels of Salvation

Taste and the Adoption of Architectural Standards in Southern Methodism during the Long Progressive Era

CHRISTOPHER M. BISHOP

In May 1870, the General Conference of the Methodist Episcopal Church, South (MECS) met in Memphis. In addition to the contentious business of running the Church, the conference directed the Southern Methodist Publishing House to produce "a manual on church-architecture, adapted to the wants and character of Southern Methodism . . . and particularly in the view of improvement in the design and construction of houses of worship, at comparatively small cost." Albert H. Redford, the head of the publishing house in Nashville, searched for an expert within MECS circles to complete this manual and quickly set his sights on William McKendree Patterson, who had just completed a tenure as pastor of the Central Methodist Church in Memphis, where he led the congregation through the construction of a Gothic sanctuary widely hailed "by ministers and laymen from various sections of the country, a '*model church*.'" After Redford tapped him for the project, Patterson guided several other congregations through building projects while he completed the manual, which assisted the writing process.[1]

Published in 1875, Patterson's *Manual of Architecture* provided expert advice on every aspect of church construction, established benchmarks and technical protocols, and included recipes for materials ranging from paint to plaster and wallpaper paste. Patterson demanded cutting-edge technology, including modern lighting, temperature control, ventilation, and acoustics that created buildings ideal for both music and the spoken word, and offered physical comfort while conforming to the latest public health standards. He stressed preparation, efficiency, and standardization. Far more than a handbook, Patterson's *Manual of Architecture* urged southern Methodists to reimagine their sacred spaces as elegant vessels of salvation that catered to ordered, liturgical worship preferred by the white middle class, while deliberately eschewing designs associated with small-town churches and rural meetinghouses.

This guidebook signaled the growing importance of the middle class to the MECS, but it is also illustrative of trends that extend beyond the realm of denominational history. Written and published amid the backdrop of Reconstruction and the Gilded Age, Patterson's manual is striking evidence that southern white evangelicals were actively engaged in the earliest phases of the Progressive movement. Conventionally understood as an urban-based reform program to ameliorate conditions associated with rapid industrialization, Progressivism has traditionally been seen to privilege actors and organizations working toward political and legislative goals addressing political corruption, morality, public health, education, economics, and social welfare. When assessing the short- and long-term results of Progressivism, historians consider the extent to which proposals ultimately became law, while simultaneously investigating the effectiveness and consequences of legislative and policy decisions. Nevertheless, scholars have long understood the connection between notions of rationalization, standardization, bureaucratization, professionalization, and reform as a broad movement led by middle-class experts to restructure American society in response to the "hierarchical needs of urban-industrial life." In this way, institutions that should be correctly identified as Progressive created bureaucracies, pursued standardization, and adopted new management techniques. Patterson's manual allows historians to pinpoint the adoption of new structures and methods in understudied institutions like the MECS and to reconsider the place of the South and southern churches within the Progressive era, in terms not only of timing but also of productivity.[2]

Patterson's manual further demonstrates ways historical actors created and codified standards of taste. Patterson leaned heavily on technology, science, and personal expertise, and presented a decidedly bourgeois aesthetic as empirical, unassailable, and universal. For Patterson, then, proper taste both defined and promoted proper religion. His manual and other church structures served notice to southern Methodists that the standards and protocols in the manual were the only way to be healthy, to be evangelical, and to be modern. As Pierre Bourdieu has demonstrated, taste for art and the cultural competency necessary to consume it are signifiers of class, privilege, and education legitimated through bourgeois institutions such as schools and universities.[3] Patterson's manual not only shows the codification of standards of taste, but also provides justifications for these bourgeois standards, a striking example of Bourdieu's thesis in action. Given the historical moment, Patterson's manual is also a discourse of modernity, rooted in the New South, of a denomination that sought to position itself relative to its northern counterpart, of an emerging urban middle class seeking to grow and maintain power, and of a church shifting from rural and extemporaneous worship to a model that was both urban and liturgical. These institutional standards of taste and aesthetics, drawn from a middle-class vision of modernity, changed practices and signified class differences.

The MECS was hardly unique in its desire to build new and sophisticated churches, and this era is regarded by architectural historians as one of the most productive in American history. Other denominations, in the North and the South, published similar guidebooks to push costs down, streamline processes, and codify institutional knowledge. These manuals were a practical necessity, because most congregations did not have laymen who understood the nuances of architecture and construction and who were able to volunteer their time and expertise. Moreover, few pastors had the necessary training or technical proficiency relevant to shepherd their flock through the construction process from beginning to end. Without a firm grasp on technical details and a clear understanding of architectural principles, money could easily be misspent and cause bitter infighting that could rock a church to its foundation. Even wealthy churches struggled to pay for architects and competent craftsmanship, and church officials nervously watched as some congregations took on dangerous levels of debt to pay for new buildings.[4]

The MECS congregation in the District of Columbia was frequently cited as a cautionary tale about the perils of debt. The congregation was comparatively small, and most Methodists in the city were affiliated with the wealthier northern branch of Methodism, the Methodist Episcopal Church (MEC). The two denominations had a longstanding rivalry, and feelings were especially raw in 1870. During the Civil War, high-ranking MEC officials leaned on connections in the War Department to turn over MECS pulpits in territory under Union control to northern Methodist missionaries in a short-lived attempt to impose religious reconstruction on the MECS. Throughout the spring of 1866, southern Methodists endured the indignity of forcing interlopers out of their pulpits, which fueled their hatred for generations. Because they were in the capital, the Washington congregation felt added pressure to live up to the standard set by their wealthier counterparts and took on heavy debt to build a new sanctuary, based on the erroneous assumption that travelers and government officials from the South would attend on Sunday mornings and provide reliable financial support. Predictably, this never materialized, the church quickly got in over its head, and eventually every dime the congregation brought in went to pay down the interest, leaving a large principal untouched, paralyzing the congregation financially. What was originally a plan to raise the profile of the MECS in the capital devolved into a conspicuous humiliation, to the extent that the 1874 and 1878 General Conferences pleaded for donations to help bail out the congregation. Progressives throughout the southern Church quivered in anger when they thought of northern Methodists in the capital snickering over the affair—they knew they had to do better.[5]

As the Washington example illustrates, middle-class Progressives longed for churchly buildings that communicated good taste to their neighbors, but there was a right way and wrong way to handle things. Certainly, Progressive clergy and laypersons within the MECS would not argue with this congregation's desire to have a building in line with prevailing bourgeois aesthetics, but projects like this could not be undertaken at the expense of their reputation. Systematic preparations and close budgeting were parts of proper taste and religion, and unwieldy debt easily could turn a tasteful building into a gauche spectacle of sinful hubris. By providing standardized templates with detailed instructions that allowed for customization, Patterson's manual would mitigate the risk that disgraced the Washington church while still providing for buildings that would garner the respect of outsiders.

Patterson perhaps felt the frustration over the Washington church more keenly than most. He was born in 1838 near St. Louis, and his father was a Methodist preacher in Missouri, where the two denominations openly (and sometimes violently) competed. Patterson graduated from St. Charles College in 1860 and matriculated to the MEC's Theological Institute in Concord, New Hampshire (now the Boston University School of Theology). Patterson returned to Missouri in the fall of 1861 and enlisted as a Confederate chaplain in General Sterling Price's brigade. He was eventually captured and spent the last year of the war in a northern prisoner camp. In 1865, Patterson took a position with the American Bible Society, headquartered in New York City, which sent him to Memphis to oversee distribution of Bibles throughout the Deep South. Patterson soon left this position, reentered full-time ministry, and was assigned to Central Methodist in Memphis, where he made his reputation in church architecture. Raised in the border region where religious and political affiliation were intertwined, educated at a northern Methodist seminary, and employed by a New York-based charity, Patterson understood how those inside and outside the southern heartland viewed the MECS. It is no accident that his manual emulated the example of mainstream institutions in the North.[6]

Patterson's overarching goal was to codify middle-class standards of taste to create a universal standard, an architectural philosophy everyone would instantly recognize and respect. In his preface, Patterson quoted Thomas O. Summers, the editor of the denomination-wide newspaper, *Christian Advocate*. Throughout his lengthy tenure at the newspaper, the English-born editor promoted a range of Progressive reforms, particularly regarding education, and he eagerly supported Patterson's plans as well. Summers asserted, "There should be a due regard to architectural beauty. The house of worship should be an attractive place. There should be no extravagance in ornamentation, but there should be no violation of the recognized principles of architecture." According to both men, a church should be easily distinguishable from a warehouse or a cotton gin, but Summers and Patterson were concerned about the message Methodists were sending to their neighbors with uninspiring architectural designs. Summers maintained that "it is not a healthy sign of public sentiment and feeling where noble and attractive buildings are devoted to commerce and amusement, to science and literature, while bald and repulsive buildings are given to the worship of God." Patterson reminded congregations that architecture would be a substantial part of their legacy and that they should put the aesthetic appeal of their buildings front and center in their plans or endure ignominy when their children would inevitably "be compelled to pull it down and build another in its place."[7]

Patterson and Summers were not merely interested in upgrading standards because of some abiding interest in architectural beauty. Progressive leaders in the Church believed that the MECS was at a crossroads and that the demands of modern evangelism required a different way of imagining sacred space. Patterson maintained "that the character of our houses of worship concerns in a great degree the success and prosperity of the Church." Citing Christ's Great Commission to spread the Gospel to everybody (Matthew 28:16–20), Patterson argued that the MECS had a biblical mandate to construct churches that would be appealing to all classes, particularly affluent professionals in growing cities and towns. This was a tacit acknowledgment that the MECS already had the loyalty of country folk and a not-so-subtle allusion to long-simmering class conflict within the Church that occasionally boiled over into nasty public spectacles. In addition to frustration with northern perceptions, Progressives in the MECS believed that southern elites in other denominations considered them to be rubes who heard fanatical ravings from circuit riders in crude meetinghouses. Progressives were sure that if the Church remained focused on its declining rural constituency, then southern Methodism would be regarded as a primitive vestige of a preindustrial society, eventually to be relegated, in the words of Bishop Holland N. McTyeire, "to the shades of oblivion." McTyeire summed up the situation: "What our enemies and patronizing friends have said of us is even so—that Methodism will do very well for rude settlements and common people, but when they have become cultivated and refined, we are to turn them over to other Churches prepared to take charge of them!"[8]

Patterson claimed that his aesthetic vision was universally beneficial. For example, splendid architecture would elevate the young, "who are taught the sublime principles of the gospel from its pulpit." These assertions of universality echoed Progressive arguments in favor of establishing a seminary to educate southern Methodist ministers, one of the most contentious issues in MECS politics. Advocates believed that seminary-trained ministers would help the MECS make inroads with the middle class while simultaneously uplifting the unsophisticated. Conservatives countered that a seminary requirement would be cost-prohibitive to most ministerial candidates, supplant the saliency of the call of God, transform the clerical fraternity into a brahmin caste, and produce preachers who delivered dry lectures instead of evangelical sermons. Landon Garland, a prominent academic, rejected these fears and defended seminary education, which would transform rustic candidates into renaissance men whose sermons would flow majestically, "like living water gushing from an inexhaustible fountain—full, clear, sparkling, and refreshing." Because such preaching would be universally beneficial, there were no drawbacks to a seminary. Similarly, elevating architectural standards could only help the Church because everybody would immediately respect a church that looked like a church. Sermons reached their full potential in churchly buildings that would "enlarge and liberalize . . . [a parishioner's] views, refine his taste, and quicken his emotional nature, and elevate intellectually and morally all who do not, through ignorance or prejudice, resist their influence." Each congregation then had a moral duty to make their church "in all respects the *best* its supporters can make it."[9]

Conservatives also feared that ostentatious buildings would alienate their traditional constituency, but Patterson brusquely dismissed the fear that codifying standards of taste would normalize class differences and turn away "plain folk" southerners. He cited the example of Roman Catholics, who had the most ornate churches but who had a higher proportion of poor congregants than other denominations. Critics also found it inconceivable that Methodists would emulate pagans and Roman Catholics in their architecture. Patterson reassured his audience that Romanesque styles did not somehow venerate pagan gods. Nor would Gothic designs mean that southern Methodists had gone soft on Catholicism, "However the Romish religion may be 'petrified,' and to whatever extent the 'cathedral' may be involved in the petrification as its cause, there is nothing in the 'Gothic' style itself that is stiff, cold, formal, or repulsive; but rather, there may be manifested in it more life, beauty, skill, and design than in any other." To underline this point, Patterson included the plans for the Gothic building he originally used when he was pastor of Central in Memphis, which also fit with the ongoing popularity of the Gothic Revival among American Protestants.[10]

In addition to the social and religious costs that conservatives dreaded, there was the practical concern that these kinds of buildings simply cost too much. To reduce expenses, Patterson stressed expertise, process, and standardization, which were consistent with the dominant strain of Progressivism in the United States. The first step of fiscally disciplined church construction was organizing a building committee made up of businessmen, merchants, and lawyers who had experience with legal paperwork and balance sheets, and who were "acquainted with the quality and value of materials, knowing how to direct labor to the best advantage, competent to detect any slight of the work or wrong execution of details by such mechanics as aim only to make their work 'pass muster' with their employer." Patterson demanded that committees maintain professionalism, elect officers with clearly defined duties, conform to rules of order, and only use itemized and legally binding contracts. No work could be done based on a handshake. They could lean on personal connections when negotiating prices, but the committee had an obligation to see that the work was completed "in accordance with strict business rules." Patterson underscored the importance of middle-class leadership in Progressivism. Specialized knowledge obliged nonexperts to defer to bourgeois professionals, who presumably knew better and could be trusted more than laypersons, which helped the middle class legitimize their aesthetic preferences.[11]

While committees should not be parsimonious, they needed to spend money wisely. "Economy," Patterson asserted, "both as a business principle and a religious duty, is never to be lost sight of in church-building." He recommended raising at least three-quarters of the projected budget before starting construction. From his experience, it was easier to raise the last quarter if the project was proceeding on budget and on time. Such donations bestowed responsibility on the committee to plan the enterprise down to the penny, but, at the same time, they should recognize their own limitations, defer to experts when necessary, and never cut corners. They ought to hire an experienced architect at the outset or purchase predesigned plans. He complained that one congregation refused to pay ten dollars for used blueprints, citing cost concerns, but "nearly that amount was paid for remodeling a door, the size of which had not been correctly *guessed*." Even after the church in question paid to have the door professionally repaired, it never looked quite right and became an eyesore. Unsurprisingly, when a committee spent money where necessary, these embarrassing mistakes did not happen.[12]

Committees had to be willing to jump into minutiae, including detailed specifications and formulas. For instance, committees had to make crucial decisions regarding seating capacity that would determine the size and potential location of the building. When weighing the potential growth of neighborhoods in discussions of ideal seating capacity, committees should ignore the optimistic speculation of boosters and rely on hard evidence and realistic appraisals of their needs. For example, churches should generally not seat more than 500 people. There was no reason to build a church so large the preacher could not be easily heard without being hoarse by the end of the sermon, and it would be an embarrassment to have a church so cavernous that it would be fully "occupied only once in five or ten years, on some extraordinary occasion." Untrained designers often overestimated how many people could comfortably sit in a room, and since most voices could only travel around eighty feet, practicality should shape these decisions. Patterson provided a formula to determine dimensions and seating capacity, "*The length of a given room (inside), multiplied by its width, and the product divided by seven (7), will give the number of regular sittings in that room.*" If, for example, a church was 35 × 50 feet in size, it could comfortably seat 250 people.[13]

After adopting comprehensive plans that considered seating, music, education, and outreach, the committee needed to select a building lot. If members could not easily get there either by foot or by streetcar, the church would suffer in the long run. A great location, however, would draw in new members. Churches often had members willing to donate land, but Patterson cautioned that such gifts (however well intentioned) were not always wise. In addition to feelings of benevolence, some might hope to offload a tax burden that they were having trouble selling. Patterson advised that churches be located away from commercial centers so that city noise would not interfere with worship, but also be within walking distance of a "public conveyance" so that people who lived at a distance or who had physical limitations could still attend. The lot should allow an edifice to be 20–40 feet from the street and, if possible, should face south to let in light from windows facing east. Patterson's insistence that churches be located away from the city center seems benign on the face, but it underlined a growing trend in American churches. Suburban communities and exclusive residential sectors tended to have homogeneous class and racial character, and Patterson's guidelines intentionally encouraged the segmentation of MECS congregations along class lines.[14]

Patterson built flexibility into his designs, highlighting the influence of standardization in Progressive management. For example, depending on budgets and preferences, a committee might choose a brick exterior or a stone façade, either of which could be used with the same basic floorplan. Through long sections detailing the benefits and drawbacks of various materials, Patterson provided formulas so committees could buy the correct amount of material and accurately plan budgets. For example, to calculate how many bricks should make up a wall, Patterson instructed: "*multiply the superficial feet of the wall by 7, and then by the number of widths (4 1/2 in.) in the thickness of the wall.*" He printed tables comparing the cost of doors and windows based on varying size and material, with charts detailing how much weight different metals and woods could support when used for ceiling support or door frames. When considering the exterior, Patterson urged committees to include a "spire, tower, or cupola" to "distinguish the building from others of common use." Although it was not appropriate to be ostentatious, "a duly-proportioned spire" was "very desirable." Churches could also consider the addition of bells. Not overlooking any detail, the manual provided specifications for belfries that would project sound to neighboring communities. All these specifications gave committees the freedom of customization to make their buildings stand out, even while using predesigned plans.[15]

Building committees had multiple options for interior walls. Patterson provided recipes for the different coats of plaster alongside instructions for their application if the congregation wanted to provide its own labor. Wooden interiors might be stained and varnished, and Patterson, true to form, detailed the process of each method alongside recipes for materials. Patterson considered paint the "finishing touch," and outlined the process for interior and exterior painting from priming all the way to the finishing coat, even including directions for specific tints ("For cream-color, add red and yellow to white"). Patterson cautioned his readers that colors needed to be well selected, which "requires both thought and taste." Churches, both old and new, could benefit from wallpaper, and "with the aid of the taste of the ladies and of the paper-seller, appropriate colors and figures can be selected." Because women had experience using wallpaper to make their homes tasteful havens from the outside world, they should be trusted as reasonable arbiters of good taste in church as well. Once selected, wallpaper was cheap, easy to maintain, and perfect to hang over old walls that might have cracks or for churches looking to refurbish a dull building with a splash of color. It was normally possible to find parishioners who could hang the wallpaper for free, reducing the cost to just the paper and the materials for the paste. Not surprisingly, Patterson had his own recipe for wallpaper paste. This level of expert detail for exterior and interior design gave Patterson's aesthetic vision credibility and did much of the hard work of institutionalizing the taste that he referenced.[16]

Patterson called for the sanctuary to be arranged like an amphitheater, emulating contemporary theaters. Charles Grandison Finney revolutionized this kind of theatrical evangelical preaching during the Second Great Awakening, and his spatial design became common in churches throughout the century. Patterson further instructed committees to approach acoustics scientifically. The pulpit should be elevated in the center of the platform so that it could be seen by everybody in the room. Because sound naturally travels up, the seats in the rear should be higher and the floor should slope downward towards the platform. This would allow people in the back to easily hear and see the preacher. Furthermore, Patterson suggested placing pews on three sides of the platform, another prominent feature in nineteenth-century theaters. While the spoken word had always been central to Methodist worship, Patterson's designs specifically appealed to middle-class audiences and imagined sacred space to feel more like a lyceum than a meetinghouse, places where both bourgeois aesthetics and erudite sermons would define the boundaries of proper religion.[17]

In addition to highlighting the spoken word, Patterson designed floorplans with music in mind. Many conservatives, however, believed that choirs and organs were an affront to Christian decency because they flaunted wealth and individual talent; further, their use sparked reprisals and, in some instances, sabotage. In 1870, for example, dissenters snuck into a church in Kokomo being used for the North Indiana Annual Conference and dumped copious amounts of pepper into the pipes of the organ. At the meeting, the playing of the organ filled the air with pepper, and an unforgettable sneezing and coughing fit seized the choir and audience, forcing everybody out to the churchyard. Patterson had no patience for this attitude and maintained that choirs and organs that led the congregation with a spirit of worship were not unseemly or flashy and were actually an essential part of modern church services. In addition to explaining that King David provided instructions to the "chief musicians" in the book of Psalms, Patterson reminded skeptical readers that John Wesley himself had said, "In all our congregations let the people learn to sing." As with other aspects of the worship environment, Patterson offered suggestions on the best ways to situate choir lofts, which should be raised but close to the floor so that parishioners could clearly see the choir members' faces and follow along.[18]

Patterson included advertisements for firms specializing in organs. Small churches could get by with cabinet organs that cost around $100, but larger congregations needed pipe organs, which ranged in price from $400 to $50,000. The organ at the Tulip Street church in Nashville is an excellent example of the type of piece common in affluent southern Methodist sanctuaries. In 1891, the Tulip Street congregation purchased an organ out of a catalogue from George Jardine and Son of New York City. Jardine sold multiple stock organs, which the firm then installed and customized based on the needs and wishes of each client. This particular organ, which cost $10,000, has 1,415 pipes, 26 different ranks or pipe "voices," and ivory keys; today it continues to serve as an impressive focal point for the sanctuary. Still, the church wanted more embellishment than Jardine provided, and it contracted a local firm to complete the white oak and cherry console. Because of the craftsmanship and expense of installation, even stock organs made up a large percentage of construction budgets. Considering the expense involved, Patterson was uncharacteristically brief on the subject, simply urging congregations to contact firms like Jardine. Because of the level of workmanship involved, however, Patterson's advice to entirely defer to experts on organs did not require extensive explanation. The Tulip Street organ is the exact type of the kind of elegant instrument Patterson envisioned for churches that could afford the expense.[19]

Patterson viewed windows and light as critical parts of church design which greatly affected their evangelical potential. Given the national trends in ecclesiastical architecture, stained glass studios thrived as never before, and southerners eagerly sought out top artists. For example, designer Nicola D'Ascenzo of Philadelphia completed windows for several southern Methodist churches, including windows at First Methodist Church in Birmingham. Patterson understood that few could hire internationally renowned artists but still demanded that congregations pay special attention to their windows. He asserted that the number of windows should be based on factors including the kind of glass, size of the room, the position of the church relative to the path of the sun, and surrounding buildings and foliage, all of which needed to be considered in advance. Patterson described the benefits and drawbacks of plain, stained, and cut glass. Plain glass was cheaper than stained or cut glass but required blinds or drapes to keep the sun out of the eyes of both preacher and parishioners. These would have to be maintained and periodically replaced. Stained glass was more expensive, but color in the designs reduced glare of the sun while creating an atmosphere suitable for worship. Cut glass provided better craftsmanship but was normally cost prohibitive for all but the most affluent of congregations. Patterson preferred stained glass not only because of how "the selection and combination of colors" could create a sacred ambiance, but for the "great durability of the work; thus bringing together the highest order of ornamentation and practical service." Patterson endorsed several firms, directing building committees toward stained glass artists such as William F. Blum of Louisville and John Hughes, who completed windows in the Broadway Methodist Church of Memphis. Patterson never commented on exactly why stained-glass windows created the ideal worship environment outside of artistry and color combinations, but Patterson was evoking the Medieval period and encouraging southern Methodists to look to the cathedrals of Europe when considering their own standards of taste and proper religion.[20]

For rainy weather, months with shorter days, or evening services, churches needed a light source besides the sun, and Patterson was particularly concerned with interior illumination. He argued that light was "a medium through which thought is conveyed and spirit communes with spirit." The audience must be able to see the preacher's face, expressions, and body language, and Patterson provided instructions to help congregations determine "the number of burners employed, and where it is best to place them," depending on the size of the room. For example, ten lamps that burned either coal oil or kerosene would adequately light a 30 × 50 foot church, although the same room needed only eight gas lamps. Chandeliers were beautiful but inefficient, and Patterson instead recommended bracket lamps along the sides of the room, which could also be placed near the pulpit for the preacher and choir. Of course, lighting contraptions gave off heat, which was generally fine in the winter, but they could make a room unbearably warm in the summer. To cut down on the need for lamps, Patterson recommended installing reflectors made of decorative corrugated glass designed to aid ventilation, amplify light, save on fuel, and beautify the room. Patterson endorsed I. P. Frink, a prominent New York artist dealing in light fixtures, when shopping for reflectors, but advised congregations to search closer to home for other light fixtures, recommending firms in Cincinnati and Memphis.[21]

Patterson considered comfort a vital aspect of ecclesiastical design. If the audience was uncomfortable or the room was unbearably warm or stuffy, the pastor stood a slim chance of preaching an effective sermon, and the church would fail in its evangelical purpose. Good comfort started with the right kind of seats. Americans have always had a strange relationship to church pews. In addition to causing a bizarre form of territorialism with the power to provoke otherwise reasonable people to storm off in a huff, pews have often been a symbol of privilege that perpetuated class differences. Pew rents have a long history in the United States, developing in the colonial era and lasting into the twentieth century. Elite families rented or purchased pews, making them heritable property, which meant that those families had guaranteed seating and bought a controlling interest in the church. In this context, pews were more than seats. Patterson discouraged but did not disavow pew rents. If congregations adopted pew rentals, "alternate ones should be reserved and kept free, so that no distinction be made in the house of God between those who possess little of this world's goods and those who have more."[22]

While Patterson claimed that churches should be open and welcoming to all, his insistence on comfortable pews highlighted his larger point of linking proper design with proper religion. Cheap pews or plank benches had no place in proper, modern worship. Some traditionalists might scoff at the expense of comfortable pews to pamper the congregation, but Patterson dismissed this concern out of hand. "The idea that a person is to do penance during the time of public worship, by sitting on a hard, rough, ill-shaped pew, when he is able to provide one of ease and comfort, finds comparatively few supporters in these days." Uncomfortable seats did nothing to enhance the spirituality of the saved, and "there is no attraction in it for the wicked to bring them to the house of God." Old-fashioned slab benches evoked a cherished era of Methodism, but such romanticism "cannot amount to an argument in favor of our adopting the same arrangement, when we have abundant means to provide a pleasant and elegant seat." Previous generations of rural Methodists might not have been able to do any better, but those days were long gone. If the MECS was going to be a modern evangelical Church, congregations needed to shell out the necessary money for proper seating. Patterson recommended congregations contact the Excelsior Church and School Furniture Company of Cincinnati and suggested their top-of-the-line Excelsior Pew made of narrow slats, which created a seat curved to fit the human form and to distribute pressure over the entire pew, obviating the need for additional cushioning. He also provided templates for churches with members capable of making pews themselves, complete with decorative flourishes and recipes for stains and varnish so that the product would be comparable to work of a major firm.[23]

Comfort extended beyond the need for ergonomic pews. Ventilation was essential to architectural design, a notion in line with prevailing public health guidelines. Patterson pleaded for proper ventilation: "Pure, fresh air is in the highest degree conducive to health, happiness, and long life." Anticipating skepticism over the expense of a proper ventilation system, Patterson quoted Joel Dorman Steele, one of the most prolific textbook authors of the nineteenth century: "The idea of drinking in at every breath the exhalations that load the atmosphere of a crowded, promiscuous assembly is as disgusting as it is noxious." Steele went on, "We shun impurity in every form; we dislike to wear the clothes of another, or to eat from the same dish; we shrink from contact with the filthy, and yet, sitting in the same room, inhale their poisonous breath." Patterson claimed that every person in a poorly ventilated space contaminated the air with carbonic acid at a rate of "5 to 10 cubic feet of air per minute," which could slow down or even stop blood circulation. In addition to carbonic acid, humans in poorly designed rooms inhaled the "putrescent excrement" others had just expelled from their lungs. The problem was worse in colder months because lighting contraptions and stoves produced heat, which caused the body temperature of parishioners to rise to such a level that they frequently caught a cold when they returned to cooler outside weather, which could "induce severe disease."[24]

Patterson's own experience in a prisoner of war camp—such camps were notoriously smelly and unhealthy—might have contributed to his advocacy for good air, but he also framed the need for good ventilation as an evangelical imperative. Parishioners in churches with poor air might leave feeling physically and mentally depleted, often suffering from terrible headaches. The preacher too was affected, felt less animated, and his audience gradually lost interest. "The sermon may fall powerless, when the blame attaches to neither preacher nor people (although the preacher frequently has it to bear); for the circumstances, the foul state of the atmosphere, and its evil influences, are averse to speaking and hearing." Patterson's demands for good ventilation were never simply about architecture or public health. He went to great lengths to frame the more expensive and intricate parts of the construction process as necessary expenses for proper religion, always returning to the argument that his methods would create an ideal atmosphere for saving lost souls.[25]

By ventilating both the floor and the ceiling with ducts to expel foul air and introduce clean air, churches could keep the atmosphere in the buildings clean and the temperature comfortable without damaging the aesthetic appearance of the room. Patterson reproduced portions of a paper delivered before the Massachusetts Medical Society (unfortunately, without proper attribution), for a "*simple and cheap plan* of ventilation" for smaller and mid-size buildings. The unknown author recommended placing a board close to the lower window sash which, when properly positioned, would direct air coming into the building downward so that it "gradually displaces the air above it until it fills the room" and a similar board along the upper sash would allow air to fill the upper part of the room, while also allowing air to escape. The author also suggested nailing pieces of pasteboard to the boards to direct air flow. While larger buildings needed a more elaborate system, Patterson believed that, "if carefully executed, this arrangement will not be objectionable in appearance." In citing Steele and the Massachusetts paper, Patterson highlighted deference to expertise, an important step in legitimizing taste. For Patterson, ventilation was not merely an aspect of architecture, it was a necessity for any congregation serious about evangelism.[26]

If ventilation was necessary for pure air, heating devices were a must to keep the congregation engaged during colder months. There was no shortage of options available, and Patterson weighed the merits and drawbacks of different contraptions. Stoves were economical but had to be periodically replaced; more ominously, they damaged "the purity of the air," which then became "unfit for pleasant and healthy respiration." Most stoves failed to evenly heat the room, "a fundamental principle of health," and they were also large, bulky, and unsightly. Exhaust pipes only added to the trouble, sometimes even running over the preacher's head, which "to a great extent disfigure[s] the room." Patterson conceded that smaller churches, especially in the country, had to use stoves, but these must be carefully placed in the room and properly ventilated. Fireplaces had distinct advantages over stoves, he felt, noting the atmosphere they created: "*hearth* has come to mean as much as *home*." Patterson printed specifications for chimneys, including both size and placement.[27]

Patterson ultimately encouraged hot air furnaces made of wrought iron as the most modern and efficient heating method. These ranged in price from $150 to $900 but were a worthwhile expense. Patterson recommended furnaces that used hot water or, somewhat less desirably, steam, with pipes that ran the length under each pew, but commented that these systems were so expensive that most congregations had to seek other options. Regardless of how churches heated their buildings, however, congregations needed to know the exact kind of fuel their furnace required. For example, "eastern furnaces are made with reference to burning anthracite, or hard, coal," which required smaller flues made of relatively light metal; such flues were not appropriate for burning bituminous coal found in western regions of the country. Improper fuel not only potentially poisoned the air but could have other serious consequences, such as fires or even explosions. Patterson recommended several foundries if churches could not purchase from a trusted blacksmith. The Eagle Foundry in Louisville, for example, sold good stoves at reasonable rates. For elaborate systems, two fine furnaces from A. Lotze and Sons of Cincinnati heated the sanctuary and Sunday School rooms for Central Methodist Church of Memphis.[28]

Finally, Patterson's manual reflected the belief among Progressive Christians that education was a vital function of the church. His smaller floorplans included a multi-use space in the back of the sanctuary that would enable churches to conveniently hold Sunday School in the main room if churches could not afford to construct dedicated classrooms. Patterson's floorplans also allowed committees to put classrooms in the basement or add an entire suite of multipurpose rooms for instruction and fellowship. However, the dimensions of these structures needed to be carefully planned. Ceilings should be 10–12 feet high and be above ground so that "it may be light, airy, and healthy." Gone, too, was the iconoclasm typical of early nineteenth-century evangelicals. Patterson suggested that churches decorate their classroom spaces. Foreshadowing advocacy of uplift through well-funded and attractive schools, Sunday School rooms were to have maps, framed pictures, and mottos or sayings hung on the walls, not only to "beautify the room, but [to] make good and lasting impressions on the minds of both teachers and pupils."[29]

Patterson used the language of evangelicalism to present his plans as unassailable to any thinking Christian, but ecclesiastical design is never theologically or socially neutral. His manual was a deliberate attempt to promote middle-class taste and aesthetics as the only legitimate way to design a church. The manual changed practices and was a major departure for the MECS, at odds with the extemporaneous worship that had long characterized southern Methodism. Printed programs with orders of worship became standard, while prayers, often written in advance, became shorter. Scripture often took the form of a responsive reading between the pastor and the congregation as sermons became brief theological treatises. Professionally arranged and performed music now openly competed with the sermon as the centerpiece of worship. Communion ware, collection plates, and other items made liturgy a defining feature of MECS worship. Although Patterson insisted that these changes were about saving lost souls, his defense of Gothic and Romanesque motifs, ergonomic pews, organs, and stained-glass windows was often accompanied by subtle jabs at rural and working-class Methodists. Patterson tapped into the ethos of professionalization and expertise to create institutional knowledge that allowed congregations to confidently navigate an admittedly difficult and fraught process, but he also extended this authority into a more subjective realm to argue for a bourgeois aesthetic more exclusive than inclusive, foreshadowing the tendency of later Progressives to project middle-class sensibilities onto the working class.

Soon after completing the manual, Patterson became an elder, but the bishops had bigger plans for him. Beginning in 1878, Patterson took over the church's missionary efforts in Mexico. Patterson's endeavors helped him achieve something approaching celebrity status in the MECS, particularly among middle-class women in mission societies. One southern Methodist waxed rapturous over Patterson's work in Mexico: "No record of missionary enterprise can compare with it since the days of the apostles." After eight years of preaching, publishing English- and Spanish-language periodicals, and carrying out heavy administrative duties, Patterson returned to the United States citing poor health. Soon thereafter, however, he took a position with the American Bible Society to oversee the distribution of Bibles in South America, based out of Venezuela. According to contemporary accounts, Patterson was the only Protestant minister in Venezuela at the time, "and the only one who has ever been here." After sixteen months, however, Patterson died of malaria in Caracas in 1889 at the age of fifty.[30]

Progressives took other aggressive action to finance church construction. Based on a model tested by the MEC, the 1882 General Conference created the Board of Church Extension to act as a creditor to MECS churches. Rather than dealing with high interest rates of banks and the terrifying prospect of legal action if donations fell short, the Board of Church Extension provided a safe option for churches that needed help paying for a portion of new facilities. The conference located the board in Louisville, and in turn it set up local auxiliary boards that coordinated preachers and elders to collect donations. Most of the money filtered back to Louisville, funds that the board then invested; proceeds were used to provide congregations with loans at low rates. The board also reserved the right to grant money that churches did not have to pay back. Churches had to formally apply to the board for assistance, describe the project, estimate costs, provide membership statistics, name their trustees, detail the breadth of their ministries, and make financial and legal disclosures. The conference created what amounted to a savings and loan for the express purpose of funding the kinds of buildings Patterson envisioned. Within four years, the board touted assets of more than $33,000, with even more vested in auxiliary boards across the South. In 1890, the board reported a four-year budget of more than $100,000. Just as Patterson had stressed the importance of expertise in building committees, individuals with specialized knowledge in banking and finance administered the board. The same impulse that led Progressives to push for a manual to standardize protocols and codify institutional knowledge and taste created a successful bureaucracy to finance Patterson's middle-class vision.[31]

Patterson's manual is a clear example demonstrating Bourdieu's theory of taste, showing how institutions draw lines that demarcate legitimate and illegitimate culture. Patterson used a discourse of modernity to convince his audience that his standards, protocols, and aesthetics were not only cutting edge but were also empirical and scientific. In this sense, Patterson positioned himself as the credentialed expert guiding his Church into a more sophisticated era. While this places Patterson squarely within the New South context, this example shows modernity and taste working in tandem to legitimize class and define the boundaries of proper Methodist worship. Finally, Patterson's manual shows that white southern evangelicals were not ancillary players in the early phases of the Progressive movement but were early leaders in standardization and creating bureaucracies to carry out reform, which stands in sharp contrast to the prevailing historiography on southern Progressivism. Scholars have fairly criticized Progressives for racist attitudes and condescension toward rural and working-class Americans. The present example is, of course, no different. In cities like Birmingham, Atlanta, and others across the region marked by increasingly rigid urban segregation and racial conflict in the late nineteenth century, ecclesiastical architecture sacralized new and growing commercial centers and all-white residential sectors, making them look and feel more religious, sadly signifying that the white southern middle class, notorious for erecting systems of Jim Crow and disenfranchisement while condoning terrorism directed at African Americans, believed they had the support of an even higher authority.

NOTES

1. Thomas O. Summers, ed., *Journal of the General Conference of the Methodist Episcopal Church, South, Held in Memphis, 1870* (Nashville: Publishing House of the Methodist Episcopal Church, South, 1870), 214; William M. Patterson, *A Manual of Architecture for Churches, Parsonages, and School-Houses: Containing Designs, Elevations, Plans, Specifications, Form of Contract, Rules for Estimating Cost of Building, with Suggestions on Acoustics, Ventilation, Seating, Lighting, Painting, Etc.* (Nashville: Publishing House of the Methodist Episcopal Church, South, 1875), 107. Patterson's manual included lengthy sections on parsonages and schoolhouses, both of which promoted the same Progressive ideals and aesthetics as the section on church architecture. These sections deserve their own extended analysis in their own right, and support the conclusions of this essay.

2. Robert H. Wiebe, *The Search for Order, 1877–1920* (New York: Hill and Wang, 1967), xiv. Wiebe linked notions of efficiency and rationalization with reform. Historians of southern Progressivism responded to the framework established by C. Vann Woodward, *Origins of the New South, 1877–1913* (Baton Rouge: Louisiana State University Press, 1951), and centered their analyses on continuities and divergences between Populists and Progressives. See Sheldon Hackney, *Populism to Progressivism in Alabama* (Princeton: Princeton University Press, 1969); Dewey W. Grantham, "The Contours of Southern Progressivism," *American Historical Review* 86, no. 5 (December 1981): 1035–59; Daniel T. Rodgers, "In Search of Progressivism," *Reviews in American History* 10, no. 4 (December 1982): 113–32; Elizabeth Sanders, *Roots of Reform: Farmers, Workers, and the American State, 1877–1917* (Chicago: University of Chicago

Press, 1999). In a synthesis of enduring importance, William A. Link, *The Paradox of Southern Progressivism, 1880–1930* (Chapel Hill: University of North Carolina Press, 1992), showed that southern Progressives successfully erected effective bureaucratic structures to support public education and, to a lesser degree, public health. Beyond this, however, Link found that weak enforcement and local resistance to reform doomed southern Progressivism to failure. See also Elna C. Green, *Southern Strategies: Southern Women and the Woman Suffrage Question* (Chapel Hill: University of North Carolina Press, 1997). Historians have expanded the usual parameters of Progressivism, both in terms of time and place. Rebecca Edwards, *New Spirits: Americans in the Gilded Age, 1865–1905* (New York: Oxford University Press, 2006), argued in favor of a "long Progressive era" that began well before the turn of the twentieth century within a larger global context. See also Daniel T. Rodgers, *Atlantic Crossings: Social Politics in a Progressive Age* (Cambridge, MA: Harvard University Press, 1998). There have a number of studies on southern evangelicals, the Social Gospel, and Progressivism, including John Patrick McDowell, *The Social Gospel in the South: The Women's Home Mission Movement in the Methodist Episcopal Church, South, 1886–1939* (Baton Rouge: Louisiana State University Press, 1982); Evelyn Brooks Higginbotham, *Righteous Discontent: The Women's Movement in the Black Baptist Church, 1880–1920* (Cambridge, MA: Harvard University Press, 1993); and Glenda Elizabeth Gilmore, *Gender and Jim Crow: Women and the Politics of White Supremacy in North Carolina, 1896–1920* (Chapel Hill: University of North Carolina Press, 1996). Historians of the twentieth century recognize that southern evangelicals have been on the forefront of technological and bureaucratic modernization; see Darren Dochuk, *From Bible Belt to Sun Belt: Plain-Folk Religion, Grassroots Politics, and the Rise of Evangelical Conservatism* (New York: W. W. Norton, 2011).

3. Pierre Bourdieu, *Distinction: A Social Critique of the Judgement of Taste*, trans. Richard Nice (Cambridge, MA: Harvard University Press, 1984).

4. For other examples of architectural manuals, see S. W. Thomas, *Fifth Annual Report of the Church Extension Society of the Methodist Episcopal Church for the Year 1870* (Philadelphia: Methodist Episcopal Book Room, 1870) and William Wallace Martin, *Manual of Ecclesiastical Architecture: Comprising a Study of Its Various Styles, the Chronological Arrangements of Its Elements, and Its Relation to Christian Worship* (Cincinnati: Curts and Jennings, 1897).

5. Thomas O. Summers, ed., *Journal of the General Conference of the Methodist Episcopal Church, South, Held in Louisville, 1874* (Nashville: Publishing House of the Methodist Episcopal Church, South, 1874), 573; Thomas O. Summers, ed., *Journal of the General Conference of the Methodist Episcopal Church, South, Held in Atlanta, Ga, 1878* (Nashville: Southern Methodist Publishing House, 1878), 238; Christopher Michael Bishop, "Methodism, the Middle Class, and the New South, 1866–1894," PhD diss., Auburn University, 2018, 42–52; Daniel W. Stowell, *Rebuilding Zion: The Religious Reconstruction of the South, 1863–1877* (New York: Oxford University Press, 1998), 130–45.

6. R. H. Mahon, ed., *Minutes of the Fiftieth Session of the Memphis Conference of the Methodist Episcopal Church, South, Held at Fulton, Kentucky, November 13–18, 1889* (Brownsville, Tenn.: States-Democrat Book and Job Office, 1889), 55–56; for sectionalism and religion in the border states, see April E. Holm, *A Kingdom Divided: Evangelicals, Loyalty, and Sectionalism in the Civil War Era* (Baton Rouge: Louisiana State University Press, 2017).

7. Patterson, *Manual of Architecture*, 21.

8. Patterson, *Manual of Architecture,* 22; *Christian Advocate* (Nashville), May 4, 1872, April 6, 1872.

9. Patterson, *Manual of Architecture,* 32; *Christian Advocate,* October 23, 1869.

10. Patterson, *Manual of Architecture,* 34.

11. Burton J. Bledstein, *The Culture of Professionalism: The Middle Class and the Development of Higher Education in America* (New York: W. W. Norton, 1976), 90; Patterson, *Manual of Architecture,* 25.

12. Patterson, *Manual of Architecture,* 20.

13. Patterson, *Manual of Architecture,* 29, 30 (original emphasis).

14. Patterson, *Manual of Architecture,* 27; Jeanne Halgren Kilde, *When Church Became Theatre: The Transformation of Evangelical Architecture and Worship in Nineteenth-Century America* (New York: Oxford University Press, 2002), 85–88.

15. Patterson, *Manual of Architecture,* 31, 38 (original emphasis).

16. Patterson, *Manual of Architecture,* 52, 57.

17. Kilde, *When Church Became Theatre,* 112–23.

18. Patterson, *Manual of Architecture,* 66; Walter W. Benjamin and Leland Scott, "The Methodist Episcopal Church in the Postwar Era," in *The History of American Methodism,* ed. Emory Stevens Bucke (New York: Abingdon Press, 1964), 2:322.

19. Patterson, *Manual of Architecture,* 31; "The 1891 George Jardine Organ," Archives, Tennessee Annual Conference, Tulip Street (closed), Davidson County, 1852–2014, Box 8, 1–4. Although Tulip Street is no longer operational as a Methodist church, the building has been repurposed for weddings and other events and the organ is a prominent feature of the room.

20. Patterson, *Manual of Architecture,* 59.

21. Patterson, *Manual of Architecture,* 72, 71; Kilde, *When Church Became Theatre,* 131.

22. Patterson, *Manual of Architecture,* 64.

23. Patterson, *Manual of Architecture,* 61; Kilde, *When Church Became Theatre,* 131; Thomas F. Rzeznik, *Church and Estate: Religion and Wealth in Industrial-Era Philadelphia* (University Park: Pennsylvania State University Press, 2013), 53–55; James Hudnut-Beumler, *In Pursuit of the Almighty's Dollar: A History of Money and American Protestantism* (Chapel Hill: University of North Carolina Press, 2007), 59–60.

24. Patterson, *Manual of Architecture,* 77. Public health advocacy became common in the South in the 1880s, particularly in large, densely populated cities that were prone to outbreaks of cholera and other diseases associated with poor sanitation and were often part of the larger trend toward racial segregation, as documented in Don H. Doyle, *New Men, New Cities, New South: Atlanta, Nashville, Charleston, Mobile, 1860–1910* (Chapel Hill: University of North Carolina Press, 1990), 278–89. Gilmore, *Gender and Jim Crow,* 163–73, documents the (sometimes interracial) efforts of white and Black women to improve sanitation and public health in the South in the early part of the twentieth century; public health advocacy in the South in those decades often focused on specific crises commonly associated with poverty, such as hookworm and pellagra. See Woodward, *Origins of the New South,* 426–27; Link, *The Paradox of Southern Progressivism,* 142–59, 216–20; and Diane C. Vecchio, "The Scourge of the South: Pellagra and Poverty in Spartanburg's Mill Villages," in *Recovering the Piedmont Past,* vol. 2: *Bridging the Centuries in the South Carolina Upcountry, 1877–1941,* ed. Timothy P.

Grady and Andrew H. Myers (Columbia: University of South Carolina Press, 2019), 58–71.

25. Patterson, *Manual of Architecture,* 77, 78; Evan A. Kutzler, *Living by Inches: The Smells, Sounds, Tastes, and Feeling of Captivity in Civil War Prisons* (Chapel Hill: University of North Carolina Press, 2019), 37–60.

26. Patterson, *Manual of Architecture,* 78, 80.

27. Patterson, *Manual of Architecture,* 73, 74.

28. Patterson, *Manual of Architecture,* 76, 77, 78; Kilde, *When Church Became Theatre,* 131.

29. Patterson, *Manual of Architecture,* 31; Charles A. Israel, *Before Scopes: Evangelicalism, Education, and Evolution in Tennessee, 1870–1925* (Athens: University of Georgia Press, 2004), 11–42.

30. Mahon, *1889 Memphis Conference,* 56, 59.

31. W. P. Harrison, ed. *Journal of the General Conference of the Methodist Episcopal Church, South, Held in Nashville, Tenn., 1882* (Nashville: Southern Methodist Publishing House, 1882), 130–32; W. P. Harrison, ed., *Journal of the General Conference of the Methodist Episcopal Church, South, Held in St. Louis, Mo., May, 1890* (Nashville: Publishing House of the Methodist Episcopal Church, South, 1890), 110.

Managing Revival

Religious Authority and Print Performances during the Great Awakening

Michael Baysa

From the 1730s through the 1740s, the New England literary public was inundated with printed accounts of fantastical visions, bodily spectacles, mass conversions, itinerant preachers, fracturing congregations, and irate ministers. Promoters of these events pointed to them as evidence of spiritual revival. According to the promoters, congregants had ceased "Drinking, Tavern-haunting, profane speaking, and Extravagance in Apparel . . . [they] that seem'd to have their Minds swallowed up with nothing but the vain Shews and Pleasures of the World, have been wonderfully altered, and have relinquished these Vanities, and are become serious, mortified and humble in their Conversations."[1]

Critics similarly turned to the press to highlight the disruptive displays of these revivals. They blamed itinerant preachers who would wander "from Town to Town, to the great Disturbance of Towns and Churches, and neglecting [their] own Church at Home."[2] When the deluge of publications about the revivals began to wane, two eminent New England ministers, First Church of Boston's Charles Chauncy and First Church of Northampton's Jonathan Edwards, tried to determine what to make of them. A staunch supporter of the revivals, Edwards published *Some Thoughts Concerning the Present Revival of Religion in New England* (1742), arguing that these events were clearly the work of God. Chauncy, the leading critic of the revivals, rushed his response to Edwards in a work aptly titled *Seasonable Thoughts on the State of Religion in New-England* (1743) to argue the contrary. At the heart of their debate was a question about categories: were these performances religion?

Scholars of American religious history who have studied these revivals have focused on the intersections of the intellectual and theological currents that led up to and followed from the debate between these two ministers. Most notably, historians such as George Marsden, Mark Noll, and Thomas Kidd examined how theological transformations during the revivals gave rise to new Protestant denominations in the eighteenth century, and how the events contributed to broader political and economic shifts in the decades leading up to the American Revolution.[3] What concerned these scholars, however, was locating a stable ideology for historians who do not study religion but could identify it as such so as to determine how Protestants may have shaped broader American social, political, and cultural currents.[4] Such attempts placed too much emphasis on published beliefs and theological claims, likely owing to the authors' own interest in tracing a consistent American Christian tradition among a loose scattering of movements and institutions over a long period of four hundred years.[5] Such confidence in belief as the locus of American Protestantism overlooked the ways that even eighteenth-century ministers themselves seemed unsure whether belief could be properly communicated and ascertained as religion. Subsequent scholarship has challenged these belief-centric frameworks by taking seriously the perspectives and experiences of non- Anglo Protestant ministers during these revivals.[6] They argued that the political dimensions of theology mattered just as much as, if not more than, the deeply held beliefs they have been understood to signify. Within the historiography, "religion" has always been a fraught term that has been made to signify anything: from the society-shifting thoughts and beliefs of remarkable figures to the authority-claiming performances by individuals who sought to assert their own power over others. It is this essay's contention that even the ministers themselves, in a pivotal moment in the history of American Protestantism, seemed unsure about the equivalence of religion to belief and themselves erred on the side that it more appropriately signified authority and performance.

This essay explores how two Protestant ministers came to debate religion as a way of managing different performances of speech. They knew that belief, an internal theological position, becomes a hypermediated form of expression when manifested in any shape or form. One could only speculate, through assertions of sincerity or authenticity, upon any direct connection between the communication of those beliefs—whether manifested orally, written, or embodied—and what the individual may have truly believed. Therefore, the only way to observe belief was to see how it was performed. By "performance," ministers did not imply insincerity but rather that such formulations are created within a complex field of social and cultural discourses and relations that always mediate and negotiate how belief is communicated. Chauncy himself would remark that this was how he understood the term. In one of his later publications, he ruminated on what it meant for his views to be written, read, understood, and published: "I am not insensible, that, in a performance of this nature, where the *proof* is of the *moral kind*, and depends upon a variety of *circumstances* duly adjusted and situated with respect to each other, there will be always room left for *difference* of sentiment in different persons."[7] Regardless of Chauncy's desire to clearly and directly communicate his beliefs to readers, the social process of writing, publication, and meaning-making always risked compromising his intentions. So instead of arguing for a particular theological position as true religion, both ministers agreed that the debate around true religion entailed managing what people did during the revivals—the way they spoke, where they preached, and how they gathered audiences.

If the revivalists' performances constituted true religion, then they should be promoted in the press and i supporters should receive the backing of local authorities. If they did not constitute true religion, then the press should not promote it and authorities should discourage any form of preaching by non registered ministers. By shifting the focus away from belief claims and toward observable social performances, ministers could better manage the revival atmosphere in eighteenth-century New England. While there are myriad approaches to analyzing theological speech as performance, I will focus on the ways performance draws out the relationship between authors, mediums, and authority. Specifically, I will argue that Chauncy and Edwards's debate about religion was really concerned with who could speak theologically in public, where they could preach, and whom their speech hailed as an audience.[8] For Anglo Protestant ministers, preaching relied on established conventions in New England Congregationalism that reinforced unidirectionality: ministers published theology through the press and preached from the pulpit, but rarely did the congregants themselves respond to the ministers. This dynamic ensured an asymmetrical relation between the two social groups, thereby maintaining ministerial authority to supply meaning-making frameworks to congregants and shape their sense of themselves as both constantly saved and needing to be saved.[9]

The first section of this essay performs a close reading of the printed exchange between Chauncy and Edwards to explore how religion was understood as a kind of performance. Illustrating J. Z. Smith's assertion that religion was not a native category, even among the most authoritative Protestants, the ministers deployed religion to arbitrate who could perform theological discourse and through what platforms and under what circumstances they could do so.[10] At the heart of their categorizations, however, was an anxiety around the ways the revivalists leveraged platforms and mediums of authority that had mostly been reserved for Anglo Protestant ministers.[11] The second section examines the consequences around their exchange. Chauncy successfully lobbied for penalties against itinerant preaching, and his connections stalled the promise of publishing non ministerial religious voices through the printing presses. His true success, however, was preserving preaching, whether printed or oral, as a strictly ministerial genre of speech. Print, in particular, was the primary platform for sermons to speak on behalf of and to an imagined religious public—imagined because it aspired to speak to more people than it may have actually reached and because it hoped to represent the thoughts of everyday readers more than it actually described them. Maintaining this power in theological discourse mattered to elite clergymen like Chauncy at a time when print became a repository for ministerial aspirations, anxiety, and failure. In other words, print was a means by which ministers could make power apparent when they felt theirs was either waning or beginning to feel as if it was not operative. These dynamics led ministers to value these platforms in ways that they needed to constrain the laity from deploying the most publicly authoritative mediums to challenge them, at least on theological matters.[12]

UNCERTAIN RELIGION

The Great Awakening was a strange time in New England. Heralded by the arrival of famous British preacher George Whitefield in the 1730s, numerous claims about spiritual revival sprang up around the New England countryside. Whitefield and his followers toured rural New England preaching fiery sermons that accused listeners of sinful behavior in ways that made them constantly question their own status as Christians. They stressed the importance of a proper conversion experience, which, at times, required an observable radical performance and a transformation in one's life and behavior. This took many forms, including fainting during the sermon and visions of the supernatural. For ministers who had only been familiar with conversions as a genre for verbally narrating a convert's transition from a life of sin to a commitment to the broader church polity, these radical performances proved too disruptive to their sensibilities. Debates ensued among the clerical class over whether they should encourage or condemn these displays. With little consensus among the ministers, they turned to the category of "religion." Representing two sides of the debate, Chauncy and Edwards grappled with evidence for true conversions, the problems of self-attestation, and the very social feature of belief itself. Clear from their discussion, however, was the certainty that religion could not be reduced to inaccessible internal beliefs. Instead, it consisted of observable performances that were open to judgment by New England's most esteemed ministers.

In his argument for the revival phenomenon to constitute religion, Edwards outlined what conversion entailed, at least as he saw it, and argued that the sensational aspects of the revival fit somewhere along this process. First, he insisted that converts must demonstrate an emotional response to shame, guilt, or conviction of their sins: "Their Sins of Life have been extraordinarily set before them: and they have also had a great Sense of their Sins of Heart; their hardness of Heart, and Enmity against that which is Good, and Proneness to all Evil; and also of the Worthlessness of their own religious Performances."[13] Second, he pointed to the importance of the emotional response giving way to more embodied spectacles: "But it has been a Thing generally supposed and allowed in the Church of GOD, till now, that there is such a Thing as being sick of Love to CHRIST, or having the bodily Strength weak'ned by strong and vigorous Exercises of Love to him. And however, kind to human Nature the Influences of the Spirit of GOD are . . . would overpower the Nature of Man in its present weak State." [14] It was important that such embodied performances themselves could be read as unnatural or uncommon to that congregant. Further emphasizing the exceptionalism of this act, he cited the b ook of Daniel: "*No Man can see me and live,* and *Flesh and Blood cannot inherit the Kingdom of GOD.* That external Glory & Majesty of CHRIST which *Daniel* saw, when *there remained no Strength in him, and his Comeliness was turned in him into Corruption.*"[15] Third, he posited that there must be positive explanations about God or other theological truths: "It seems to me that the very Life and Soul of all true Religion consists in [affections]."[16] By "affections," he gestured toward various examples from scripture equating it to the concept of the fruits of the Spirit, which could be observed as "rejoicing with Joy," "believing in and loving an unseen Saviour," "having the Love of God shed abroad in our Hearts," and "having the Day-Star arise in our hearts." Finding the importance of scriptural support for his formulation, Edwards challenged his critics: "And what Notions have they of Religion, that reject what has been described as not true Religion? What shall we find to answer those Expressions in Scripture . . .?"[17] For his fourth criterion, Edwards stressed a radical change in congregants' demeanor in public after the point of conversion: "And now instead of Meetings at Taverns and drinking Houses, and Meetings of young People in Frolicks and vain Company, the Country is full of Meetings of all

Sorts and Ages of Persons, Young and Old, Men, Women and little Children, to read and pray, and sing Praises, and to converse of the Things of GOD and another World." Altogether, these acts, consisting of outward expressions of shame and guilt, exceptional embodied performances, positive affections, and behavioral changes, constituted, for Edwards, religion. If the actions of revivalists could be fitted into his scheme, then the revivals were "a glorious WORK OF GOD" and thus, constituted religion.[18]

Chauncy was not convinced by Edwards's criteria, since they seemed focused on ephemeral performances rather than consistent, day-to-day actions. For example, while Edwards emphasized that public displays of positive affections were a crucial way of performing one's love for God, Chauncy insisted that true love was enacted through "*Obedience to the Commandments of GOD;* and the *stronger* the Love, the more uniform, steady and pleasant will be this *Obedience*."[19] In other words, demonstrations of love rely on consistent observance rather than ephemeral emotionality. Similarly, Edwards argued that joy was itself manifested through audibly loud cries, which Chauncy rebutted could "meerly [be] an *animal Passion*, a free *Flow of Spirits*." Instead, true joy consisted of an observable *"Complacence* of *Soul* in GOD, a holy Satisfaction and Chearfulness of Mind . . . mixt with a becoming *Fear* and *Caution*, so will it express itself in as low an *Abasement* of our selves, as *high* Adorations of the free and rich Grace of GOD."[20] For Chauncy, joy was manifested through quiet stability and not through loud outbursts. His emphasis on stability better fit Edwards's understanding of peace: "Calm and Serenity of the Soul, without any Cloud to interrupt it; a continual rejoicing in all the Works of GOD's Hands."[21] However, the Boston minister corrected Edwards's understanding of peace, proposing that peace is "not so much a holy Serenity of Mind" as it is a "State of *outward Quietness*, and *good Order*" that prevented "Strife and Contention, and go[ing] into the like mutinous and divisive Methods."[22] Through concepts like obedience, complacence, and quietness, Chauncy provided alternative criteria for performed religion. While the two ministers differed on the temporality and proper execution of how to properly perform their faith, they seemed in clear agreement that whatever warranted religion was a series of performances.

The observability of these acts was important precisely because ministers knew they could not ascertain a person's salvation. This is reflected in the ways ministers tried to interpret actions as signifying something invisibly situated within the mentality, psychology, or other terms of interiority of a converted individual. When Edwards was making his argument about how love, joy, and peace were evidenced through converts' actions, Chauncy's responses were appropriate not because he himself could peer into the minds and hearts of the observer, but because his assertion that they were "animal passions" was an equally unvalidatable interpretation. In the end, ministers could only adjudicate religion by their social function: how do these acts perform for and affect the community of visible saints?[23] Edwards himself was forced to acknowledge the risk of relying on invisible criteria because it was difficult to discern motive. He confessed that "the Influences of the Spirit, for Instance, may be an Occasion of new Ways of the Exercise of *Pride*, as has been acknowledged by orthodox Divines in general."[24] At best, Edwards could only guess at belief, and even his qualifiers suggested a caution toward any strong claims about interiority. While Edwards's publications would famously come to represent the strong position held by revivalists that the performances of revival constituted true religion, they may actually better evidence the minister's hopeful optimism that the events of the revival were religion. Chauncy likely picked up on Edwards's cautious tone and may have been encouraged in his own position that these performances were not religion.

Given the ambiguities of the question of the performances around revival as religion, the debate turned toward the politics of categorization itself: who could claim these performances as religion? Edwards placed the onus of description on the individual who performed those actions. This implied that religion constituted a self-determined performance that evidenced spiritual conversion, often wrought by divine intervention into the natural world to raise the affections of an individual. As he wrote: "Things of Religion take Place in Men's Hearts, no further than they are *affected* with them."[25] However, the phrase "affected with them " gestured toward the importance of external catalysts that initiated religious experiences. For Edwards, these included hearing the preaching of God's Word, praying, and worshipping. Within his scheme, these catalysts were activated through invisible divine intervention and traceable by the conscious attestation of the experiencer themselves. With proper guidance from ministers, the experiencer could then identify these signs as: "Exercises of Love to GOD, Delight and Complacence in GOD, Desires and Longings after GOD, Delight in the Children of GOD, Love to Mankind, Brokenness of Heart, Abhorrence of Sin, and Self-abhorrence for Sin; and the Peace of GOD which passeth all Understanding, and Joy in the Holy Ghost, Joy unspeakable and full of Glory; admiring Thoughts of GOD, exulting and glorying in GOD."[26] In other words, whatever acts took place, the experiencer must also be able to frame and narrate them through theological language. *Some Thoughts* only slightly hinted at Edwards's anthropology of this interiority as a kind of process: "All Acts of the Affections of the Soul are in some Sense Acts of the Will, and all Acts of the Will are Acts of the Affections."[27] Put another way, "true religion consists in the sensory encounter itself, as grace becomes actualized as the immanent 'indwelling principle' of the human soul."[28] It was important that individuals lacked the agency to create this process within themselves and that their primary role as experiencer was to simply be a rational witness. The process of making theological meaning of internal transformation required guidance, but the decision still fell on the conscious individual. This evidenced Edwards's confidence in the experiencer's capacity to adjudicate their own interiority because of their conscious and otherwise rational mind.[29]

Chauncy did not share Edwards's confidence in the individual's rational faculties to observe their own interiority, at least when it came to categorizing it as religion. For the Boston minister, performances of religion must be understood with regard to their social function. He implies that the discursive act of categorization relied on a certain level of sociality and empiricism. Since the idea of the social or public could not be situated within Edwards's scheme of self-knowledge, any categorical claims made on the basis of self-knowledge could not be shared by others. As he wrote in his introduction, "From whence it follows, by the Way, that the *Work of God*, as an *internal* Thing, can be judged of by others, only from the *outward* Discoveries of it. One Man can't look into the Heart of another: This is the Prerogative of him who has said, *I am he that searcheth the Heart, and trieth the Reins of the Children of Men*. If therefore we would judge of the *interior* State of *others*, we must do it from some *external Manifestations* of it."[30] In other words, Chauncy stressed that categorization must be an act external to the event or person itself. This difference between categorization as a self-determined act as opposed to a social one pointed to the ways in which Chauncy and Edwards were disagreeing on the nature of epistemology itself: how do people know what they know? Chauncy insisted that individuals cannot truly know the state of their own soul without proper attestation from others. Hence, any process of classification must itself rely on some form of social consensus.

Although Chauncy critiqued Edwards for trusting too much in individuals' self-knowledge, Edwards also identified a weakness in the antirevivalists' position in assuming that the performances were not religion. He believed that they were making a key epistemological mistake in classifying performances *a priori*. By this he meant that their refusal to recognize revival performances as religion might not imply some indeterminable essence, but might nevertheless posit an undeterminable cause. To put it another way, antirevivalists should only classify religion based strictly on what can be clearly observed and measured, and not on what they can hypothesize, *a posteriori*: "We are to observe the Effect wrought; and if, upon Examination of that, it can be found to be agreeable to the Word of GOD, we are bound without much more ado to rest in it as God's work."[31] Here, Edwards was making a sophisticated argument about the politics of categorization itself. When Chauncy posited "animal passion" and "hysteria" as equally valuable explanations for the performances, he was making an implicit argument that the catalysts for them were strictly natural or biological. Chauncy did not claim that he knew the causes or catalysts for these performances, but Edwards's critique suggested that there was a tricky slippage between mere description and positing cause. As he reminded his antirevivalist foes, humanity cannot "resolve that we will first be satisfied how GOD brought this or the other Effect to pass, and why he hath made it thus, or why it has pleased him to take such a Course, and to use such and such Means, before we will acknowledge his Work, and give him the Glory of it. This is too much for the *Clay* to take upon it with respect to the *Potter. GOD gives not Account of his Matters.*"[32] Edwards's critique was a double-edged sword. While his opponents could not assert that the causes were strictly natural, neither could Edwards confidently claim that they were supernatural. Hence, Edwards could only feign total ignorance when it came to the true cause or nature and essence of the revivals.

In their debates about the revivals as religion, both Edwards and Chauncy turned to the performance because they could not manage inaccessible knowledge and information. Neither Edwards nor Chauncy could ascertain with full confidence the sincerity of converts or the nature of the revivals themselves. Nevertheless, their continued struggle and uncertainty over the category of "religion" evidenced Smith's contention that religion was not "a first-person term of self-characterization" and instead was "a category imposed from the outside of some aspect of native culture."[33] The two ministers' attempts to make meaning from the revivals relied on "religion" as a category that promised some semblance of order and hierarchy. "Religion" as a concept was not entirely foreign to New England Protestants, yet when it came to self-descriptions of fantastical visions, bodily spectacles, and mass conversions, it was nevertheless unstable and, as Chauncy asserted, must be a term imposed upon the event itself. However, this raised a different question. Given that neither the individual nor the observer could adjudicate the nature or cause of the revival performances so as to render them "religion," then who might have the authority to make a claim about it to others? Ministers already disagreed on whether the revivals constituted "religion" or not, which made it even more difficult for the clergy to assert some authoritative consensus toward a larger public. Furthermore, the public spectacle of the revivals had already published the fractured state of clerical authority to congregants. Chauncy knew that authority lay at the heart of the process of categorization, and, for the Boston minister, the questions around the category of "religion" were bound up in larger questions about performance, speech, and mediums.

PUBLISHING AUTHORITY

The debate around religion was ultimately a disagreement about who was authorized to speak publicly about religion. This question mattered, precisely because the revivals raised the important issue of ministerial authority: should the clergy be the primary public religious voice if they themselves might not yet have had a proper conversion experience, at least one like what Edwards laid out in *Some Thoughts*? Both Edwards and Chauncy acknowledged that authority was at stake and proffered different ways of managing revival's disruptions to the congregational order. Edwards promoted the racially and gendered egalitarianism of the revivals, at least when it came to producing religious speech, but with ample support and guidance from the established Anglo Protestant ministers so as to rein in some of the radical proponents who sought to completely undo the congregational hierarchy. Chauncy, however, saw the process of upending social hierarchies and disrupting congregational order as inherent to the revivals themselves. As he complained in *Seasonable Thoughts*: "Nay, there are many among these Exhorters, Babes in Age, as well as Understanding. They are chiefly indeed young Persons, sometimes Lads, or rather Boys: Nay, Women and Girls; yea, Negroes, have taken up on them the Business of Preachers."[34] Given his concerns, his solution was to constrain who could preach theology across different mediums.

In this section I explore how the use of religion as a means of managing performance was part of a broader initiative to arbitrate who could speak and where. Given that public displays of religious speech had previously been reserved for ministers, it was not surprising that Edwards and Chauncy located authority within one's ability to speak for and to a public on matters of religion. To put it another way, there was a sense that ministerial authority was itself a product of the very platforms and mediums available to them that rendered ministers' speech exceptional from other theological voices. Preserving ministerial privileges when it came to oral preaching and print production was crucial at a time when ministers grew anxious over their ability to properly manage their congregations. These platforms for gathering a listening or reading public allowed them to make power apparent when it was otherwise waning or beginning to seem as if it was no longer operative.[35] The stakes were even higher when print became the primary way that performances of religion were mediated between congregants and ministers, whether it was to sustain asymmetries between parties or to subvert existing power relations.

When Edwards and Chauncy debated their criteria for what constituted "religion," their concern about its "truth" and implicit singularity evidenced a particular anxiety about an observable diversity and fracture in Christianity writ large. To reinforce this sense of a timeless orthodoxy, both ministers turned to historical examples as a way of naturalizing their own positions onto an imagined unchanging past. Edwards, relying on an eighteenth-century version of *sola scriptura* whereby he cited extensively from the Christian Bible instead of learned scholars throughout Church history, argued for a parallel between the events of the revival and those of the movement of Christians in the earliest centuries. Meanwhile, Chauncy turned to the works of prominent Reformation clergymen to argue that his antirevivalist position shared a continuity with the one and true Christian Church. Both attempted to establish the notion that there was a singular, unfractured Christianity that they were hoping to either resuscitate or preserve against broader social and political forces of their time. Such moves said more about the fractured reality and diverse Christianities within New England Puritanism in the eighteenth century than it did about a transhistorical theological consistency that both ministers wanted to assert and establish.

Recognizing the growing number of voices performing public theology during the revivals, Edwards sought to create a governing principle that reined in its seemingly universal scope, which transcended learning, ability, gender, and race. Marveling at the revivals' egalitarian promise, he wrote: "All Sorts of Persons, throughout the whole Congregation of Israel, Great and Small, Rich and Poor, Men and Women, helped to build the Tabernacle in the Wilderness . . . Everyone whose Heart stirred him up, and every one whom his Spirit made willing; all Sorts contributed, and all Sorts were employed in that Affair, in Labours of their Hands, both Men and Women."[36] He observed that children were also "remarkably enlighten'd, and their Hearts wonderfully affected and enlarged, and their Mouths open'd, expressing themselves in a Manner far beyond their Years."[37] Even among converted Africans and Native Americans who he believed were "ignorant and barbarous," he noticed that the revival was "very glorious in its Influences and Effects."[38] Through these observations, Edwards was laying the foundation for a Protestantism that would necessitate his social vision in this work. Even if he did not explicitly say so, the dynamics between his speech and its medium nevertheless hinted at one. Edwards followed up *Some Thoughts* with a continuing study on the nature of true religion: *A Treatise on Religious Affections* (1746), *The Life and Narrative of David*

Brainerd (1749), and more famously *An Inquiry into the Modern Prevailing Notions Respecting That Freedom of the Will* (1754). These works analyzed the continuing revival spirit among the missionary efforts to Native Americans, but his approach evidenced a clear audience for his study: fellow Anglo Protestant ministers. They were the ones in need of convincing that these conversions were legitimate and that the performances during the revivals should continue to be remembered as religion. In a material and literary sense, Edwards's texts were also only accessible to members of certain segments of society who could afford to purchase his works and whose interests would consist of shoring up their knowledge and authority across a wide array of audiences.[39] Edwards's fascination with the growing diversity of voices performing theology publicly across a wide demographic might not necesarily conflict with his own slaveholding practices because his inquiry into religion was less invested in what it promised politically and spiritually for marginalized communities, and more in the ways it provided a method for theologically managing the broader and increasingly diversifying Church. It was through non-Anglo Protestants that Christianity could seemingly thrive, and those very Anglo Protestant ministers that needed to prepare for that future. In perhaps more cynical terms, a more inclusive theology opened room for more voices and bodies for ministers to eventually manage.

Although Edwards's social vision was more implicit in his work, Chauncy had little reservations about sharing his concerns over losing ministerial authority. As he addressed fellow ministers in his pamphlet: "We, who have been made Overseers of the Flocks in this Land, are peculiarly oblig'd to use our Endeavours, in all suitable Ways, within our proper Sphere, to suppress these Disorders."[40] In response to Edwards's encouragement for ministers to take seriously the religiosities of the marginalized, Chauncy complained that preachers outside the ministerial class were simply "vain enough to think themselves fit to be Teachers of others." While Edwards was optimistic that newer voices could be managed, Chauncy disagreed because the ministers who were the most confident in their abilities to rein in these voices could barely manage themselves. He complained about those who were bold enough, "who, though they have no Learning, and but small Capacities, yet imagine they are able, and without Study too, to speak to the Spiritual Profit of such as are willing to hear them."[41] Furthermore, Chauncy did not celebrate the various audiences that itinerants gathered through their preaching. He complained that itinerants boasted too much about the overwhelming diversity of their audiences: "The Number of those who were thought to have received the KING of GLORY into their Souls, in eight Days, in three Towns, was computed to be about one

Hundred; among which, some were Negros; and, I think, about twenty Indians; besides a vast Multitude, who were left under Hopeful Convictions."[42] Given Chauncy's criteria for religion, it was likely that he saw little promise and staying power within non-Anglo Protestant conversions. Perhaps more worryingly, however, itinerants were setting a dangerous precedent: if they, without the proper vetting of the New England ministerial training, could speak authoritatively on matters of religion, then laity's entry into the public sphere to talk about religious matters might dilute the specialized authority of ministers who had previously held that distinct role in the public sphere.[43]

The debate over religion decided who could perform public speech through two mediums: itinerant preaching and print publication. The most successful attempt was made by the Connecticut Assembly, which banned itinerant preaching in 1742, resulting in revivalists like Eleazar Wheelock losing their pastoral funding from their local congregation. In addition, clerical and educational institutions also began signing declarations against itinerants, leading some congregations to remove their local minister. Some clergymen had to relocate to adjacent colonies like New York and Pennsylvania, outside of the Congregational ministers' jurisdictions.[44] Through a variety of means, revivalists felt the weight of Chauncy's publication and the ways it rallied antirevivalists to penalize their fellow clergymen. However, even though established ministers felt the consequences of supporting revival, dissenting laity continued its spirit through their preaching. Mohican preachers like Samson Occom and Joseph Johnson continued their ministries among Native American converts with support from Edwards's supporters, such as Wheelock. Women like Sarah Osborn also kept the revival spirit alive by preaching within their local contexts.[45] By the 1770s, heterodox preachers, such as Jemimah Wilkinson and universalist John Murray, moved about throughout the New England countryside with few repercussions. At best, the ministers could only rebuke them through the press and debate how they might discourage their congregants from listening to these preachers.

Preaching's authority came from the ways it seeped through much of seventeenth- and eighteenth-century Congregationalist life. As historian Harry Stout observed about sermons, "the sermon stood alone in local New England contexts as the only regular (at least weekly) medium of public communication. As a channel of information, it combined religious, educational, and journalistic functions, and supplied all the key terms necessary to understand existence in this world and the next."[46] Sermon culture permeated New England life to the extent that it oriented much of congregants' listening and note-taking habits, and at times even informed their many ritualized habits around scripture.[47] Chauncy worried that itinerancy challenged the ways sermons were localized to speak to the daily rhythms of a local congregation. Ministers often crafted weekly sermons by relying on close proximity to and familiarity with congregants and tailoring their message to address regular congregational needs. In contrast, itinerancy proffered a universalizing and alluring message that was unmoored from the day-to-day minister-congregation relations, which grounded all religious performances within a community. As Chauncy saw it, disrupting this rhythm threatened the very fabric of New England religious life.

Much as Chauncy achieved some success in limiting itinerant preaching, he also succeeded with constraining print access for new religious voices. For thirty years after the revivals, racialized and heterodox authors struggled to publish their work through the British American printing press, with some having to circumvent New England's minister-printer relations by printing overseas in London. For most of the eighteenth century, religious printing was conducted on behalf of or with substantial support from published ministers, missionary organizations, and local congregations. Chauncy himself confessed that he was the primary editor for many of the antirevivalists' publications during the revivals of the 1740s. As he wrote, "there is scarce a piece against the times but was sent to me and I had the labour sometimes of preparing it for the press, and always of correcting the press."[48] Even without the power to actively censor the press, the complicated process of publishing, which balanced printers' and booksellers' market aspirations with ministers' and missionary organizations' goals of preserving an orthodox public sphere, maintained the prominence of Anglo Protestantism in print, at least in the British colonies.[49] Tools that promised sales, such as subscription lists and letters of support, transformed market logics into religious barriers to entry for non-Anglo Protestant authors in a largely Anglo Protestant market. The ways an imagined public sanctioned the publication of a text through salability and the way texts spoke to and on behalf of that imagined public replicated the minister-laity dynamic within New England Congregationalism. Whether it was by design or not, the effect these facets of print had on marginalized authors would contribute to reflecting Chauncy's social vision well into the 1770s.

Chauncy's involvement in the publications of marginalized authors appeared most prominently in the publication of Phyllis Wheatley's *Poems on Various Subjects, Religious and Moral* (1772). As the first print- published African American woman in the British c olonies, she was vetted by Boston's most esteemed magistrates and ministers, including Chauncy himself, to gain their approval that she was indeed the author of her work.[50] Such an effort was often required of racialized authors, given ministers' and Anglo Protestant readers' persistent doubts about racialized Protestants' abilities to perform English literacy in a manner worthy of the press. The attestation read: "WE whose Names are under-written, do assure the World, that the Poems specified in the following Page, *were (as we verily believe) written by Phillis, a young Negro Girl, who was but a few Years since, brought an uncultivated Barbarian from *Africa*." It continued: "She has been examined by some of the best Judges, and is thought qualified to write them."[51] The attestation itself was not a sign of approval for publication but merely a confirmation that Wheatley was the author of the text. This may partly explain why the text risked being printed across the Atlantic in London and not in the colonies where it might have been more convenient.[52] Outside of the first Native American–authored publication by Occom, titled *A Sermon Preached at the Execution of Moses Paul* (1772), there were barely any print publications by racialized authors within British America, likely owed to the continuing influence of Anglo Protestant ministers on the printing process. With the assistance of benefactors in London, the text would be published in London, away from the curatorial relationships that printers maintained with ministers like Chauncy whose history with religious speech and the press has demonstrated an investment in curating the religious public sphere. Remarking on Wheatley's publication, and perhaps echoing Chauncy's own bewilderment about non-Anglo Protestant public presence and voices during the Great Awakening revivals, Thomas Jefferson famously wrote: "Religion indeed has produced a Phyllis Whatley [*sic*]; but it could not produce a poet. The compositions published under her name are below the dignity of criticism."[53] As Jefferson so put it in a demeaning manner, the question of religion in the press revolved around expectations on who could speak to an Anglo Protestant public.

Why was print so important? Similar to oral preaching, print was an important medium of New England culture, so much so that it undergirded any performance that could be understood as religion. As historian David Hall wrote, "Lay men and women learned far more from spoken than from written sermons and got most of what they had to know from custom and face-to-face conversation. Yet the ways they viewed the world were sustained by print culture, and in turning to the books that circulated widely we encounter structures of belief, or as I prefer to say, the stories that lay people knew and used to understand the world."[54] However, one way to understand print as a medium for authority was through those who abstained from it altogether. Consider an exchange between Philadelphia printer Benjamin Franklin and Michael Wohlfahrt, a member of the Ephrata Cloister in Lancaster County, Pennsylvania.

Franklin, who had grown up among New England Puritans and was one of the primary printers who promoted revival through the publication of itinerant George Whitefield's sermons, wondered why they had not yet printed their theological views despite their access to a printer, investments in literacy and education, and even reliance on printed hymnals.[55] Wohlfahrt responded: "we fear that if we should once print our confession of faith, we should feel ourselves as if bound and confined by it, and perhaps be unwilling to receive further improvement; and our successors still more so, as conceiving what we their elders and founders had done to be something sacred, never to be departed from." Franklin was surprised, deeming their fear as modesty. Observing other denominations, especially the New England Puritans from whom he descended, he opined on "every other sect supposing itself in possession of all truth, and that those who differ are so far in the wrong."[56] This exchange captured how print naturalized discourse through the way it asserted permanence in New England's literary culture. Through its less perishable form compared to fragile manuscripts or ephemeral speech, and its authority to speak to and on behalf of an imagined public, print functioned differently from other modes of communication. It naturalized classification of the revivals onto the literary public sphere, and both published and authorized these ministers' interpretations for future generations. It was likely these features that Chauncy wanted to reserve strictly for ministers' uses.

CONCLUSION

Debates about whether the 1740s revivals constituted "religion" ultimately revolved around how the clergymen should manage performances. They were well aware that one could not interrogate beliefs unless they were appropriately performed, and they were well attentive to the ways such forms were mediated through itinerant preaching or publication via the printing press. It was through a particular understanding of religion as performance that Chauncy successfully leveraged his position and networks to manage revival during the 1740s and well into the 1770s. He knew that it was never simply about what people believed, but about what they purported to say, how they said it, where they proclaimed it, and to whom they spoke. Perhaps most strategically, Chauncy knew that whatever authority audiences lent to revivalists' performances was inherently tied to the mediums that carried their message. Perhaps it was on these eighteenth-century grounds that religion would continue to be used by Anglo Protestants as a way of managing acts and bodies, knowing full well that belief was never about an inaccessible interiority, but rather about assessing how one performed theology in a public setting.

NOTES

1. Jonathan Edwards, *Some Thoughts concerning the Present Revival of Religion in New-England* (Boston: S. Kneeland and T. Green, 1742), 53.

2. Charles Chauncy, *Seasonable Thoughts on the State of Religion in New-England, a Treatise in Five Parts* (Boston: Rogers and Fowle, 1743), 50.

3. See George Marsden, *Jonathan Edwards: A Life* (New Haven: Yale University Press, 2004); Mark Noll, *America's God* (New York: Oxford University Press, 2002); and Thomas Kidd, *The Great Awakening: The Roots of Evangelical Christianity in Colonial America* (New Haven: Yale University Press, 2007).

4. Historians have relied on a theological formulation called "Bebbington's Quadrilateral" which outlined the thread that united evangelicals across American history: Biblicism, Crucicentrism, Conversionism, and Activism. The criterion was coined by British historian of evangelicalism David Bebbington. See David Bebbington, *Evangelicalism in Modern Britain: A History from the 1730s to the 1980s* (London: Unwin Hyman, 1989). It is worth noting that these four characteristics all revolve around "belief": belief in the authority of scripture, belief in the atoning work of Jesus Christ, belief in the importance of converting others to Christianity, and a belief that the gospel must be lived out in the world. Among scholars who successfully made an argument for the Protestant religion's contribution to broader American intellectual traditions, perhaps the most influential was Nathan Hatch, *Democratization of American Christianity* (New Haven: Yale University Press, 1991), whose work shaped the works of other historians. See Daniel Walker Howe, *What Hath God Wrought: The Transformation of America, 1815–1848* (New York: Oxford University Press, 2009); and Sean Wilentz, *The Rise of American Democracy: Jefferson to Lincoln* (W. W. Norton, 2005). Specifically, historians like Marsden and Hatch successfully demonstrated the importance of nineteenth-century revivalists to many other democratizations in the nineteenth century and the rise of American institutions.

5. This has been a recurring critique of these historians' work. See Michael J. Altman, "'Religion, Religions, Religious,' in America: Toward a Smithian Account of Evangelicalism," *Method and Theory in the Study of Religion* 31 (2019): 71–82.

6. A range of books have examined different communities' experiences with the revivals. For a sampling of works (and this is by no means exhaustive), see Susan Juster, *Disorderly Women: Sexual Politics and Evangelicalism in Revolutionary New England* (Ithaca: Cornell University Press, 1996); Linford Fisher, *The Indian Great Awakening: Religion and the Shaping of Native Cultures in Early America* (New York: Oxford University Press, 2014); Christopher Cameron, *To Plead Our Own Cause: African Americans in Massachusetts and the Making of Antislavery Movement* (Kent, OH: Kent State University Press, 2014); and Douglas Winiarski, *Darkness Falls on the Land of Light* (Williamsburg, VA: Omohundro Institute of Early American History and Culture, 2017).

7. Charles Chauncy, *The Mystery Hid from Ages and Generations, Made Manifest by the Gospel-Revelation* (London: Printed for C. Dilly, 1784), vii.

8. Much of my readings on authority and speech relies on Bruce Lincoln, *Authority: Construction and Corrosion* (Chicago: University of Chicago Press, 1995). I read printed objects, both text and paratext, as comprising what Lincoln describes as "the whole theatrical array of

gestures, demeanors, costumes, props, and stage devices through which one may impress or bamboozle an audience" (7).

9. At least discursively. Scholars have looked for ways that congregants negotiated the contents of the sermon. The most notable work on this was Meredith Neuman, *Jeremiah's Scribes: Creating Sermon Literature in Puritan New England* (Philadelphia: University of Pennsylvania Press, 2011). However, I read mediated space more along the lines of Althusser's interpellation: subject formation could occur one way but not the other, and with the various cultural meanings that congregations have attributed to print, it was even more important that congregants could not simply print their own theologies. On subjecthood and sermons as genre, see Michael Warner, "The Evangelical Public Sphere," A. S. W. Rosenbach Lectures in Bibliography, Van Pelt Library, University of Pennsylvania, March 23–26, 2009. On scripture's role in mediating this process, also see Seth Perry, *Bible Culture and Authority in the Early United States* (Princeton: Princeton University Press, 2018).

10. J. Z. Smith, "Religions, Religious," in *Critical Terms for Religious Studies,* ed. Mark C. Taylor (Chicago: University of Chicago Press, 1998), 269–84, 269. "Religion" itself was a term familiar to many of the participants in and opponents of the revival. Smith's idea of it as a nonnative category, however, is helpful because it brings to the surface the instability of the term even among those for whom it could be argued to be native. Even the fact that Edwards and Chauncy were debating it suggested that there was no consensus for what it might mean.

11. My argument about the revivals joins a larger historiography that has focused on its material forms and emphasized its disruptive effects on ministerial authority. It's a position aligned with the historiography that includes Jon Butler, Frank Lambert, and most recently Douglas Winiarski. It stands in stark contrast to the more traditional approach, which described the revivals through their proto-democratic religiosities as told through the experience of supporters of the revivals themselves: evangelicals. See Noll, *America's God;* and Kidd, *Great Awakening*. See also Jon Butler, "Enthusiasm Described and Decried: The Great Awakening as Interpretative Fiction," *Journal of American History* 69, no. 2 (September 1982), 305–25; Frank Lambert, *Inventing the Great Awakening* (Princeton: Princeton University Press, 2001); Douglas Winiarski, *Darkness Falls on the Land of Light.*

12. Some of the earliest critiques of interpreting print as the sole form of publication came from scholars who turned to manuscript sources to make arguments about correspondence networks, orality, and other embodied means of enacting public theology. See Harry Stout, "Religion, Communications, and the Ideological Origins of the American Revolution," *William and Mary Quarterly* 34, no. 4 (October 1977): 519–41; Stout, *The New England Soul: Preaching and Religious Culture in Colonial New England* (Oxford: Oxford University Press, 1986); and Catherine Brekus, "Writing Religious Experience: Women's Authorship in Early America," *Journal of Religion* 92, no. 4 (October 2012): 482–97.

13. Edwards, *Some Thoughts*, 55.

14. Edwards, *Some Thoughts*, 15.

15. Edwards, *Some Thoughts*, 16 (original emphasis).

16. Edwards, *Some Thoughts*, 8.

17. Edwards, *Some Thoughts*, 79.

18. Edwards, *Some Thoughts*, 1.

19. Chauncy, *Seasonable Thoughts*, 26 (original emphasis).

20. Chauncy, *Seasonable Thoughts*, 27.

21. Edwards, *Some Thoughts*, 76.

22. Chauncy, *Seasonable Thoughts*, 28–29 (original emphasis).

23. For more on this notion of visible saints and the role of covenant, see John Winthrop, "A Modell of Christian Charity," *Collections of the Massachusetts Historical Society*, 3rd ser., no. 7 (1838): 31–48. For more on covenant as a social agreement among individuals, see Perry Miller, "The Marrow of Divinity," in *Errand into the Wilderness* (Cambridge, MA: Harvard University Press, 1952), 48–98; and John von Rohr, *The Covenant of Grace in Puritan Thought* (Atlanta: Scholars Press, 1986).

24. Edwards, *Some Thoughts*, 35.

25. Edwards, *Some Thoughts*, 9 (original emphasis).

26. Edwards, *Some Thoughts*, 11.

27. Edwardsd, *Some Thoughts*, 8.

28. Sarah Rivett, *Science of the Soul in Colonial New England* (Chapel Hill: University of North Carolina Press, 2011), 325.

29. This is an important point about the revivalists who themselves seemed to emphasize this kind of self-knowledge. Historian Catherine Brekus has connected this feature of the revivalists to broader currents in the early modern European Enlightenment. On this front, Edwards's confidence in self-knowledge harkens back to some of philosopher John Locke's own work on the matter. See Catherine Brekus, *Sarah Osborn's World: The Rise of Evangelical Christianity in Early America* (New Haven: Yale University Press, 2013).

30. Chauncy, *Seasonable Thoughts*, 7 (original emphasis).

31. Edwards, *Some Thoughts*, 2.

32. Edwards, *Some Thoughts*, 3 (original emphasis).

33. Smith, "Religions, Religious," 269.

34. Chauncy, *Seasonable Thoughts*, 200.

35. Ministerial anxiety and the ever-looming threat of fracture has been an important through-line for historians of New England Puritanism. See Miller, *Errand into the Wilderness*. Miller already tracked this anxiety through the tensions between New England colonists and their European counterparts. The main concern for ministers, as scholars have argued but I'm a bit wary about, was their waning influence on political authorities whose interests had shifted toward accommodating economic and political interests rather than theological ones. For example, see Christopher Grasso, *A Speaking Aristocracy: Transforming Public Discourse in Eighteenth-Century Connecticut* (Chapel Hill: University of North Carolina Press, 1999).

36. Edwards, *Some Thoughts*, 139.

37. Edwards, *Some Thoughts*, 59.

38. Edwards, *Some Thoughts*, 86.

39. For more on Edwards's pursuit of "true religion" outside of the revivals, see Rivett, *Science of the Soul*. For more on Native American revivals, see Linford Fisher, *The Indian Great Awakening: Religion and the Shaping of Native Cultures in Early America* (Oxford: Oxford University Press, 2014). For more on Edwards himself, see Marsden, *Jonathan Edwards: A Life*

40. Chauncy, *Seasonable Thoughts*, 334.

41. Chauncy, *Seasonable Thoughts*, 226.

42. Chauncy, *Seasonable Thoughts*, 200. Chauncy did not write much about his skepticism around the scale of revival accounts outside of his general assessment that the event itself sensationalized. For more on the limits on the revival, see Linford Fisher, "It Provd but Temporary, & Short Lived: Pequot Affiliation in the First Great Awakening," *Ethnohistory* 59, no. 3 (2012): 465–88.

43. On this front two works have argued for this democratization narrative; see Hatch, *Democratization of American Christianity*; and Grasso, *A Speaking Aristocracy*. Both works charted the declension narrative that ministers feared: different voices could now enter print and assert themselves as authorities on theological matters. Whether that phenomenon should be called "democratization" or "secularization" has been the primary contention since, rather than flattening authority structures, access to the printing press may have just created new hierarchies that mirrored traditional hierarchical structures. See Amanda Porterfield, *Conceived in Doubt: Religion and Politics in the New American Nation* (Chicago: University of Chicago Press, 2012). I opt for the term "dilute," acknowledging that in a print market, publications at best crowded out ministers' publications rather than necessarily signaling a decline in religious interest.

44. For more on institutional fracturing, see Winiarski, *Darkness Falls on the Land of Light*.

45. On Native American religiosities that coincided with the revivals, see Fisher, *The Indian Great Awakening*. On Sarah Osborn, see Brekus, *Sarah Osborn's World*.

46. Stout, *The New England Soul*, 3. For more on the ways sermons functioned as a way of connecting local towns with each other, see Richard Brown, *Knowledge Is Power: The Diffusion of Information in Early America, 1700–1865* (Oxford: Oxford University Press, 1991).

47. See Neuman and Matthew Brown, *The Pilgrim and the Bee: Reading Rituals and Book Culture in Early New England* (Philadelphia: University of Pennsylvania Press, 2007).

48. Charles Chauncy, "A Sketch of Eminent Men in New England," *Collections of the Massachusetts Historical Society*, 1st ser., no. 10 (1809): 73.

49. Most famously, Benjamin Franklin himself balanced the politics of printing during the revivals. He gladly printed for famous revivalist George Whitefield, due to its profitability and perhaps as a way to also bother his Congregationalist peers. For the best overview of colonial print, see Hugh Amory and David D. Hall, eds., *A History of the Book in America, Vol. 1: The Colonial Book in the Atlantic World* (Cambridge: Cambridge University Press, 1999).

50. See Henry Louis Gates Jr., *The Trials of Phyllis Wheatley* (New York: Basic Books, 2009).

51. Phyllis Wheatley, *Poems on Various Subjects, Religious and Moral* (London: A. Bell, Aldgate, 1773). For more on Wheatley, see Vincent Carretta, *Phillis Wheatley: Biography of a Genius in Bondage* (Athens: University of Georgia Press, 2011).

52. There were many other reasons why the text was published in London, but there's a lot to be said about Wheatley having to travel across the Atlantic and meet with her sponsors who connected her to publishers there, rather than meeting with the publishers in the colonies.

53. Thomas Jefferson, *Notes on the State of Virginia* (Philadelphia: Prichard and Hall, 1788), 150.

54. David D. Hall, *Worlds of Wonder, Days of Judgment: Popular Religious Belief in New England* (Cambridge, MA: Harvard University Press, 1990), 70.

55. On Franklin's upbringing and how it shaped his own views, see Thomas Kidd, *Benjamin Franklin: The Religious Life of a Founding Father* (New Haven: Yale University Press, 2017).

56. The actual quotation appears in Franklin's autobiography, where he recounted an encounter with Michael Wohlfahrt, a follower of Johann Conrad Beissel, the leader who founded the Ephrata Cloister. Benjamin Franklin, *Franklin's Autobiography*, ed. Frank Woodworth Pine (New York: Henry Hold and Co., 1916).

Bibliography

Aborn, Sasha. N.d. "The Truth about the Duggars Dresscode." *The List.*

Adorno, Theodor W. *Prisms.* Cambridge, MA: MIT Press, 1981.

Agrippa, Henry Cornelius, and L. W. de Laurence. *The Philosophy of Natural Magic.* Chicago: de Laurence Co., 1913.

Ahmed, Sara. *The Cultural Politics of Emotion.* London: Routledge, 2004. 2nd ed., Edinburgh: Edinburgh University Press, 2014.

———. *The Promise of Happiness.* Durham, NC: Duke University Press, 2010.

Aidi, Hisham D. *Rebel Music: Race, Empire, and the New Muslim Youth Culture.* New York: Pantheon, 2014.

Alempijevic, Djordje, et al. "Statement on Conversion Therapy." *Journal of Forensic and Legal Medicine* 72 (2020): 1–6.

Alfaro, Olmedo. *El peligro antiallano en la America Central: La defensa de la raza.* 2d ed. Panama: Imprenta Nacional, 1925.

Allen, Ted. "Longtime Campus Counselor and Mentor Leaves Legacy of Love at Liberty." January 13, 2021.

Altman, Michael J., ed. *American Examples: New Conversations about Religion.* Vol. 1. Tuscaloosa: University of Alabama Press, 2021.

———. *Heathen, Hindoo, Hindu: American Representations of India, 1721–1893.* Oxford: Oxford University Press, 2017.

———. "'Religion, Religions, Religious' in America: Toward a Smithian Account of 'Evangelicalism.'" *Method and Theory in the Study of Religion* 31, no. 1 (2019): 71–82.

American Sermons: The Pilgrims to Martin Luther King Jr. New York: Library of America, 1999.

Amory, Hugh, and David Hall, eds. *A History of the Book in America, Vol. 1: The Colonial Book in the Atlantic World.* Cambridge: Cambridge University Press, 1999.

Ampadu, Lena. "Maria W. Stewart and the Rhetoric of Black Preaching: Perspectives on Womanism and Black Nationalism." In *Black Women's Intellectual Traditions: Speaking Their Minds,* edited by Kristin Waters and Carol B. Conaway, 38–54. Burlington: University of Vermont Press, 2007.

Andrews, William L., ed. *Sisters of the Spirit: Three Black Women's Autobiographies of the 19th Century.* Bloomington: Indiana University Press, 1986.

"The Annual Report of the American and Foreign Anti-Slavery Society, Presented at New York." William Harned, for the American and Foreign Anti-Slavery Society, May 7, 1850. American Congregational Library.

Another Assault on the South. *Charleston Mercury*, January 27, 1843.

"The Anti-Slavery Assaults on Mr. Calhoun and the South—Again." *Charleston Mercury*, January 28, 1843.

Appelfeld, Aharon. "After the Holocaust." In *Writing and the Holocaust*, edited by Berel Lang, 83–92. New York: Holmes and Meier, 1988.

Appleby, R. Scott, and Martin E. Marty. *Fundamentalisms Observed*. Chicago: University of Chicago Press, 2004.

Asad, Talal. *Formations of the Secular: Christianity, Islam, Modernity*. Stanford: Stanford University Press, 2003.

Auston, Donna. "Prayer, Protest, and Police Brutality: Black Muslim Spiritual Resistance in the Ferguson Era." *Transforming Anthropology* 25, no. 1 (2017): 11–22.

Bachman, John. *The Doctrine of the Unity of the Human Race Examined on the Principles of Science*. Charleston, 1850.

Baker, Paula. "The Domestication of Politics: Women and American Political Society, 1780–1920." *American Historical Review* 89, no. 3 (1984): 620–47.

Bald, Vivek. *Bengali Harlem and the Lost Histories of South Asian America*. Cambridge, MA: Harvard University Press, 2013.

Baldwin, James. *The Cross of Redemption: Uncollected Writings*. New York: Vintage, 2010.

———. "Here Be Dragons." In *The Price of the Ticket: Collected Nonfiction, 1948–1985*, 677–90. New York: St. Martin's Press, 1985.

Baraka, Amiri (LeRoi Jones). "Expressive Language." In Baraka, *Home: Social Essays* (1963). Reprint. New York: Akashic Books, 2009.

Barkun, Michael. "Conspiracy Theories as Stigmatized Knowledge." *Diogenes* 62, nos. 3–4 (2015): 114–20.

———. *Religion and the Racist Right: The Origins of the Christian Identity Movement*. Chapel Hill: University of North Carolina Press, 1997.

Barnum, Phineas T. *The Life of P. T. Barnum*. New York: Redfield, 1855.

Bartkowski, John P. "Debating Patriarchy: Discursive Disputes over Spousal Authority among Evangelical Family Commentators." *Journal for the Scientific Study of Religion* 36, no. 3 (1997): 393–410.

———. *The Promise Keepers: Servants, Soldiers, and Godly Men*. New Brunswick, NJ: Rutgers University Press, 2003.

Bartky, Sandra L. "Foucault, Femininity, and the Modernization of Patriarchal Power." In *Feminist Social Thought: A Reader*, edited by Diana Tietjens Meyers, 93–111. New York: Routledge, 1990.

Bayart, Jean-François. *The Illusion of Cultural Identity*. Trans. Steven Rendall, Janet Roitman, Cynthia Schoch, and Jonathan Derrick. Chicago: University of Chicago Press, 2005.

Begum, Sultan Jahan. "We Sinful Women ('Hum Guneghaar Aurtain'): Transgressing Temporality and Poetic Form." *Literature and Transgression*, April 17, 2014.

Bell, Catherine M. *Ritual Theory, Ritual Practice*. New York: Oxford University Press, 2009.

Bendroth, Margaret Lamberts. "Fundamentalism and the Family: Gender, Culture, and the

American Pro-family Movement." *Journal of Women's History* 10, no. 4 (1999): 35–54.

Benjamin, Walter W., and Leland Scott. "The Methodist Episcopal Church in the Postwar Era." In *The History of American Methodism*, edited by Emory Stevens Bucke, 2:315–90. New York: Abingdon Press, 1964.

Bennett, Jeffrey A. "Love Me Gender: Normative Homosexuality and 'Ex-gay' Performativity in Reparative Therapy Narratives." *Text and Performance Quarterly* 23, no. 4 (2003): 331–52.

Berbrier, Mitch. 2000. "The Victim Ideology of White Supremacists and White Nationalists in the United States." *Sociological Focus* 33, no. 2 (2000): 175–91.

Berger, Peter L. *The Sacred Canopy: Elements of Sociological Theory of Religion*. New York: Anchor Books, 1990.

Berger, Peter L., and Thomas Luckmann. *The Social Construction of Reality*. New York: Doubleday, 1967.

Berlant, Lauren. "Cruel Optimism." In *The Affect Theory Reader*, edited by Melissa Gregg and Gregory J. Seigworth, 93–117. Durham, NC: Duke University Press, 2010.

Berlet, Chip. "Christian identity: The Apocalyptic Style, Political Religion, Palingenesis and Neo-fascism." *Totalitarian Movements and Political Religions* 5, no. 3 (2004): 469–506.

Berry, Daina Ramey, and Leslie M. Harris, eds. *Sexuality and Slavery: Reclaiming Intimate Histories in the Americas*. Athens: University of Georgia Press, 2018.

Berzon, Todd. *Classifying Christians: Ethnography, Heresiology, and the Limits of Knowledge in Late Antiquity*. Berkeley: University of California Press, 2016.

Besson, Jean. *Martha Brae's Two Histories: European Expansion and Caribbean Culture-Building in Jamaica*. Chapel Hill: University of North Carolina Press, 2002.

Best, Stephen, and Saidiya Hartman. "Fugitive Justice." *Representations* 92, no. 1 (Fall 2005): 1–15.

Bey, Marquis, and Jesse A. Goldberg. "Queer as in Abolition Now!" *GLQ: A Journal of Lesbian and Gay Studies* 28, no. 2 (April 2022): 159–63.

"Big Family Meets Big Apple." *Seventeen Kids and Counting*, E01S01. TLC, September 28, 2008.

Birth, Kevin. "Most of Us Are Family Some of the Time: Interracial Unions and Transracial Kinship in Eastern Trinidad." *American Ethnologist* 24, no. 3 (1997): 585–601.

Bishop, Christopher Michael. "Methodism, the Middle Class, and the New South, 1866–1894." PhD diss., Auburn University, 2018.

"Black Vomit." *Gazette of the United States*, September 14, 1793.

Blakely, Johanna. "Liberals and Conservatives Have Wildly Different TV-Viewing Habits—But These Five Shows Bring Everyone Together." *The Conversation*, July 1, 2019.

Bledstein, Burton J. *The Culture of Professionalization: The Middle Class and the Development of Higher Education in America*. New York: W. W. Norton, 1976.

Blockett, Kimberly. "Disrupting Print: Emigration, the Press, and Narrative Subjectivity in the British Preaching and Writing of Zilpha Elaw, 1840–1860s." *MELUS: Multi-Ethnic Literature of the United States* 40, no. 3 (September 2015): 94–109.

Blumberg, Antonia. "What You Need to Know about the 'Quiverfull' Movement." *HuffPost*, May 26, 2015.

Boggs, Carl. "Marxism, Prefigurative Communism, and the Problem of Workers' Control." *Radical America* 6 (Winter 1977).

Boivin, Michel. *The Hindu Sufis of South Asia: Partition, Shrine Culture and Sindhis in India.* London: I. B. Tauris, 2019.

"Bombshell Duggar Police Report." *InTouch*, September 22, 2016.

Bourdieu, Pierre. *Distinction: A Social Critique of the Judgement of Taste.* Translated by Richard Nice. Cambridge, MA: Harvard University Press, 1984.

Breines, Wini. 1989. *Community and Organization in the New Left, 1962–1968: The Great Refusal.* New Brunswick, NJ: Rutgers University Press.

Brekus, Catherine A. *Sarah Osborn's World: The Rise of Evangelical Christianity in Early America.* New Haven: Yale University Press, 2013.

———. *Strangers and Pilgrims: Female Preaching in America, 1740–1845.* Chapel Hill: University of North Carolina Press, 1998.

———. "Writing Religious Experience: Women's Authorship in Early America." *Journal of Religion* 92, no. 4 (October 2012): 482–97.

Brown, Kathleen M. *Good Wives, Nasty Wenches, and Anxious Patriarchs: Gender, Race, and Power in Colonial Virginia.* Chapel Hill: University of North Carolina Press, 1996.

Brown, Matthew. *The Pilgrim and the Bee: Reading Rituals and Book Culture in Early New England.* Philadelphia: University of Pennsylvania Press, 2007.

Brown, Richard. *Knowledge Is Power: The Diffusion of Information in Early America, 1700–1865.* Oxford: Oxford University Press, 1991.

Bryce, Benjamin. "Undesirable Britons: South Asian Migration and the Making of a White Argentina." *Hispanic American Historical Review* 99, no. 2 (2019).

Buckland, Michael. *Information and Society.* Cambridge, MA: MIT Press, 2017.

Burke, Edmund. *Reflections on the Revolution in France.* London, 1790.

Burke, Sean D. *Queering the Ethiopian Eunuch: Strategies of Ambiguity in Acts.* New York: Fortress Press, 2013.

Burton, Tara Isabella. "Christianity Gets Weird." *New York Times*, May 8, 2020.

Butler, Jon. "Enthusiasm Described and Decried: The Great Awakening as Interpretative Fiction." *Journal of American History* 69, no. 2 (September 1982): 305–25.

Cabico, Regie. ed. *Stoked Words: An Anthology of Queer Poetry from the Capturing Fire Slam and Summit.* Washington, DC: Capturing Fire Press, 2018.

Camp, Stephanie M. H. *Closer to Freedom: Enslaved Women and Everyday Resistance in the Plantation South.* Chapel Hill: University of North Carolina Press, 2004.

Campt, Tina Marie. *Listening to Images.* Durham, NC: Duke University Press, 2017.

Cannon, Katie G. "Hitting a Straight Lick with a Crooked Stick: The Womanist Dilemma in the Development of a Black Liberation Ethic." *Annual of the Society of Christian Ethics* 7 (1987): 165–77.

Carbajal, Alberto Fernández. *Queer Muslim Diasporas in Contemporary Literature and Film.* Manchester, UK: Manchester University Press, 2019.

Carretta, Vincent. *Phillis Wheatley: Biography of a Genius in Bondage.* Athens: University of Georgia Press, 2011.

Chan-Malik, Sylvia. *Being Muslim: A Cultural History of Women of Color in American Islam.* New York: New York University Press, 2018.

Chauncy, Charles. *The Mystery Hid from Ages and Generations, Made Manifest by the Gospel-Revelation.* London: Printed for C. Dilly, 1784.

———. *Seasonable Thoughts on the State of Religion in New-England, a Treatise in Five Parts.* Boston: Rogers and Fowle, 1743.

———. "A Sketch of Eminent Men in New England." *Collections of the Massachusetts Historical Society*, 1st ser., no. 10 (1809).

Choudhury, Samah, Prea Persaud, and Michael J. Altman, eds. *American Examples: New Conversations about Religion*. Vol. 2. Tuscaloosa: University of Alabama Press, 2021.

Cohen, Cathy. "Punks, Bulldaggers, and Welfare Queens: The Real Radical Potential of Queer Politics?" In *Black Queer Studies: A Critical Anthology*, edited by Mae Henderson and Patrick E Johnson, 21–51. Durham, NC: Duke University Press, 2005.

———. "The Radical Potential Of Queer? Twenty Years Later." *GLQ: A Journal of Lesbian and Gay Studies* 25, no. 1 (January 1, 2019): 140–44.

Coley, Jonathan S. *Gay on God's Campus: Mobilizing for LGBT Equality at Christian Colleges and Universities*. Chapel Hill: University of North Carolina Press, 2018.

"The Constitution of the United States with All the Acts of Congress in Relation to Slavery." D. M. Dewey: Arcade Hall, Rochester, NY, 1854. Boston Athenaeum.

Cook, James. 2001. *The Arts of Deception: Playing with Fraud in the Age of Barnum*. Cambridge, MA: Harvard University Press.

Corinealdi, Kaysha. "Envisioning Multiple Citizenships: West Indian Panamanians and Creating Community in the Canal Zone Neocolony." *Global South* 6, no. 2 (Fall 2012): 87–106.

Cornish, F., J. Haaken, L. Moskovitz, and S. Jackson. "Rethinking Prefigurative Politics: Introduction to the Special Thematic Section." *Journal of Social and Political Psychology* 4, no. 1 (2016): 114–27.

Craig, Shelley L., et al. "Fighting for Survival: The Experiences of Lesbian, Gay, Bisexual, Transgender, and Questioning Students in Religious Colleges and Universities." *Journal of Gay and Lesbian Social Services* 29, no. 1 (2017): 1–24.

Crawley, Ashon T. *The Lonely Letters*. Durham, NC: Duke University Press, 2020.

Critchlow, Donald T. *Phyllis Schlafly and Grassroots Conservatism: A Woman's Crusade*. Princeton: Princeton University Press, 2008.

Crosson, J. Brent. *Experiments with Power: Obeah and the Remaking of Religion in Trinidad*. Chicago: University of Chicago Press, 2020.

———. "Own People: Race, 'Altered Solidarities,' and the Limits of Culture in Trinidad." *Small Axe* 45 (November 2014): 18–34.

———. "What Obeah Does Do: Healing, Harm, and the Limits of Religion." *Journal of Africana Religions* 3, no. 2 (2015): 151–76.

Crumley, Jaimie D. "Tried as by Fire: Free African American Women's Abolitionist Theologies, 1789–1880." PhD diss., UCLA, 2022.

C-SPAN. "Q and A with Paul Weyrich." March 22, 2005.

C-SPAN. "Roundtable with Bill McCartney." September 30, 1997.

Cuneo, Michael W. *The Smoke of Satan: Conservative and Traditionalist Dissent in Contemporary American Catholicism*. Baltimore: Johns Hopkins University Press, 1999.

Daly, Gabriel. "Catholicism and Modernism." *Journal of the American Academy of Religion* 53 (1985): 773–96.

Das, Veena. *Life and Words: Violence and the Descent into the Ordinary*. Berkeley: University of California Press, 2007.

de Laurence, L. W. *The Great Book of Magical Art, Hindu Magic and East Indian Occultism.* Chicago: de Laurence Co., 1915.

———. *The Sacred Book of Death, Hindu Spiritism, Soul Transition and Soul Reincarnation.* Chicago: de Laurence, Scott and Co., 1905.

DiBranco, Alex. "Before the Alt-Right: Anita Hill and the Growth of Misogynist Ideology." Institute for Research on Male Supremacism, August 13, 2018.

Dochuk, Darren. *From Bible Belt to Sun Belt: Plain-Folk Religion, Grassroots Politics, and the Rise of Evangelical Conservatism.* New York: W. W. Norton, 2011.

"Document 21: General Association of Massachusetts Congregational Churches, 'Pastoral Letter,' 28 June 1837." Alexander Street Documents.

"The Domestic Institutions of the South." *Charleston Mercury*, January 14, 1843.

Donoghue, Michael E. *Borderland on the Isthmus: Race, Culture, and the Struggle for the Canal Zone.* Durham, NC: Duke University Press, 2014.

Douglas, Kelly Brown. *Sexuality and the Black Church: A Womanist Perspective.* Maryknoll, N: Orbis Books, 1999.

Douglas, Mary. *Purity and Danger: An Analysis of Concepts of Pollution and Taboo.* London: Routledge and Kegan Paul, 1978.

Doyle, Don H. *New Men, New Cities, New South: Atlanta, Nashville, Charleston, Mobile, 1860–1910.* Chapel Hill: University of North Carolina Press, 1990.

Durkheim, Émile. *The Elementary Forms of Religious Life.* New York: Free Press, 1965.

Durkin, Tish. "The Catholics Who Hate Joe Biden—and Pope Francis." *The Atlantic*, October 21, 2020.

Edwards, Jonathan. *Some Thoughts concerning the Present Revival of Religion in New-England.* Boston: S. Kneeland and T. Green, 1742.

Edwards, Rebecca. *New Spirits: Americans in the Gilded Age, 1865–1905.* New York: Oxford University Press, 2006.

Elaw, Zilpha. "Memoirs of the Life, Religious Experience, Ministerial Travels, and Labours of Mrs. Elaw." In *Sisters of the Spirit: Three Black Women's Autobiographies of the Nineteenth Century*, edited by William L. Andrews, 49–160. Bloomington: Indiana University Press, 1986.

Erzen, Tanya. *Straight to Jesus: Sexual and Christian Conversions in the Ex-Gay Movement.* Berkeley: University of California Press, 2006.

Falzon, Mark-Anthony. *Cosmopolitan Connections: The Sindhi Diaspora.* Leiden: Brill, 2004.

Farber, David. 2012. *The Rise and Fall of Modern American Conservatism: A Short History.* Princeton: Princeton University Press.

Feminist Critical Hindu Studies Collective. "Feminist Critical Hindu Studies in Formation." *Religion Compass* (2021): e12392.

Fisher, Linford. *The Indian Great Awakening: Religion and the Shaping of Native Cultures in Early America.* Oxford: Oxford University Press, 2014.

FitzGerald, David Scott, and David Cook-Martín. *Culling the Masses: The Democratic Origins of Racist Immigration Policy in the Americas.* Cambridge, MA: Harvard University Press, 2014.

Fitzgerald, Tim. "Religion, Philosophy, and Family Resemblances." *Religion* 26 (1996): 215–36.

Floyd-Thomas, Stacey M. *Mining the Motherlode: Methods in Womanist Ethics*. Cleveland: Pilgrim Press, 2006.

Flynn, J. D. Twitter post, February 13, 2021.

Forman, Murray, and Mark Anthony Neal, eds. *That's the Joint! The Hip-Hop Studies Reader*. New York: Routledge, 2004.

Foucault, Michel. "About the Beginning of the Hermeneutics of the Self (1980)." In *Religion and Culture*, edited by Jeremy R. Carrette, 158–81. New York: Routledge, 1999.

———. "Docile Bodies." In *The Foucault Reader*, edited by Paul Rabinow, 179–87. New York: Pantheon, 1984.

———. "Panopticism." In *The Foucault Reader*, edited by Paul Rabinow, 206–13. New York: Pantheon, 1984.

———. *Power/Knowledge: Selected Interviews and Other Writings 1972–1977*. Edited by Colin Gordon. New York: Pantheon, 1980.

———. "Sexuality and Power (1978)." In *Religion and Culture*, edited by Jeremy R. Carrette, 115–30. New York: Routledge, 1999.

Frank, Lambert. *Inventing the Great Awakening*. Princeton: Princeton University Press, 2001.

Frank, Priscilla. "Welcome to the Bizarre and Beautiful World of Purity Balls." *HuffPost*, December 6, 2017.

Franklin, Benjamin. *Franklin's Autobiography*. Edited by Frank Woodworth Pine. New York: Henry Holt and Co., 1916.

Freeman, Elizabeth. "Queer Belongings: Kinship Theory and Queer Theory." In *A Companion to Lesbian, Gay, Bisexual, Transgender, and Queer Studies*, edited by George E. Haggerty and Molly McGarry. Malden, MA: Blackwell, 2007.

Freitas, Stéphane de, dir. *On est ensemble/We Are One*. Netflix, 2020.

Gates, Henry Louis, Jr. *The Trials of Phyllis Wheatley*. New York: Basic Books, 2009.

Geertz, Clifford. *The Interpretation of Cultures: Selected Essays*. New York: Basic Books, 1973.

Generations of Light. "The Pledge."

Gerber, Lynne. "Grit, Guts, and Vanilla Beans: Godly Masculinity in the Ex-Gay Movement." *Gender and Society* 29, no. 1 (2015): 26–50.

Gilmore, Glenda Elizabeth. *Gender and Jim Crow: Women and the Politics of White Supremacy in North Carolina, 1896–1920*. Chapel Hill: University of North Carolina Press, 1996.

Gjelten, Tom. "For Trump, Conservative Catholics Are the New Evangelicals." NPR, October 26, 2020.

Glatshteyn, Yankev. "A gute nakht, velt" [Good Night, World]. *Inzikh* 8, no. 3 (April 1938): 66–67.

———. "A gute nakht, velt." In *Gedenklider* [In Remembrance], 41–42. New York: Yidisher Kemfer, 1943.

Gordon, Linda. *The Moral Property of Women: A History of Birth Control Politics in America*. Chicago: University of Chicago Press, 2007.

"Grand Exhibition!" *Charleston Mercury*, January 17, 1843.

Grantham, Dewey W. "The Contours of Southern Progressivism." *American Historical Review* 86, no. 5 (December 1981): 1035–59.

Grasso, Christopher. *A Speaking Aristocracy: Transforming Public Discourse in Eighteenth-Century Connecticut*. Chapel Hill: University of North Carolina Press, 1999.

Green, Elna C. *Southern Strategies: Southern Women and the Woman Suffrage Question.* Chapel Hill: University of North Carolina Press, 1997.

Greenberg, Kenneth S. "The Nose, the Lie, and the Duel in the Antebellum South." *American Historical Review* 95, no. 1 (1990): 57–74.

Greene, Julie. "Spaniards on the Silver Roll: Labor Troubles and Liminality in the Panama Canal Zone, 1904–1914." *International Labor and Working-Class History* 66 (Fall 2004): 78–98.

Greene-Hayes, Ahmad. "'Queering' African American Religious History." *Religion Compass* 13, no. 7 (2019): e12319.

Guy-Sheftall, Beverly. "The Combahee River Collective." In *Words of Fire: An Anthology of African-American Feminist Thought*, 231–40. New York: New Press, 1995.

Hackney, Sheldon. *Populism to Progressivism in Alabama.* Princeton: Princeton University Press, 1969.

Halberstam, Jack. *Trans*: A Quick and Quirky Account of Gender Variability.* Berkeley: University of California Press, 2018.

Hall, David. *Lived Religion in America: Toward A History of Practice.* Princeton: Princeton University Press, 1997.

———. *Worlds of Wonder, Days of Judgment: Popular Religious Belief in New England.* Cambridge, MA: Harvard University Press, 1990.

Hall, Stuart. "Cultural Identity and Diaspora." In *Identity: Community, Culture, Difference*, edited by Jonathan Rutherford. London: Lawrence and Wishart, 1990.

———. "Fantasy, Identity, Politics." In *Cultural Remix: Theories of Politics and the Popular*, edited by Erica Carter, James Donald, and Judith Squires, 63–69. London: Lawrence and Wishart, 1995.

———. "Introduction: Who Needs 'Identity'?" In *Questions of Cultural Identity*, edited by Stuart Hall and Paul Du Gay, 1–17. London: Sage Publications, 1996.

———. "Race, Articulation and Societies Structured in Dominance." In *Sociological Theories: Race and Colonialism.* Paris: UNESCO, 1980.

Hallinan, Blake, and Ted Striphas. "Recommended for You: The Netflix Prize and the Production of Algorithmic Culture." *New Media and Society* (2014).

Harding, Susan. "Representing Fundamentalism: The Problem of the Repugnant Cultural Other." *Social Research* 58, no. 2 (1991): 373–93.

Hardisty, Jean. *Mobilizing Resentment: Conservative Resurgence from the John Birch Society to the Promise Keepers.* Boston: Beacon Press, 1999.

Harris, Neil. *Humbug: The Art of P. T. Barnum.* Chicago: University of Chicago Press, 1981.

Harrison, Laura, and Sarah B. Rowley. "Babies by the Bundle: Gender, Backlash, and the Quiverfull Movement." *Feminist Formations* 23, no. 1 (Spring 2011): 47–69.

Harrison, W. P., ed. *Journal of the General Conference of the Methodist Episcopal Church, South, Held in Nashville, Tenn., 1882.* Nashville: Southern Methodist Publishing House, 1882.

———. *Journal of the General Conference of the Methodist Episcopal Church, South, Held in St. Louis, Mo., May, 1890.* Nashville: Publishing House of the Methodist Episcopal Church, South, 1890.

Hartman, Saidiya V. *Lose Your Mother: A Journey along the Atlantic Slave Route.* New York: Farrar, Straus, and Giroux, 2007.

———. *Scenes of Subjection: Terror, Slavery, and Self-Making in Nineteenth Century America.* New York: Oxford University Press, 1997.

———. "Venus in Two Acts." *Small Axe* 26 (June 2008): 1–14.

Hatch, Nathan. *The Democratization of American Christianity.* New Haven: Yale University Press, 1991.

Herman, Didi. "'Then I Saw a New Heaven and a New Earth': Thoughts on the Christian Right and the Problem of 'Backlash.'" In *Dangerous Territories*, edited by Leslie G. Roman and Linda Eyre. New York: Routledge, 1997.

Higginbotham, Evelyn Brooks. *Righteous Discontent: The Women's Movement in the Black Baptist Church, 1880–1920.* Cambridge, MA: Harvard University Press, 1993.

Hilberg, Raul. *Perpetrators Victims Bystanders: The Jewish Catastrophe, 1933–1945.* New York: HarperPerennial, 1993.

Hine, Darlene Clark. "Rape and the Inner Lives of Black Women in the Middle West." *Signs* 14, no. 4 (1989): 912–20.

Holm, April E. *A Kingdom Divided: Evangelicals, Loyalty, and Sectionalism in the Civil War Era.* Baton Rouge: Louisiana State University Press, 2017.

Hong, Grace Kyungwon. *Death beyond Disavowal: The Impossible Politics of Difference.* Minneapolis: University of Minnesota Press, 2015.

hooks, bell. *Yearning: Race, Gender, and Cultural Politics.* New York: Routledge, 2014.

Horowitz, Jason. "Steve Bannon Carries Battles to Another Influential Hub: The Vatican." *New York Times*, February 7, 2017.

Hudnut-Beumler, James. *In Pursuit of the Almighty's Dollar: A History of Money and American Protestantism.* Chapel Hill: University of North Carolina Press, 2007.

Hunt, Stephen. *Christian Millenarianism: From the Early Church to Waco.* Bloomington: Indiana University Press, 2001.

Hunter, James Davison. *Culture Wars: The Struggle to Define America.* New York: Basic Books, 1991.

Immerwahr, Daniel. *How to Hide an Empire: A History of the Greater United States.* New York: Farrar, Straus, and Giroux, 2020.

Israel, Charles A. *Before Scopes: Evangelicalism, Education, and Evolution in Tennessee, 1870–1925.* Athens: University of Georgia Press, 2004.

Jefferson, Thomas. *Notes on the State of Virginia.* Philadelphia: Printed and Sold by Prichard and Hall, 1788.

Johnson, E. Patrick. *Honeypot: Black Southern Women Who Love Women.* Durham, NC: Duke University Press, 2019.

"Joice Heth." *Charleston Mercury*, February 7, 1843.

Joyce, Kathryn. "Arrows for the War." *The Nation*, November 9, 2006.

———. "Deep State, Deep Church: How Qanon and Trumpism Have Infected the Catholic Church." *Vanity Fair*, October 30, 2020.

———. *Quiverfull: Inside the Christian Patriarchy Movement.* Boston: Beacon Press, 2009.

Kelly, Annie. "The Housewives of White Supremacy." *New York Times*, June 1, 2018.

Khabeer, Su'ad Abdul. *Muslim Cool: Race, Religion, and Hip Hop in the United States.* New York: New York University Press, 2016.

Khan, Aisha. "Caucasian, Coolie, Black, or White? Color and Race in the Indo-Caribbean

Diaspora." In *Shades of Difference: Why Skin Color Matters*, edited by Evelyn Nakano Glenn. Stanford: Stanford University Press, 2009.

———. "Dark Arts and Diaspora." *Diaspora: A Journal of Transnational Studies* 17, no. 1 (Spring 2008): 40–63.

Kidd, Thomas. *Benjamin Franklin: The Religious Life of a Founding Father*. New Haven: Yale University Press, 2017.

———. *The Great Awakening: The Roots of Evangelical Christianity*. New Haven: Yale University Press, 2008.

Kiersz, Andy, and Hunter Walker. "These Three Charts Confirm Conservatives' Worst Fears about American Culture." *Business Insider*, November 3, 2014.

Kilde, Jeanne Halgren. *When Church Became Theatre: The Transformation of Evangelical Architecture and Worship in Nineteenth-Century America*. New York: Oxford University Press, 2002.

Kloß, Sinah Theres. "Manifesting Kali's Power: Guyanese Hinduism and the Revitalisation of the 'Madras Tradition.'" *Journal of Eastern Caribbean Studies* 41, no. 1 (April 2016): 83–110.

Knepper, Timothy D., and Leah E. Kalmanson, eds. *Ineffability: An Exercise in Comparative Philosophy of Religion*. Vol. 1. Cham, Switzerland: Springer, 2017.

Kobes Du Mez, Kristin. *Jesus and John Wayne: How White Evangelicals Corrupted a Faith and Fractured a Nation*. New York: Liveright Publishing, 2021.

Kutzler, Evan A. *Living by Inches: The Smells, Sounds, Tastes, and Feeling of Captivity in Civil War Prisons*. Chapel Hill: University of North Carolina Press, 2019.

LaMothe, Kimerer L. "What Bodies Know about Religion and the Study of It." *JAAR* 76, no. 3 (2008): 573–601.

Langer, Lawrence L. *The Holocaust and the Literary Imagination*. New Haven: Yale University Press, 1975.

Lanouette, William J. "The New Right—'Revolutionaries' Out after the 'Lunch-Pail' Vote." *National Journal*, January 21, 1978. Weyrich Scrapbooks, 1978, box 6, folder 7, vol. 22, Library of Congress.

"Latest from the Exploring Squadron—Massacre of Two of the Peacock at the Eeejee Islands." *Richmond Enquirer*, February 23, 1841.

Latrobe, John H. B. *The History of Mason and Dixon's Line*. Philadelphia: Lippincott, Grambo, and Co., 1855.

"Lectures on Mesmerism." *Charleston Mercury*, February 11, 1843.

Lederman, Doug. "The Biggest Movers Online." *Inside Higher Ed*, December 17, 2019.

Lefebvre, Henri. *Critique of Everyday Life: The One-Volume Edition*. Translated by John Moore and Gregory Elliott. New York: Verso, 2014.

Lepselter, Susan. *The Resonance of Unseen Things: Poetics, Power, Captivity, and UFOs in the American Uncanny*. Ann Arbor: University of Michigan Press, 2016.

"The LGBTQ+ Student Divide: The State of Sexual and Gender Minority Students at Taxpayer-Funded Christian Colleges." Report. Religious Exemption Accountability Project (REAP), 2021.

"The Liberty Way: Student Honor Code." Liberty University, August 8, 2019.

Lincoln, Bruce. *Authority: Construction and Corrosion*. Chicago: University of Chicago Press, 1995.

Link, William A. *The Paradox of Southern Progressivism, 1880–1930.* Chapel Hill: University of North Carolina Press, 1992.

Long, Carolyn Morrow. *Spiritual Merchants: Religion, Magic, and Commerce.* Knoxville: University of Tennessee Press, 2001.

"Lord Morpeth on Slavery." *Charleston Mercury,* January 12, 1843.

Lorde, Audre. "Poetry Is Not a Luxury." In Lorde, *Sister Outsider: Essays and Speeches.* Berkeley: Crossing Press, 2007.

———. *Sister Outsider: Essays and Speeches.* Berkeley: Crossing Press, 2007.

Lowe, Lisa. *The Intimacies of Four Continents.* Durham, NC: Duke University Press, 2015.

"Lunatic Asylum." *Charleston Mercury,* January 31, 1843.

Lyle Morgan, Jennifer. *Laboring Women: Reproduction and Gender in New World Slavery.* Philadelphia: University of Pennsylvania Press, 2004.

Mahmood, Saba. "Rehearsed Spontaneity and the Conventionality of Ritual: Disciplines of 'Ṣalāt.'" *American Ethnologist* 28, no. 4 (2001): 827–53.

Mahon, R. H., ed. *Minutes of the Fiftieth Session of the Memphis Conference of the Methodist Episcopal Church, South, Held at Fulton, Kentucky, November 13–18, 1889.* Brownsville, TN: States-Democrat Book and Job Office, 1889.

Markovits, Claude. *The Global World of Indian Merchants, 1750–1947: Traders of Sind from Bukhara to Panama.* Cambridge: Cambridge University Press, 2000.

Marsden, George. *Jonathan Edwards: A Life.* New Haven: Yale University Press, 2003.

———. *Understanding Fundamentalism and Evangelicalism.* Grand Rapids, MI: William B. Eerdmans Publishing Co., 1991.

Martin, James. "Steve Bannon vs. the Pope." *AM Joy,* MSNBC, February 12, 2017.

Martin, William Wallace. *Manual of Ecclesiastical Architecture: Comprising a Study of Its Various Styles, the Chronological Arrangements of Its Elements, and Its Relation to Christian Worship.* Cincinnati: Curts and Jennings, 1897.

"The MASGD." Muslim Alliance for Sexual and Gender Diversity (MASGD).

"Masjid Al-Rabia." Masjid Al-Rabia, Chicago.

Mason, Carol. 2009. *Reading Appalachia from left to Right: Conservatives and the 1974 Kanawha County Textbook Controversy.* Ithaca: Cornell University Press, 2009.

Masuzawa, Tomoko. *The Invention of World Religions Or, How European Universalism Was Preserved in the Language of Pluralism.* Chicago: University of Chicago Press, 2005.

McCammon, Sarah. "Evangelical Writer Who Influenced Purity Culture Announces Separation from Wife." NPR, July 21, 2019.

McCandless, Peter. "Mesmerism and Phrenology in Antebellum Charleston: 'Enough of the Marvellous.'" *Journal of Southern History* 58, no. 2 (1992): 199–230.

McDowell, John Patrick. *The Social Gospel in the South: The Women's Home Mission Movement in the Methodist Episcopal Church, South, 1886–1939.* Baton Rouge: Louisiana State University Press, 1982.

McGirr, Lisa. 2015. *Suburban Warriors: The Origins of the New American Right.* Princeton: Princeton University Press.

McKittrick, Katherine. *Dear Science and Other Stories.* Durham, NC: Duke University Press, 2021.

Medinger, Alan. *Growth into Manhood: Resuming the Journey.* Colorado Springs, CO: WaterBrook Press, 2000.

"The Mermaid." *Charleston Mercury*, January 20, 1843.

"The Mermaid." *New York Herald*, July 17, 1842.

Mesaro-Winckles, Christy Ellen. "Christian Patriarchy Lite: TLC's *19 Kids and Counting*." In *Media Depictions of Brides, Wives, and Mothers*, edited by Alana Amato Ruggerio. Lanham, MD: Lexington Books, 2012.

"Mesmerism." *Charleston Mercury*, February 24, 1843.

"Mesmerism Confirmed." *Charleston Mercury*, April 1, 1843.

"Mesmerism—Important Circumstances." *Charleston Mercury*, March 29, 1843.

Miller, James. *Democracy Is in the Streets: From Port Huron to the Siege of Chicago*. New York: Simon and Schuster, 1987.

Miller, Perry. *Errand into the Wilderness*. Cambridge, MA: Harvard University Press, 1952.

———. *Jonathan Edwards*. Lincoln: University of Nebraska, 1949.

"Millerism in Brooklyn." *Charleston Mercury*, March 10, 1843.

"Millerism—The Comet—Signs and Wonders." *Charleston Mercury*, March 16, 1843.

Mills, C. Wright. *The Power Elite*. Oxford: Oxford University Press, 2000.

Mintz, Alan L. *Ḥurban: Responses to Catastrophe in Hebrew Literature*. New York: Columbia University Press, 1984.

Molodovsky, Kadye. *Der meylekh dovid aleyn iz geblibn* [Only King David Remained]. New York: Papirene Brik, 1946.

———. "El Khanun" [God of Mercy]. In *Der meylekh dovid aleyn iz geblibn* [Only King David Remained]. New York: Papirene Brik, 1946.

———. "Havdole." In *Der meylekh dovid aleyn iz geblibn* [Only King David Remained]. New York: Papirene Brik, 1946.

Muller, Lauren, and June Jordan, eds. *June Jordan's Poetry for the People: A Revolutionary Blueprint*. London: Taylor and Francis, 1995.

Muñoz, José Esteban. *Cruising Utopia: The Then and There of Queer Futurity*. New York: New York University Press, 2009.

———. *Disidentifications: Queers of Color and the Performance of Politics*. Minneapolis: University of Minnesota Press, 2009.

"The Muslim Protagonist: Centering the Margin." PEN America, March 6, 2017.

"Naval General Court Martial on Board of the U.S. Ship North Carolina." *New York Herald*, August 23, 1842.

Neuman, Meredith. *Jeremiah's Scribes: Creating Sermon Literature in Puritan New England*. Philadelphia: University of Pennsylvania Press, 2011.

Newton, Velam. *The Silver Men: West Indian Labour Migration to Panama 1850–1914*. Kingston, Jamaica: Ian Randle Publishers, 2004.

Nicolosi, Joseph. "A Developmental Model for Effective Treatment of Male Homosexuality." *American Journal of Pastoral Counseling* 3, nos. 3–4 (2001): 87–100.

Nixon, Richard. Veto of the Economic Opportunity Amendments of 1971. December 9, 1971. The American Presidency Project, University of California, Santa Barbara.

"No Humbug." *Charleston Mercury*, April 19, 1843.

Noll, Mark. "Common Sense Traditions and American Evangelical Thought." *American Quarterly* 37, no. 2 (1985): 216–38.

———. *The Rise of Evangelicalism: The Age of Edwards, Whitefield, and the Wesleys*. Westmont,

IL: Intervarsity Academic, 2010.

Noll, Mark, David Bebbington, and George M. Marsden. *Evangelicals: Who They Have Been, Are Now, and Could Be.* Grand Rapids, MI: William B. Eerdmans Publishing Co., 2019.

Norich, Anita. *Discovering Exile: Yiddish and Jewish American Culture during the Holocaust.* Stanford: Stanford University Press, 2007.

Nott, Josiah C. *Two Lectures, on the Natural History of the Caucasian and Negro Races.* Mobile: Dade and Thompson, 1844.

Ogden, Emily. *Credulity: A Cultural History of US Mesmerism.* Chicago: University of Chicago Press, 2018.

Olson, Carl E. "Father Dwight Longenecker Let's 'Er Rip!" Blog post. Insight Scoop, The Ignatius Press Blog, April 16, 2008.

O'Neill, Kevin L. "Beyond Broken: Affective Spaces and the Study of American Religion." *JAAR* 81, no. 4 (2013): 1093–1116.

"The Orang Outang of Malacca." *Farmers' Gazette and Cheraw Advertiser,* April 19, 1842.

Orlick, Annelise. *Rethinking American Women's Activism.* New York: Routledge, 2015.

Ozick, Cynthia. "Roundtable Discussion: Cynthia Ozick." In *Writing and the Holocaust,* edited by Berel Lang, 277–84. New York: Holmes and Meier, 1988.

Pandey, Gyanendra. "Which of Us Are Hindus?" In *Hindus and Others: The Question of Identity in India Today,* edited by Gyanendra Pandey, 238–72. New Delhi: Viking, 1993.

Paton, Diana. *The Cultural Politics of Obeah: Religion, Colonialism and Modernity in the Caribbean World.* Cambridge: Cambridge University Press, 2015.

Patterson, William M. *A Manual of Architecture for Churches, Parsonages, and School-Houses: Containing Designs, Elevations, Plans, Specifications, Form of Contract, Rules for Estimating Cost of Building, with Suggestions on Acoustics, Ventilation, Seating, Lighting, Painting, Etc.* Nashville: Publishing House of the Methodist Episcopal Church, South, 1875.

Perry, Samuel L., and Andrew L. Whitehead. *Taking America Back for God.* Oxford: Oxford University Press, 2020.

Piela, Anna. *Muslim Women Online: Faith and Identity in Virtual Space.* New York: Routledge, 2012.

"Practical Millerism." *Charleston Mercury,* March 29, 1843.

Promise Keepers. Website.

Putnam, Lara. *Radical Moves: Caribbean Migrants and the Politics of Race in the Jazz Age.* Chapel Hill: University of North Carolina Press, 2013.

———. "Rites of Power and Rumors of Race: The Circulation of Supernatural Knowledge in the Greater Caribbean, 1890–1940." In *Obeah and Other Powers: The Politics of Caribbean Religion and Healing,* edited by Diana Paton and Maarit Forde. Durham, NC: Duke University Press, 2012.

———. "Undone by Desire: Migration, Sex across Boundaries, and Collective Destinies in the Greater Caribbean, 1840–1940." In *Connecting Seas and Connected Ocean Rims: Indian, Atlantic, and Pacific Oceans and China Seas Migrations from the 1830s to the 1930s,* edited by Donna R. Gabaccia and Dirk Hoerder. Leiden: Brill, 2011.

"Radical Traditional Catholicism." Southern Poverty Law Center.

Ramey, Steven W. *Hindu, Sufi, or Sikh: Contested Practices and Identifications of Sindhi Hindus in India and Beyond.* New York: Palgrave Macmillan, 2008.

Rashid, Hussein. "Qawwālī in America: Making Space." *Muslim World* 107, no. 2 (2017): 271–86.

"Reconstructed." *Reconstructed Magazine.*

Reese, David M. *Humbugs of New-York: Being a Remonstrance against Popular Delusion; Whether in Science, Philosophy, or Religion.* New York: John S. Taylor, Brick-Church Chapel, 1838.

"Report of the Boston Female Anti-Slavery Society with a Sketch of the Obstacles Thrown in the Way of Emancipation by Certain Clerical Abolitionists and Advocates for the Subjugation of Woman." Boston, 1837. American Congregational Library.

"The Return of the Exploring Expedition." *Camden Journal,* June 22, 1842.

Ribuffo, Leo P. "Family Policy Past as Prologue: Jimmy Carter, the White House Conference on Families, and the Mobilization of the New Christian Right." *Review of Policy Research* 23 (April 2006): 311–38.

Riley, Krista Melanie. "'You Don't Need a Fatwa': Muslim Feminist Blogging as Religious Interpretation." PhD diss., Concordia University, 2016.

Ritter, Luis Pulido. "Armando Fortune y la identidad cultural Panameña." *Tareas* 140 (January–April 2012): 83–106.

Rivett, Sarah. *Science of the Soul in Colonial New England.* Chapel Hill: University of North Carolina Press, 2011.

Robinson, Christine M., and Sue E. Spivey. "The Politics of Masculinity and the Ex-Gay Movement." *Gender and Society* 21, no. 5 (2007): 650–75.

Rocklin, Alexander. *The Regulation of Religion and the Making of Hinduism in Colonial Trinidad.* Chapel Hill: University of North Carolina Press, 2019.

Rodgers, Daniel T. *Atlantic Crossings: Social Politics in a Progressive Age.* Cambridge, MA: Harvard University Press, 1998.

———. "In Search of Progressivism." *Reviews in American History* 10, no. 4 (December 1982): 113–32.

Roose, Kevin. *The Unlikely Disciple: A Sinner's Semester at America's Holiest University.* New York: Grand Central Publishing, 2009.

Rosenfeld, Alvin H. *A Double Dying: Reflections on Holocaust Literature.* Bloomington: Indiana University Press, 1980.

Roskies, David G. *Against the Apocalypse: Responses to Catastrophe in Modern Jewish Culture.* Cambridge, MA: Harvard University Press, 1984.

Roskies, David G., and Naomi Diamant. *Holocaust Literature: A History and Guide.* Waltham, MA: Brandeis University Press, 2012.

Rzeznik, Thomas F. *Church and Estate: Religion and Wealth in Industrial-Era Philadelphia.* University Park: Pennsylvania State University Press, 2013.

Sanders, Elizabeth. *Roots of Reform: Farmers, Workers, and the American State, 1877–1917.* Chicago: University of Chicago Press, 1999.

Schaefer, Donovan O. *Religious Affects: Animality, Evolution, and Power.* Durham, NC: Duke University Press, 2015.

———. *Wild Experiment: Feeling Science and Secularism after Darwin.* Durham, NC: Duke University Press, 2022.

Schlozman, Daniel. *When Movements Anchor Parties: Electoral Alignments in American History*. Princeton: Princeton University Press, 2015.

Schneider, David M. *American Kinship: A Cultural Account*. Chicago: University of Chicago Press, 1980.

Sedgwick, Eve K., and Adam Frank. *Shame and Its Sisters: A Silvan Tomkins Reader*. Durham, NC: Duke University Press, 1995.

———. *Tendencies*. London: Taylor & Francis, 2014.

———. *Touching Feeling: Affect, Pedagogy, Performativity*. Durham, NC: Duke University Press, 2003.

Sellers, Charles. *The Market Revolution in Jacksonian America, 1815–1846*. New York: Oxford University Press, 1991.

"The Sequel to the Mermaid Controversy." *Charleston Mercury*, March 29, 1843.

Sharma, Nitasha Tamar. *Hip Hop Desis: South Asian Americans, Blackness, and a Global Race Consciousness*. Durham, NC: Duke University Press, 2010.

Sheingate, Adam D. "Political Entrepreneurship, Institutional Change, and American Political Development." *Studies in American Political Development* 17, no. 2 (2003): 185–203.

Smith, Jonathan Z. *Drudgery Divine: On the Comparison of Early Christianities and the Religions of Late Antiquity*. Chicago: University of Chicago Press, 1990.

———. *Map Is Not Territory: Studies in the History of Religions*. Chicago: University of Chicago Press, 1993.

———. "Religions, Religious." In *Critical Terms for Religious Studies*, edited by Mark C. Taylor, 269–84. Chicago: University of Chicago Press, 1998.

Smith, Mitzi. "'Unbossed and Unbought': Zilpha Elaw and Old Elizabeth and a Political Discourse of Origins." *Black Theology* 9, no. 3 (June 2011): 287–311.

Sottile, Leah. *Bundyville: The Remnant*. Podcast series. Longreads and Oregon Public Broadcasting. July 2019.

"The South Proscribed." *Charleston Mercury*, January 19, 1843.

Spillers, Hortense. "Mama's Baby, Papa's Maybe: An American Grammar Book." *Diacritics* 17 (Summer 1987): 65–81.

Spivey, Sue E., and Christine M. Robinson. "Genocidal Intentions: Social Death and the Ex-Gay Movement." *Genocide Studies and Prevention* 5, no. 1 (2010): 68–88.

Stanley, Amy Dru. "Conjugal Bonds and Wage Labor: Rights of Contract in the Age of Emancipation." *Journal of American History* 75, no. 2 (1988): 471–500.

Stearns, Carol Z., and Stearns, Peter N. *Anger: The Struggle for Emotional Control in America's History*. Chicago: University of Chicago Press, 1986.

Steiner, George. *Language and Silence: Essays on Language, Literature, and the Inhuman*. New York: Atheneum, 1967.

———. "The Long Life of Metaphor: An Approach to the 'Shoah.'" In *Writing and the Holocaust*, edited by Berel Lang, 154–71. New York: Holmes and Meier, 1988.

Stern, Alexandra Minna. *Proud Boys and the White Ethnostate: How the Alt-Right Is Warping the American Imagination*. Boston: Beacon Press, 2020.

Stewart, Kathleen. *Ordinary Affects*. Durham, NC: Duke University Press, 2007.

Stewart, Maria W. "Religion and the Pure Principles of Morality, the Sure Foundation on

Which We Must Build." In *America's First Black Woman Political Writer: Essays and Speeches*, edited by Marilyn Richardson. Bloomington: Indiana University Press, 1987.

Stoler, Ann Laura. *Race and the Education of Desire: Foucault's History of Sexuality and the Colonial Order of Things*. Durham, NC: Duke University Press, 1995.

Stout, Harry. *The New England Soul: Preaching and Religious Culture in Colonial New England*. Oxford: Oxford University Press, 1986.

———. "Religion, Communications, and the Ideological Origins of the American Revolution." *William and Mary Quarterly* 34, no. 4 (October 1977): 519–41.

Stowell, Daniel W. *Rebuilding Zion: The Religious Reconstruction of the South, 1863–1877*. New York: Oxford University Press, 1998.

Striphas, Ted. "Algorithmic Culture." *European Journal of Cultural Studies* 18, nos. 4–5 (2015): 395–412.

Summers, T. O., ed. *Journal of the General Conference of the Methodist Episcopal Church, South, Held in Atlanta, Ga, 1878*. Nashville: Southern Methodist Publishing House, 1878.

———. *Journal of the General Conference of the Methodist Episcopal Church, South, Held in Louisville, 1874*. Nashville: Publishing House of the Methodist Episcopal Church, South, 1874.

———. *Journal of the General Conference of the Methodist Episcopal Church, South, Held in Memphis, 1870*. Nashville: Publishing House of the Methodist Episcopal Church, South, 1870.

Taberski, Dan. *Running from Cops*. Podcast. April–May 2019.

Tchen, John Kuo Wei, and Dylan Yeats. "Introduction: Yellow Peril Incarnate." In *Yellow Peril! An Archive of Anti-Asian Fear*, edited by John Kuo Wei Tchen and Dylan Yeats. London: Verso, 2014.

Tentler, Leslie Woodcock. 2009. *Catholics and Contraception: An American History*. Ithaca, New York: Cornell University Press.

Thakur, U. T. *Sindhi Culture*. Bombay: University of Bombay, n.d.

"That Mermaid." *Charleston Mercury*, January 20, 1843.

Thomas, S. W. *Fifth Annual Report of the Church Extension Society of the Methodist Episcopal Church for the Year 1870*. Philadelphia: Methodist Episcopal Book Room, 1870.

Thomas, Todne. *Kincraft: The Making of Black Evangelical Sociality*. Durham, NC: Duke University Press, 2021.

Tipton, Steven M. 1982. *Getting Saved from the Sixties: The Transformation of Moral Meaning in American Culture*. Berkeley: University of California Press, 1982.

Tomkins, Silvan. "Shame-Humiliation and Contempt-Disgust." In *Shame and Its Sisters: A Silvan Tomkins Reader*, edited by Eve Kosofsky Sedgwick and Adam Frank, 133–78. Durham, NC: Duke University Press, 1995.

Tønnessen, Alf Tomas. *How Two Political Entrepreneurs Helped Create the Conservative Movement, 1973–1981*. Lampeter, Wales, UK: Edwin Mellen Press, 2009.

"To the Editor of the *Charleston Courier*." *Charleston Mercury*, February 1, 1843.

"To the Editor of the *Mercury*." *Charleston Mercury*, January 26, 1843.

Treudly, Mary. "The United States and Santo Domingo 1789–1866." *Journal of Racial Development* 7, no. 2 (1916): 226.

21Studios.com. The 22 Convention: Make Women Great Again.

Uricchio, William. "Recommended for You: Prediction, Creation and the Cultural Work of Algorithms." *Berlin Journal* 28 (2015): 6–9.

Valencia, Heather. "Only King David Remained: Reactions to the Holocaust in the Poetry of Kadya Molodowsky." In *The Fourteenth Avrom-Nokhem Stencl Lecture in Yiddish Studies, Occasional Papers* 7. Oxford: Oxford Centre for Hebrew and Jewish Studies, 2006.

Van Geuns, Suzanne. "Mothers for a Christian Nation." *Exchange* 43, no. 2 (2014): 192–206.

Vecchio, Diane C. "The Scourge of the South: Pellagra and Poverty in Spartanburg's Mill Villages." In *Recovering the Piedmont Past*, vol. 2: *Bridging the Centuries in the South Carolina Upcountry, 1877–1941*, edited by Timothy P. Grady and Andrew H. Myers, 58–71. Columbia: University of South Carolina Press, 2019.

Viguerie, Richard. "Ends and Means." In *The New Right Papers*, edited by Robert Whitaker. New York: St. Martin's Press, 1982.

"Vital Statistics of Negroes and Mulattoes." *Boston Medical Journal*, October 12, 1842.

"Vital Statistics of Negroes and Mulattoes." *Charleston Mercury*, March 3, 1843.

Von Rohr, John. *The Covenant of Grace in Puritan Thought*. Atlanta: Scholars Press, 1986.

Walker, Alice. *In Search of Our Mothers' Gardens: Womanist Prose*. New York: Harcourt, 1983.

Weaver, Mary Jo, and R. Scott Appleby, eds. *Being Right: Conservative Catholics in America*. Bloomington: Indiana University Press, 1995.

Weber, Max. *The Protestant Ethic and the Spirit of Capitalism*. Trans. Stephen Kalberg. New York: Oxford University Press, 2011.

Welter, Barbara. "The Cult of True Womanhood: 1820–1860." *American Quarterly* 18, no. 2 (1966): 151–74.

Weyrich, Paul M. Papers. American Heritage Center, University of Wyoming, Laramie.

Weyrich, Paul M. Scrapbooks. Library of Congress, Washington, DC.

Wheatley, Phyllis. *Poems on Various Subjects, Religious and Moral*. London: A. Bell, Aldgate, 1773.

Wheeler, Kayla Renée. "Remixing Images of Islam: The Creation of New Muslim Women Subjectivities on YouTube." *Online—Heidelberg Journal of Religions on the Internet* 6 (2014).

White, Mel. *Stranger at the Gate: To Be Gay and Christian in America*. New York: Plume, 1995.

Whitehead, J., and J. Conlan. "The Establishment of the Religion of Secular Humanism and Its First Amendment Implications." *Texas Technical Law Review* 10, no. 1 (1978–79): 1–66.

Wiebe, Robert H. *The Search for Order, 1877–1920*. New York: Hill and Wang, 1967.

Wiesel, Elie. "Why I Write." In *Confronting the Holocaust: The Impact of Elie Wiesel*, edited by Alvin H. Rosenfeld and Irving Greenberg, 200–206. Bloomington: Indiana University Press, 1978.

Wieviorka, Annette. *The Era of the Witness*. Ithaca: Cornell University Press, 2006.

Winiarski, Douglas. *Darkness Falls on the Land of Light: Experiencing Religious Awakenings in Eighteenth-Century New England*. Williamsburg, VA: Omohundro Institute of Early American History and Culture, 2017.

Winthrop, John. "A Modell of Christian Charity." *Collections of the Massachusetts Historical Society*, 3rd ser., no. 7 (1838): 31–48.

Woodward, C. Vann. *Origins of the New South, 1877–1913*. Baton Rouge: Louisiana State University Press, 1951.

Wynter, Sylvia. "Jonkonnu in Jamaica: Towards the Interpretation of Folk Dance as a Cultural Process." *Jamaica Journal* (June 1970): 34–48.

Youngblood, Denise. "Rainbow Family, Rainbow Nation: Reflections on Relatives and Relational Dynamics in Trinidad." In *The Ethics of Kinship: Ethnographic Inquiries*, edited by James D. Faubion. Lanham, MD: Rowman and Littlefield, 2001.

Zenger, Robin Elizabeth. "West Indians in Panama: Diversity and Activism, 1910s–1940s." PhD diss., University of Arizona, 2015.

Zien, Katherine A. *Sovereign Acts: Performing Race, Space, and Belonging in Panama and the Canal Zone*. New Brunswick, NJ: Rutgers University Press, 2017.

Contributors

MICHAEL J. ALTMAN is a professor in the Department of Religious Studies at the University of Alabama. He researches and teaches courses about the category "religion" in American history and culture, using examples ranging from Hinduism to professional wrestling to American evangelicalism. His most recent book is *Hinduism in America: An Introduction* (Routledge, 2022). He is also the director of the American Examples program.

MICHAEL BAYSA is a PhD candidate in the Department of Religion at Princeton University. He is finishing his dissertation, titled "Unpublishing Religion: How Anglo-Protestant Printing Constrained Public Speech in Early America," which explores how eighteenth-century ministers, printers, and booksellers continued to curate the production of public religion beyond outright censorship. He specializes in the intersection of religion, economy, and media, and he is the past recipient of the E. Rhodes and Leona B. Carpenter Fellowship in Early American Religious Studies at the McNeil Center at the University of Pennsylvania.

CHRISTOPHER M. BISHOP completed his PhD in American history at Auburn University in 2018. He currently teaches US and world history surveys and is revising his dissertation for publication. He lives with his wife in Birmingham, Alabama.

JAIMIE D. CRUMLEY is an assistant professor at the University of Utah. She is a Black feminist intellectual historian who studies Black Christian women's contributions to the antislavery movement in eighteenth- and nineteenth-century New England.

CHELSEA EBIN is an assistant professor of political science at Drew University and a co-founder of the Institute for Research on Male Supremacism. She studies the development of right-wing movements in the United States, with a particular focus on the Christian Right.

LAUREN HORN GRIFFIN is an assistant professor in the Department of Philosophy and Religious Studies at Louisiana State University. Her research and teaching focus on religion, media, and technology. Her current project navigates discourses on tradition and modernity in Catholic communities around the globe.

ERIK KLINE is an assistant professor of American literature at the University of Wisconsin, River Falls. He received his PhD in American literature from the University of Alabama. His research interests include twentieth-century American fiction and autobiography, addiction studies, and word-image studies. His work has appeared in the *F. Scott Fitzgerald Review* (Duke University Press) and *Let Us Now Praise Famous Men at 75: Anniversary Essays* (University of Tennessee Press), and he is currently working on a monograph that examines intersections of travel, intoxication, and religious experience in postmodern American autofiction.

DANA LLOYD is an assistant professor of global interdisciplinary studies at Villanova University. She holds a PhD in religion from Syracuse University and a law degree from Tel Aviv Law School. Her scholarship has been published in *Journal of Law and Religion*; *Law, Culture, and the Humanities*; *Canopy Forum*; and *Political Theology Network*. Her first book, with the working title "Arguing for This Land: Rethinking Indigenous Sacred Sites," is under contract with the University Press of Kansas.

HINASAHAR MUNEERUDDIN is a doctoral candidate at the University of North Carolina, Chapel Hill, in the Islamic studies track of the religious studies program, with a graduate certificate in women's and gender studies. Her research lies at the intersections of Islam(s), gender, race, affect, and performativity.

CODY MUSSELMAN is a postdoctoral fellow at the John C. Danforth Center on Religion and Politics at Washington University, St. Louis. She is a scholar of contemporary American religion with degrees in religious studies from Yale University, Harvard Divinity School, and Kalamazoo College. Her work focuses on the intersections of health, capitalism, and religion in everyday life. Her current research examines how religion and spirituality became embedded in the fitness and wellness industry.

ALEXANDER ROCKLIN received his PhD in the history of religions from the University of Chicago. His work examines the politics of the category "religion" in the interactive making of Hinduism, Islam, and Afro-Atlantic religions in the colonial Caribbean. His first book, *The Regulation of Religion and the Making of Hinduism in Colonial Trinidad*, was published in spring 2019 by University of North Carolina Press. His current research analyzes the co-production of the categories "race" and "religion" in the nineteenth and twentieth centuries through a series of case studies of various individuals passing as "Hindu" in and between the circum-Caribbean region, the United States, and beyond.

Sean Sidky works on American Judaism, Yiddish literature and culture, and literatures written in response to disaster and catastrophe. His current research examines Yiddish-language poetry written in the United States during the Holocaust. He received his PhD in comparative literature and religious studies from Indiana University, Bloomington, and currently coordinates the university's writing center.

Joshua Urich is an assistant professor of religious studies at Colby College. His current research explores the ways in which the physical and emotional experience of suspicion has generated religious categories of social difference throughout American history.

Lucas F. W. Wilson is the Justice, Equity, and Transformation Postdoctoral Fellow at the University of Calgary. He is currently writing a queer history of Liberty University. In addition to being featured in several edited volumes, his work has been published in *Flannery O'Connor Review*, *Canadian Jewish Studies*, and *Journal of Jewish Identities*. He is also the co-editor of a forthcoming volume of essays on the descendants of Holocaust survivors and perpetrators, which is under contract with Lexington Books.

Index